Medieval and Renaissance Series
Number 4

MEDIEVAL

AND

RENAISSANCE STUDIES

Proceedings of the Southeastern Institute
of Medieval and Renaissance Studies
Summer, 1968

Edited by John L. Lievsay

Duke University Press, Durham, N. C.

© *1970, Duke University Press*
L.C.C. card no. 66-25361
I.S.B.N. 0-8223-0227-6
Printed in the United States of America
by the Seeman Printery, Inc.

Foreword

If one sometimes has the impression that the Middle Ages had no beginning and the Renaissance no ending, he should feel right at home with the lectures comprising this volume. For the topics discussed range back into pre-Christian times and forward to the concerns of day after tomorrow. Which is another way of saying, I think, Courteous Reader, that the distinguished men responsible for them are men who think in the very broadest of Humanistic terms about the human condition: nothing that concerned, concerns, or will concern their fellow men is without its interest to them. Our roots are in the past, and a little intelligent cultivation of those roots is among our best of guarantees that the old family tree will continue to stand and flourish.

The occasion that brought these amiable and learned gentlemen together and placed them behind the lectern before delighted audiences of their fellow students (and a sprinkling of enlightened community residents) was the Fourth Session of the Southeastern Institute of Medieval and Renaissance Studies, held on the campus of Duke University during July and August, 1968. Here, for the five weeks of the session, on a sort of scholarly busman's holiday, freed from the mounting pressures and tensions of Academia, the members of the Institute pursued their individual and communal interests and communicated their findings publicly and privately. The lectures are the record of the public powwows—with one exception: an eighth address, delivered by M. Jean-Claude Margolin, noted Erasmian scholar then visiting this country, has not been available for inclusion. M. Margolin spoke with Gallic charm and enthusiasm on "Erasmus and Music."

Otherwise, the lectures are here printed in the order of delivery and pretty much *as* they were delivered. The speakers have felt free to make minor alterations, but the content and temper remain unchanged. If something of their original oral pattern has been left over, that is pure gain; for one of the most delightful aspects of the Institute is its companionable informality. The scholars who address you here are not unimpressed by greatness: they are simply unawed by reputations, their own or those of others. Shakespeare knew that a man might smile and smile and be a villain; his great contemporary, Montaigne, knew that he might laugh and laugh—and be a philosopher.

The editor has, perforce, introduced a minimum of consistency in mechanical details. He will be satisfied if it proves not to be a foolish one.

John L. Lievsay
Chairman, 1968 Institute
Durham, N. C.

Contents

MEDIEVAL
AND
RENAISSANCE STUDIES

The Renaissance Antiquarian and Allegorical Interpretation

Don C. Allen
Johns Hopkins University

From the histories of Arrian,[1] Diodorus Siculus,[2] and Justinus,[3] Renaissance men learned that Alexander crossed from Sestos to Abydos to visit at Ilium the tombs of heroes, one of whom was Protesilaus, first of the warriors to disembark from Agamemnon's ship in the Bay of the Achaeans. At the Temple of Athena, Alexander exchanged his own armor for a fine coat of dedicated mail; and when later he was attacking a city of the Mallians, the companion Peucestas carried the shield of Athena before him. Plutarch informs us that Alexander not only poured libations on the heroes' graves but also anointed the tombstone of Achilles, running naked round the sepulchre, crowning it with garlands, and "declaring how happy he esteemed Achilles, in having while he lived so faithful a friend, and when he was dead, so famous a poet to proclaim his deeds."[4] After these rites, Alexander was informed he could see the harp of Paris, but thought it not worth the trouble, preferring to see that of Achilles "to which he used to sing the glories and great actions of brave men."

Strabo, who wandered over the plains of Troy and saw the grave of Hector, the sanctuary of Protesilaus, the shrines of Achilles and Patroclus, and similar hallowed places, knew that Alexandria Troas was not the site of Priam's Troy "if we judge from Homer." Thirty stades from this coastal city, a flourishing Roman colony, was the "Ilians' village," standing above the Scamander; "but no trace survives of the ancient city . . . Ilium was absolutely rooted out."[5] Strabo also tells of the visit of Julius Caesar to the ruins of Troy, but his plain prose tale

[3]

is not nearly so fascinating as Lucan's poetic account. After the defeat and death of Pompey, Caesar, Lucan writes, came to the Sigean sands and the waters of Simois and Rhoeteum, places ennobled with "Grecian tombs and ghosts owing much to the poets." Walking through "the name" of burned Troy, he sought for memorial remnants, but the temples were overgrown with trees. "Even the ruins are gone." Nonetheless, he identified the rock of Hesione, the bower of Anchises, the seat of Paris, the place of Ganymede's kidnapping, and where Oenone disported. As he was crossing unknowingly the Xanthus, a native urged him not to tread on the ghost of Hector. After erecting altars, he prayed for the Julians and promised that the Ausonians would restore the Phrygian walls "and a Roman Pergamus shall rise."[6]

The belief that Alexandria Troas was Priam's Ilium persisted during the Middle Ages. The historian Zozimus writes that anyone sailing across the Hellespont could see the ruins with "parts of the walls standing."[7] Saewulf, coursing near Tenit, saw on the coast of Romania the remains of Troy "still apparent over the space of many miles";[8] and a few centuries later, Johann Schiltberger, on a voyage to Constantinople, describes the "fine plain . . . where the city stood."[9] Sir John Mandeville did not avoid this point of ancient interest,[10] but the Levantine tourists of the sixteenth and seventeenth centuries naturally examined the ruins more closely.

In 1553, Pierre Belon visited the ruined walls, towers, and tombs of Troy. Inside the city was desolation, and the soil for a mile about was sterile, sandy, and treeless.[11] Edward Barton, Elizabeth's ambassador to Turkey, also saw Troy on the Asia side as he passed through the Hellespont. Two hills rose in pyramidal form, "not unlikely to be the tombs of Achilles and Ajax."[12] John Sanderson[13] and Richard Wrag[14] passed by the same ruins, and somewhat later George Sandys, who was enough of a classicist to have read Strabo and hence knew, standing amid the ruins of Roman baths and a somewhat better preserved Christian church, that he was not on Trojan soil.[15] On the other hand, Thomas Coryat was overwhelmed with classical nostalgia when he stood amid the same debris. He paused in reverence before the Tomb of Priam, admired a "delicate trough of white marble" and ten "faire gray Marble Pillars," measured with his carpenter's rule a thirty-foot pillar lying among the detritus, walked the road to the king's palace, and estimated the ruined walls to be thirty feet in height. He attempted to read some Latin inscriptions and made out the word "Numinid" on one, but found the other in "such exoticke characters" as to be unintelligible. He viewed the remains of a heathen temple and entered a vault only to find it full of "ordure and dung of Cattle." He describes the palace in some detail and reports its front as the best preserved remains of old Troy. At this point, Master Robert Rugge drew his sword and standing on a great stone, knighted Coryat as a "True Trojane from Aeneas' race descended." Coryat acknowledged the honor with verses and an oration to his *Commilitones* in which he found in the ruin of the city and the palace of Ilus an example of Jehovah's revenge on adulterers.[16]

The visitors to the plains of windy Troy during the reigns of Elizabeth and James provide Shakespeare's *Troilus* or Garnier's plays on the Trojan stories with an immediacy we have not realized. The supposed ruins are a realistic gloss on the false oath of Cressida:

> When time is old and hath forgot itself,
> When waterdrops have worn the stones of Troy,
> And blind oblivion swallow'd cities up
> And mighty states characterless are grated
> To dusty nothing.
>
> (III, 2, 193-196)

But besides these accounts, graphic enough in detail, was the presence in places like England, far from the Phrygian terrain, of material relics presumably Homeric. Thomas Dallam, who visited the ruins of Troy in 1600, returned to London with "a peece of whyte marble piller, the which I broke with my owne handes";[17] and Coryat, after surveying the altitude of the front arch of Priam's palace "brake of certaine stones to carrie with mee into my Countrey, and to reserve them in my safe custodie for memorable Antiquities while I live."

These curious inspectors of the scene of the *Iliad* were, in a modern sense, souvenir hunters and hardly what the Renaissance called "antiquarians." They had been preceded by the mediaeval pilgrims who furnished themselves with guides to the churches and ruins of Rome. More immediately, they were like Petrarch, who wandered ecstatically through the Eternal City imagining he saw the palace of Evander, the shrine of Carmentis and the cave of Cacus.[18] Poggio Bracciolini may, in a sense, have fathered modern antiquarianism when he sat on the Tarpeian Hill with his friend Antonio Lusco and attempted, on the basis of classical texts and half-effaced inscriptions, to mark the notable monuments among the ruin spread below.[19] In due course, the topographical studies of Biondi of Forli, Andrea Fulvio, Bartolommeo Marliani, and, particularly, the sketches of Palladio made the ancient stones of Rome live; moreover, with the publication in 1534 of Peter Apian's *Inscriptiones Sacrosanctae Vetustatis*, the stones began to speak.

But it was a long way to Troy, to Athens, and to Rome; and were it not for the acquisitive inclinations of the human heart, antiquarianism as a professional art might have been delayed. The great masters of Europe, Francis I, Philip II, and Rudolf II, adorned their palaces with statues and busts, bas-reliefs and sarcophagi, cabinets of coins and gems garnered from the classical past. The royal infection became in half a century so endemic on the Continent that anyone with a little wealth and a little love of the past had a classical head in his study, which, fitted with a recent nose, seemed likely to be a bust of Socrates or Pericles. Antiquarianism as such, however, found its first English exponents in the Earl of Arundel and the Duke of Buckingham. It is reported that Francis Bacon, on first seeing the nude statues in the Earl's garden started back and exclaimed, "The Resurrection!" The Earl's greatest achievement was, of course, the collection of broken marbles "raked together" by his agent William Petty in Greece. The publication of thirty-nine of these inscriptions by John Selden in 1628 as the *Marmora Arundelliana* was the first great moment in British archaeology. The fever spread to such a degree that when Henry Peacham published the second edition of his *Compleat Gentleman* in 1634, he added advice on collecting antiquities and suggested, now Italy was supervising its classical exports, that Greece, where "the barbarous religion of the Turks" forbade the representation of living things, was the place to collect objects usually "headlesse and lame, yet most of them venerable for antiquitye and elegancy."

When John Selden died, he left his heads and statues of Greek workmanship and the Greek marble inscriptions about his house in Whitefriars to Oxford, but most antiquarians, particularly the great virtuosi, were not so modest. Etchers were engaged to copy the coins, intaglios, inscriptions, and other objects of art. Scholars then supplied the illustrations with texts which attempted to identify and date the item, compare it with similar objects, and illuminate it with quotations from Greek and Latin authors. Some of these explanations were purely historical, and a coin of Augustus could be easily supplied with the historical event it memorialized, but the bull, the flaming altar, the five ears of wheat on the reverse required something more than history. To the elucidation of these symbols, the antiquarians often brought a mode of explanation they had learned from poets and literary explicators.

By the middle of the sixteenth century, readers of Homer were able to understand baffling contradictory or sacrilegious episodes in the epics thanks to the publication of allegorical readings found in Proclus, Porphyry, Eustathius, Heraclitus of Pontus, and other ancient interpreters. The moralizations of the *Aeneid*, which begin with Servius, and the Christian readings of Ovid's *Metamorphoses* were passed on by the Middle Ages, copied, and augmented by Renaissance exegetes. When the symbolic lexicon of the presumed Egyptian Hor Apollo was in print, it begot further symbolic dictionaries like that of Piero Valeriano and promoted the vogue of the emblem-book. Boccaccio, first of modern mythographers, began where the mediaeval allegorizers of myth, Fulgentius and Albricus, left off and found windfalls of moral and physical meanings under his genealogical tree. His methods were avidly followed by Conti, Cartari, and Pomey, whose mythologies were standard works of reference. The eager search for degenerated Adamic truths or distorted biblical history in Greek poets and philosophers inaugurated by Ficino of Florence and Steuco of Gubbio was almost insanely pursued by sixteenth- and seventeenth-century interpreters. The custom of reading classical texts as Christian or quasi-Christian allegories was quickly applied to the understanding of the monuments and objets d'art beginning to crowd public and private museums.

An early application of this means of reading monuments can be found in the commentary of Girolamo Ferrucci on a now lost Mithraic bas-relief (Plate I). The entablature had been found in a vineyard and brought down to Rome where there were, according to its publisher, others like it in the Palazzi di S. Marco and the house of Cardinal Gesis. Ferrucci understood it as a series of symbolical figures surrounding the central representation of Agriculture, who is surveyed in his efforts by the crow of Diligence, the dog of Fidelity, the serpent of Providence, the scorpion of Generation, the lion of Strength while he plunges the knife of Labor in the bull of Earth releasing the blood of Fruitfulness. The lateral figures with torches stand for Day and Night; whereas the superior frieze displays the diurnal phases of the sun, the nocturnal manifestations of the moon, and Nature in her chariot. Thirty-eight years later, Lorenzo Pignoria published another Mithraic group which he properly identified from its half-effaced inscription and ancient texts. He took this occasion to denounce Ferrucci's interpretation as "out of the question,"[20] but his criticism went unheeded and Ferrucci's interpretation was reprinted for many years in popular guidebooks to Rome. It was the sort of mysterious misunderstanding the Renaissance cherished, and it could be abandoned only with regret.

Although Pignoria was hostile to nonhistorical and allegorical commentaries by other antiquaries, he embraced the process when he published a series of letters on classical symbolism

▲ AGRICOLTVRA ▲

Plate I

Plate II

in 1629, each of which was dedicated to a famous devotee of the procedure. One went to Aleander, who had discovered the allegory of the *Tabula Heliaca*;[21] another was assigned to Thomas Dempster, an authority on Latin symbols.[22] Pignoria had earlier shown his civic virtue by discovering in an ancient marble clear proof Padua had been founded by Antenor.[23] In the *Symbolic Letters* he revealed why the hawk is the sign of God, why Diana is accompanied by bees, why Isis represents the earth, and why the arm of Aesculapius is entwined by a serpent. It must be admitted, however, that he always finds a suite of Greek or Latin texts to support his symbolical or allegorical readings.

By adapting the techniques of this master, Pighius,[24] Pignoria adapted the methods of literary interpreters to antiquarian studies. In short order, the same form of exposition was used by numismatists like Augustin,[25] Falconieri,[26] Foy-Valliant,[27] Gros de Boze,[28] Oisel,[29] and Patin.[30] Specialists in figurines, painting, statues, and other artistic remains—Buonarroti,[31] De la Chausse,[32] Oliva,[33] and Spoor[34]—looked for allegory and symbol in whatever they examined. Some of these antiquarians were generalists, but others, like Niçaise, who wrote on the Sirens,[35] Bracci, who studied the Phoenix,[36] and Cuper, whose masterpiece on elephant symbolism[37] was preceded by a study of pagan cults[38] and a book on Harpocrates,[39] centered their efforts on single themes. Many antiquarians contented themselves with monographs on single items. Aulisio read the hidden meaning of an embossing on a wine filter[40] and was criticized by Menestrier,[41] who had studied the Ephesian Diana and her conventional symbols.[42] It should not be overlooked that the first book on ancient painting,[43] written by Francis Junius at the request of the Earl of Arundel, did not shirk the heraldic devices by which the Greeks and Romans identified their gods and heroes.

The discipline of archaeological study was unified, if not systematized, toward the end of the seventeenth century when Jacques Spon, who had written a history of Geneva and collected his separate antiquarian papers in a *Recherches Cur-*

ieuses, gathered a tentative handbook in which the various forms of investigative endeavor are defined and illustrated by papers reprinted from the works of virtuosi.[44] Great folios edited by Gruter, Gronovius, Sallengre, and Poleni soon appeared to furnish the world with printed and until then unprinted antiquarian treatises; and in 1719-1724, the Abbé Montfaucon issued the fifteen volumes of his *L'Antiquité Expliquée* which summarized the archaeological discoveries of the sixteenth and seventeenth centuries.

Troy, its heroes, and poet were, of course, not forgotten. Feith, Allacci, and other scholars made the life, times, and text of the *Iliad* and *Odyssey* more comprehensible than they had been. The *Tabula Iliadis* was published by Fabretti in 1683[45] with a historical-literary exposition expanded in 1709 by Laurence Beger. The eminent antiquary Cuper published the monument and discoursed on the *Apotheosis Homeri*, a basrelief by Archelous of Priene; and though his exposition was far better than that invented by Athanasius Kircher,[46] it was corrected and improved by Schott,[47] official antiquarian to the King of Prussia. But the allegorical interpretations of the antiquarians, similar in many respects to those of men of letters, can be illustrated by pausing on the *Hieroglyphica sive antiqua schemata gemmarum anularium quaesita moralia, politica, historica, medica, philosophica et sublimiora* of Fortunio Liceti.

Liceti wrote his autobiography in 1634 and published his correspondence with other scholars in 1640. At the age of nineteen, he had written a book on the nature of the soul; hence, after taking his doctorate in the next year, he naturally became Professor of Logic at Pisa. In 1609 he transferred to Padua, succeeding the famous Cremonini as Professor of Philosophy. From here he migrated to Bologna, returning to Padua as Professor of Medicine shortly before his death in 1657. He wrote controversial books on diet, spontaneous generation, and comets, but his antiquarian interests early resulted in a profusely illustrated book on ancient lamps followed by one on rings. The research involved in composing these books undoubtedly led to the *Hieroglyphica*, which was finished in 1653. Sixty etchings of engraved stones are published in this volume dedicated to the illustrious bluestocking, Christine, Queen of Sweden, who is addressed as Minerva, Bellona, Camilla, Penthesilea, Semiramis, Diotima, but more frequently as "virgo." The Swedish female Maecenas is informed that the devices on the gems were improvised to shield philosophical truth from vulgarization. Liceti admits he was not always able to penetrate to their true meaning and that he is, consequently, sometimes audacious; but he reminds his patroness that texts he might have employed for exact expositions have vanished with the passage of time.

Since he was now far too elderly to be engaged with the passion, Liceti prints eight essays—more than a quarter of his volume—on the myths of Eros and the Greek theories of love as graphically expressed by the lapidaries. In his first essay, he comments on a gem displaying three Cupids; in his fifth chapter, he follows the theme of Eros as a warrior. He is impressed by Love as a Weeper, Love quenching his torch, and Love deprived of his dart by Venus. In his second essay of almost thirty folios, he explains a gem depicting Cupid as a boy birdcatcher (Plate II), a juxtaposition of bird and human which has enchanted the imagination of men for two thousand years.

Liceti agrees with Plato and Aristotle that love is a desire to possess the beautiful and that this is the proper desire of the wise man. The youthfulness and the nudity of the Eros on the gem portray the basic simplicity of mind required for this intellectual pursuit. The aspiring nature of rational love is implied by the wings and the uplifted arms and hands—also an old symbol of prudence—of the Cupid, whose primary posture reminds the antiquarian of the contemplative attitude of angels. Certain of Christian undertones in pagan letters, Liceti often finds the true doctrine in these pagan objects. Although it is plain to most beholders that the Eros is intent on snaring the bird with limed reeds, Liceti sees these instruments as two ropes by means of which his winged boy or the "avid intellect" seeks through "seeing" and "hearing" to elevate himself to the bough on which the bird perches.

[11]

As a consequence of his imaginative assumption, he finds the bird, the tree, and the depending cage more than they seem. After an extended discourse on the true meaning of the Homeric moly and and Scriptural trees of the Knowledge of Good and Evil and of Life, Liceti concludes that this tree represents that of Human Wisdom. He identifies it as the laurel which symbolizes knowledge, not imbued by God in men, but secured by labor. The bitter taste of the laurel's leaf is an attribute of this labor. The lapidary has properly added no flowers to the tree, "because the end of human wisdom is bare truth, unpleasant, and sometimes unflattering; only poetry, which has verisimilitude for its end, mixes the useful with the charming." Flowerless, "the tree bears fruit, the unreal fruit of symbol, allegory, and metaphor," the fruit of doctrine or signified wisdom.

The allegorical tree and its symbolic fruit are emphasized by the emblematic bird and the cage. "The little Cupid, who stands for the love of learning, a desire placed in mankind by Nature, attempts to pull himself towards the summit of the ancient tree of Knowledge . . . so that he may be closer to the bird and the cage." The bird is essentially the *word* which Homer had called both "winged" and "birdlike." Liceti considers the possibility that the bird is a swan, but rejects this identification and decides it is a nightingale, the ancient sign of men "conspicuous for learning and eminent in the world of letters." Through their singing, youthful Cupids are instructed. The cage, a prison for birds, symbolizes the book in which the accumulated singing of wise men is preserved. The meaning of the gem can now be epitomized in Liceti's words: "Our little gem shows, under the type of a young Cupid, youth desirous of instruction and eager to rise to the tall top of the ancient tree of knowledge in order to take the melodious nightingale of learning . . . and the cage containing the writings of wise men."[48] To support this explanation, Liceti quotes or refers to the Bible, Galen, Plato, Aristotle, Julius Capitolinus, Diogenes Laertius, Boethius, Lucian, Lactantius, Seneca, Horace, Plotinus, Proclus, and several score other ancient and contemporary nightingales of learning. His interpretation is, consequently, not entirely the product of his own peculiar insights.

Although Liceti brought a great library to the aid of the theme established by the carver of his symbolic gem, he overlooked two essential texts—both Greek—which would have come closer to the true explanation of the obvious theme of "the boy and the bird." The first of these is the second eclogue (sometimes numbered as the fourth) of Bion, and the second, stemming originally from the Orient, was given to the West by St. John Damascene in his account of the conversion and ministry of Joasaph.[49] Since the lapidary who engraved the gem probably had Bion's theme in mind, we may turn first to this poem.

In Bion's eidyllion we are shown a youthful birdcatcher who sees Eros perching in a box tree and attempts to snare the "big bird" with his limed reeds. The bird easily avoids the boy, who, vexed by ill-success, goes to the old farmer "who taught him his art" and shows him the bird in hopes of aid. The presbyter smiles and says,

"Refrain from this hunting and stay away from this bird!
Fly far! This is a bad bird! You will be happy
As long as you do not catch him. But when you have man's measure
This thing which now flees and hops away of its own accord
Will come suddenly and perch on your head."

Bion's intent is clear. The boy birdcatcher, who represents the anticipatory aspects of life as opposed by the presbyter, who has, to use the Greek expression, "turned the page of love," is not completely inexperienced. He has gone into the world, the "grove filled with trees," to hunt birds, the symbols of mature amorous activity, carrying with him implements necessary to manhood but not yet adequate for the creature he encounters. He has undoubtedly speculated on the grown-up preoccupation with love; it has come before his eyes, but he does not fully understand it. It is, consequently, like a bird, singing and fluttering, but masked in its true and curious nature by the dense foliage of adult life. Bion's eclogue is, therefore, a sensitive study of how an adolescent and a man impotent with age look forward and backward on sexual experience.

The birdlike figure of winged Eros is visible throughout classical literature. Three hundred years after Bion wrote his poem, Longus asks Philetas, a rural Orpheus, to repeat it to the young lovers, Daphnis and Chloe. This time the presbyter relates his own experience, not in a dense wood, but in a pleasant garden made by his own hands. As a young man, he, too, had come upon Eros and mistaking him for a nightingale attempted his capture. But the bird eluded him and said, "I may not be taken though an eagle or hawk be flown at me; I am not a boy, though I seem to be one, but am older than Saturn and all this universe." He then informed Philetas that when he met his beloved wife, Amaryllis, "I was at her side, but you did not see me." Contrary to Bion, Longus seems to imply that Eros, the feathered thing, reveals himself best to those who, like Daphnis and Chloe, stand on the edge of maturity or to ancients, like Philetas, who have passed beyond the limits of love but remember it as a sunny land.

Bion's theme was rephrased by Ronsard in his "Un enfant dedans un bocage," a poem in which the presbyter is replaced by a sour "vielle mere," a gray-haired Medea, whose cousins are the witchlike inspirers and quellers of love who move menacing through the verses of the Roman elegiac poets. She is patterned on La Vielle of the *Romance of the Rose* or on Villon's Belle Heaulmière. For her, Eros is a cruel conqueror, a maker of martyrs, and she warns the "enfant" to stay off the register of lovers and predicts that someday Love will "trample" not just "perch" on his head. With Ronsard's poem antieroticism begins to creep like a clammy mist into modern literature; nevertheless, it is an emotional mode, the germ of which is found when Socrates, a bearer of limed twigs, interrogated Cephalus about the nature of love. "Never," said that old man, "lament the passing of love, but say with Sophocles: 'Hush to my great delight, I have escaped it and feel free of a despot who was both desperate and angry.'"

Spenser, moved by Ronsard's poem, fashioned his "March

Eclogue" on the same motif. In this poetic episode, it was the father of Willye who assumed the role of the boy birdcatcher and took Cupid in a net spread to catch the crows that devastated his pear tree. Eros bided his time; but after Willye's mother died, the father married a woman whom the young shepherd (who sees love as a kind of animal passion prevalent during the spring mating season) described as "a stepdame eke as whott as fire." In other words, in his second wife, the father who had insulted love has taken Ronsard's "vielle mere" or Dido's witch of Atlas for a bride. But the central victim of Spenser's poem is Thomalin, the sensitive religious shepherd of the "July Eclogue."

In the "March Ecologue," Thomalin has like Bion's boy gone into the wood, the field of life; he is no boy, but an aggressive hunter, and seeing the bush move, he knows it is not a nightingale but rather "faerie feend, or snake." When the god shines forth, he knows whom he faces. There is no question of catching the bird, or securing a specimen for his aviary. He discharges his arrows, and once they are exhausted, he hurls stones. His purpose is clear; he will avenge the "martyrs of love" and shoot Eros down. But Eros cannot be subdued; he looses an arrow in turn which strikes Thomalin, not in the heart, but in the heel. The wounding of Thomalin would be a mystery to us if Spenser's glossator, "E. K.," had not annotated it with an allegorical explanation of the wounding of Achilles. The head of the arrow cut those veins, he writes, that lead to the "previe partes" and then "the partie straighte becommeth cold and unfruitful." With one pull of his bowstring, Eros changes Thomalin, a somewhat older hunter than Bion's adolescent, but not yet ready for marriage, into an impotent presbyter.[50]

There is no question that in this branch of the "boy and the bird" legend instruction is given by winged Eros to the inquisitive. In the second branch, the theme is more in accord with the pedagogical explanation invented by Liceti. In the Greek original, Barlaam tells Joasaph about a fowler who released a captured nightingale in return for three lessons beneficial to life. The precepts offered by the bird are "Never try to attain the unattainable; never regret past matters; and never believe the unbelievable." The bird, released and safely sheltered in a high tree, informs the fowler "I have inside me a pearl larger than an ostrich egg." When the fowler immediately forgets all the precepts and avariciously tries to lure the bird from the bough, the nightingale points out he is a pure fool so quickly to lose all the benefits of his lesson. "Have you not the sense to see," asks the bird, "that my whole body is not so large as an ostrich egg?" Barlaam does not tell this tale frivolously, but to illustrate the stupidity of pagan idolatry.

As the tale spread like a flood over the Western world and was recited in almost every language, including Old Norwegian, it was sometimes used for a moral purpose. The Philosopher of Petrus Alphonsus' *Disciplina Clericalis* uses it to instruct his Disciple to read everything but not to believe all he reads. In the *Récit d'un Menestrel de Reims*, Archbishop Rigaut of Rouen uses the plight of the trapped bird to comfort a king whose son has died. In the *Scala Celi*, the nightingale is equated with worldly prosperity and the hunter with man panting after wealth or fame, vices to which the precepts can be piously adjusted. The *Gesta Romanorum* follows this interpretation of the *Scala*, but also equates the sweet-singing nightingale with Christ and finds in his utterances parallels to the bird's three advices. Most other recensions closely follow the original Greek text although the species of bird and its secret gem are sometimes different. In the *Lai d'Oiselet* there is superb revision. The garden in which the bird dwells is represented as the former delight of a knight whose feckless heir had sold it to a *vilain*; nevertheless, the bird still sang her song about the duty man owes God, who is also Love, a love upheld by loyalty, courtesy, and honor. When she sees the new possessor of the garden, the annoyed nightingale praises the knights and ladies once her auditors and so enrages the evil-minded, covetous *vilain* that he traps her. Escaping by the traditional ruse, she leaves the garden, which immediately decays and vanishes as a magic garden should.

The version of the fable best known in England was "The Churl and the Bird," a poem usually assumed to be Lydgate's, which the poet admits is "out of the Frenssh." The English churl has naturally made himself a fine garden with alleys and streams; in the midst of it is a laurel tree in which a bird with feathers brighter than gold sings a heavenly melody at dawn and sunset. Trapping the bird, the churl puts it in a cage so he can better hear the singing; but the bird quickly informs him that even if the cage were of gold, beryl, and crystal, captives sing no songs. The churl responds to this ultimatum by informing the bird that unless it sings, he will take it to his kitchen, pull off its feathers, and roast and bake it for his dinner. The bird offers to exchange its wisdom for freedom, is released, describes the jacinth in its entrails with an extensively erudite lecture on precious stones, and finally makes sport of the churl. The poet concludes by advising his readers to take the advice of the bird seriously.

In all these poetic versions man is instructed, as Liceti supposed, by birds. The boy birdcatcher of Bion has exchanged places in Liceti's gem design with Eros himself, but the admonitory relationship between the creature of the skies and earthbound mortals is retained and extended. As we move through Western literature, we find the motif of "the boy and the bird" repeated with nuances. The boy Wordsworth learns about the unsubstantial nature of a world made real only in youth's "golden time" when he hears the cuckoo call. The young poet Shelley takes metaphors from the song of a Platonic skylark that knows more of death "than we mortals dream." Keats recognizes the eternity of art as opposed to the ephemerality of the artist as the nightingale pours forth its soul "in such an ecstasy." In nineteenth-century America, a boy walking by Paumanok's shore heard the mockingbirds, visitors from Alabama, as first they sang of love, a song that changed into the single refrain of "Death, death, death, death, death."[51] The chanting of the Greek nightingale perched on the bough of Liceti's Tree of Human Wisdom had no better lesson to teach than this.

I now find myself in recent times, and I could move even closer than I have, but my center of interest is the manner in which the sixteenth and seventeenth centuries understood the literary and artistic remains of their great classical ancestors. The bare surface of things was not satisfactory enough and the adepts felt an inner pressure to seek the hidden meaning, to see beyond the letter, to touch more than the flesh. To support what must first have been a private impulsion begotten by learning, they sought further aid and comfort from their revered predecessors. In this way they suggest to men of our generation a means of penetrating more learnedly and deeply into the works of art and letters they have left us. It is advice which we heed to our own joyful profit.

Notes

1. I, 11, 55; VI, 9, 3.
2. XVII, 17-18; XVIII, 5.
3. XI, 5.
4. *Alexander*, XV.
5. XIII, 1-70.
6. *Pharsalia*, IX, 950-995.
7. *Historia*, ed. I. Bekker (Bonn, 1837), p. 95.
8. T. Wright, ed., *Early Travels to Palestine* (London, 1848), p. 49.
9. *The Bondage and Travels in Europe, Asia, and Africa, 1396-1427*, ed. J. B. Telfer (London, 1889), p. 79.
10. *Travels*, ed. M. Letts (London, 1953), p. 11.
11. *Les Observations de plusieurs singularitez et choses mémorables trouvées en Grèce, Asie, Judée, Egypte, Arabie et autres pays estranges* summarized in the article *Troy* in Hoffman's *Lexicon*, and mentioned by both Sandys and Coryat.
12. Richard Hakluyt, *The Principal Navigations* (London, 1911), I, 12.
13. *Purchas his Pilgrims* (Glasgow, 1905), IX, 413.
14. Hakluyt, VI, 107.
15. Purchas, VIII, 102-105.
16. *Ibid.*, X, 399-412.
17. J. T. Bent, ed., *Voyages and Travels in the Levant* (London, 1893), pp. 49-50.
18. *Opera* (Basel, 1554), p. 731.
19. *De Fortunae Varietate Urbis Romae et de Ruina eiusdem* in A. H. de Sallengre, *Novus Thesaurus Antiquitatum Romanarum* (The Hague, 1716), I.
20. V. Cartari, *Delle Imagini degli Dei delli Antichi* (Padua, 1626), pp. 464-465.
21. *Antiquae Tabulae Marmoreae Solis Effigie, Symbolisque Explicatio* (Paris, 1617).
22. See his mythological addenda to J. Rosinus, *Antiquitatum Romanarum corpus*, beginning with the 1613 impression.
23. *L'Antenore* (Padua, 1625).
24. Pighius was the author of *Mythologiae* ΕΙΣ ΤΑΣ ΩΡΑΣ, *vel in Anni Partes* (Antwerp, 1568); *Themis Dea seu de Lege Divina* (Antwerp, 1568).
25. *Dialogos de las Medallas* (Tarragon, 1587), trans. Dionigi Sada as *Dialoghi intorno alle medaglie, inscrittioni, et altre antichità* (Rome, 1592).
26. *De Nummo Apamensi, Deucalionei diluvii typum exhibente*, in P. Seguin, *Selecta Numismata Antiqua* (Paris, 1655).
27. Foy-Valliant's numismatic publications are too numerous to list, but his method comes clear in *Numismata Selectiora in Aere Maximi Moduli* (Paris, 1694), a selection of coins and medals from the museum of François de Camps.
28. *Dissertation sur le Janus des Anciens et sur quelques Médailles qui ont rapport* (Paris, 1705).
29. *Thesaurus Selectorum Numismatum Antiquorum* (Amsterdam, 1677).
30. *Imperatorum Romanorum Numismata* (Strassburg, 1671).
31. *Osservazioni sopra alcuni Frammenti di Vasi Antichi di Vetro Ornati di Figure, trovati ne'Cimiteri di Roma* (Florence, 1716).
32. *Deorum Simulacra Idola, aliaeque Imagines Aereae*, in Graevius, *Thesaurus*, V.
33. *Exercitationes in Marmoribus Isiacum Romae nuper Effossum* (Rome, 1719).

Don C. Allen

34. *Deorum et Heroum, Virorum et Mulierum Illustrium Imagines Antiquae Illustratae Versibus et Prosa* (Amsterdam, 1715).

35. *Les Sirènes ou Discours sur leur Forme et Figure* (Paris, 1691).

36. *Phoenicis Effigies in Numismatis et Gemma quae in Museo Gualdino Asservantur* (Rome, 1637).

37. *De Elephantis in Nummis Obviis*, in Sallengre, *Novus Thesaurus*, I.

38. *Observationum liber quartus in quo Antiqui Ritus Eruuntur* (Daventry, 1678).

39. *Harpocrates* (Amsterdam, 1676).

40. *De Colo Mayerano*, in Sallengre, III.

41. *De Colo Antiquo ad Cl. V. Mayerum*, in *ibid.*

42. *Symbolica Dianae Ephesiae Statua* (Rome, 1657); an expert in these matters Menestrier wrote many books on blazons, devices, emblems, and decorations.

43. *De Pictura Veterum libri tres* (Amsterdam, 1637).

44. *Miscellanea Eruditae Antiquitatis in quibus Marmora, Statuae, Musiva, Toreumata, Gemmae, Numismata . . . aliisque Antiquorum Monumentorum . . . referuntur ac illustrantur* (Lyons, 1685).

45. *De Columna Traiani Syntagma* (Rome, 1683), pp. 315-384.

46. *Latium* (Amsterdam, 1671), pp. 81-85.

47. *Explication Nouvelle de l'Apothéose d'Homère* (Amsterdam, 1714).

48. *Hieroglyphica sive antiqua schemata gemmarum anularium quaesita moralia, politica, historica, medica, philosophica, et sublimiora omnigenam eruditionum, et altiorum sapientiam attingentia, diligenter explicata* (Padua, 1663), pp. 38-76.

49. *Barlaam and Joasaph*, trans. G. R. Woodward and H. Mattingly (London, 1914), X, 79-81. The history of the transmission of the story of the boy and the nightingale has been traced with reprinted texts by Gaston Paris, *Légendes du Moyen Age* (Paris, 1903), pp. 225-291, and Franz Tyroller, *Die Fabel von dem Mann und dem Vogel in ihrer Verbreitung in der Weltliteratur* (Berlin, 1912). A more recent bibliographical history and text is found in Jean Sonet, *Le Roman de Barlaam et Josaphat* (2 vols.; Namur and Paris, 1949, 1950).

50. D. C. Allen, *Image and Meaning* (Baltimore, 1968), pp. 1-19.

51. Leo Spitzer, "Explication de Texte Applied to Walt Whitman's Poem 'Out of the Cradle Endlessly Rocking,'" *ELH*, XVI (1949), 229-249.

Ancient Books and the Biblical Texts

Kenneth Willis Clark
Duke University

The Lord God did not speak Hebrew to Jeremiah, nor did he speak Greek to John of Patmos; though perhaps it would be quite as true to say that God knows all languages and has always spoken to any prophet in his own tongue. God's Word to Jeremiah was recorded in Hebrew words, and his Word to John was recorded in Greek words. However God may reveal truth to a prophetic mind, the proclamation of that truth in turn to God's people must use the words of human language. Although God's Word may transcend all human language, the prophet's message must be transmitted in the particular language of his own time and place.

This is a gnomic truth that underlies man's historic problem: How may a man recognize the Word of God? How may a mortal distinguish divine truth? How may a man identify a true spokesman for God? In which historic documents may the Word of God be found? Is there a common inspiration in all the sacred scriptures of men: the Bhagavadgita, the Torah, the Bible, the Koran? All these questions may converge for us in the one immediate question: Wherein lies the authority of the Christian's Bible?

Prophets have not always recorded the revelation of a divine message; indeed, most religions of history have had no written word. The ancient prophet was the religious counterpart of the medieval troubador, as an itinerant singer of divine songs implanting them in the memory of his hearers. The oldest religious texts extant, from Egypt and Babylonia, reach back beyond 3000 B.C.; and the oldest Semitic writings are the proto-Sinaitic inscriptions in the peninsula of Sinai, before the time of Moses. The first substantial religious literature recorded among the Hebrews comes from the major prophets of the eighth and seventh centuries, and all the books of the Old Testament were written in the following six hundred years. However, the oldest complete copy of the Hebrew Old Testament in existence today is a medieval manuscript now in a synagogue in Aleppo having been copied near the end of the ninth century, which leaves a gap of 1150-1650 years since the original composition of the books.[1] It is true that for us the written word does come much closer in time to the autographs, because the original Hebrew documents were translated for Greek-speaking Jews in Egypt well before the Christian era, and copies of this Greek text nearly complete are now again extant from as early as the fourth century, which is five hundred years earlier than our Hebrew witness.[2] The case is similar for the Greek writings of the New Testament, since the oldest complete copies upon which we have relied come from the fourth century and therefore are centuries later than the original compositions.[3]

I

When man commits an inspired message to record he gives it explicit form and limit. The problem of authority then pertains especially to his written Bible, which for him is the Word of God complete and final and true. The man with a Bible affirms that God has spoken to him therein as he has not spoken elsewhere. He affirms that a divine rule or canon of truth has tested and selected the contents. Yet in the Judaeo-Christian tradition these basic affirmations have often been disturbed by debate and disagreement. Which authors, which books may be considered truly inspired? Is Esther the equal of Deuteronomy? Is the Epistle of James the equal of the Gospel of John? Are the prophets as authoritative as Moses; or Paul, as the Evangelists? Is the Word of God better revealed in the Old or New Testament? Indeed, why should there be an "old covenant" and a "new covenant?" Such questions assume sharp pointedness when the sacred word is put in writing.

We may well recall the historical expansion of the Christian Bible. Its earliest limits were the five books of Moses, the Torah, and it contained nothing more as late as 200 B.C. It was next enlarged by the addition of the Corpus of the Prophets, though the Samaritans would have none of this (and never have, to this day). The Jews themselves held the Torah and Prophets on different levels of authority, considering the Prophets merely as interpreters of the Law. Furthermore, Pharisaic Judaism supplemented the Book with an oral tradition whereas Sadducees insisted upon exclusive adherence to the Book.

The Christian movement had already grown beyond its "apostolic age" when Judaism once again enlarged the Bible by adding the Writings, yet on a subordinate level of authority. All this Jewish scripture was accepted by Christians although it was relegated to a secondary position as an "old covenant" when Christian writers recorded the "new covenant." Even within the New Testament the books were accorded different degrees of authority. The Gospels of John and Matthew were held to be superior to those of Luke and Mark. The four Gospels were exalted above the letters of Paul. The Apocalypse of John was doubtfully accepted, and never by the Syrian Church. The Shepherd of Hermas was barely rejected, although accepted for some time in the Egyptian Church. Manuscript copies of the New Testament surviving today show considerable variety in their contents, especially within the first five centuries, and such variety persists in different branches of the Church even today.

Another result of recording the Word of God in a book is that it raises the question of scribal accuracy. If we are to understand what God would say to man through the prophet, the prophet's message must be carefully expressed and the reader is then required to interpret the written phrase in order to capture the divine idea.

At this point we come to the fundamental task of the textual critic, whose responsibility is to preserve or to recover the exact textual expression, of the prophet or of the evangelist. When a prophetic message is committed to writing, the book

[23]

takes on great significance as its medium. The very form and limitation of this physical medium must be studied and understood because the textual transmission is affected by it. Today we think of a book as a volume of printed pages in a neat binding containing in one unit a complete text, with duplicate copies on all hands. But ancient writers never had such an instrument, and this circumstance had critical results for the text recorded. The earliest materials used by the Hebrews were durable stone and baked clay tablets. Inscriptions on stone were difficult to accomplish and were intended for the preservation of brief texts only. Certainly they were not portable nor suited for dissemination, especially among nomadic and illiterate Hebrews. The clay tablets were more easily inscribed (before the baking) and more readily transportable, but these were not suitable for extended text nor as durable as a stone inscription. It seems most probable that when the Hebrew prophet's message and the legal codes were first recorded in Palestine they were inscribed on rolls of crude leather, like certain of the Dead Sea scrolls rediscovered only in this generation. The Dead Sea Isaiah scroll is twenty-four feet long, and the prophecy of Jeremiah would be of equal length, while that of Ezekiel is shorter. A seventeenth-century roll of the five books of Torah, in the library of Duke University is seventy feet long. It is therefore clear that the ancient leather roll could well accommodate a lengthy single document, and it is probable that each of the Old Testament writings was first recorded alone, on its own leather roll.

With New Testament times conditions were different. Stone inscriptions belong to rock country, clay tablets belong to the Tigris-Euphrates valley, leather belongs to pastoral country, and papyrus belongs to Egypt. But in early Christian times, papyrus was exported as the paper of the Mediterranean world. There is no doubt that Paul wrote his letters on papyrus rolls, and little question that the papyrus roll was used originally for each separate Gospel, for the Apocalypse, and for all the later New Testament documents; and consequently these were subject to the vicissitudes of papyrus.[4] Except for a few single "books" or fragments of the Old Testament text we must still rely upon the complete Hebrew codices of the ninth and tenth centuries. The oldest self-dated Hebrew manuscript, which contains only the Later Prophets, was written in A.D. 916, and is today in Leningrad (MS B 3). Although the original Hebrew witness is much to be preferred, the Greek translation is here an important source because its extant copies are five centuries older and therefore partially bridge the gap.

Of the New Testament also all original papyrus autographs have perished, and it was not until the late nineteenth century (1877) that continuous finds of early papyrus text began to be made in Egypt.[5] We do know that in the ninth century Irish scholars in European monasteries produced fresh copies of the Greek New Testament, several of which survive today.[6] In the Byzantine East or the Medieval West the New Testament was consulted either in Greek or in translation in copies of the tenth century or later. It is surprising to note that hundreds of Greek texts surviving today were used and even copied in institutions of the West as early as the Medieval centuries, thus testifying to the widespread use of the Greek language throughout the Middle Ages. It was these later Byzantine texts which, though corrupted by time and scribe, served later as exemplars in format and text for the first printed editions; and therefore the press served to establish the long hiatus between the lost primitive text and the later traditional forms. No Byzantine copy was ever made without alteration of its exemplar, great or small. Of course unintentional scribal changes were inevitable, but sheer error constitutes only a small proportion of change. It was quite deliberate that the scribe-theologian took the opportunity to correct, improve, or clarify his text. The ancient manuscripts preserved in our libraries today without exception exhibit this phenomenon of change and difference, and it is therefore a safe conclusion that similar change has occurred between the lost autographs and the earliest surviving copies now available to us.

The scribe often considered himself more an editor and reviser. No document was ever copyrighted, and legal protection was not sought, since authorship yielded no royalties in those days. A book carried no title page, and usually no author's name appeared—except with an epistle or an apocalypse. When thought was once committed to writing it became common property and it might be freely copied in whole or in part, or revised, or compounded with other works. Many parts of the Bible illustrate relationships like this and none better than the revision to which the Gospel of Mark was subjected at the hands of Luke and "Matthew," for here we find some literal copying, and also deliberate revising, reinterpretation, omission, addition, and rearrangement within the later Gospels.

For the New Testament as a whole there survive today some five thousand manuscript copies of various portions, and of all these a few hundred have been examined to date. Within these few hundred copies, it may be estimated that there are found at least three hundred thousand textual differences, small and large. The vast majority of these differences are merely orthographic, but it is the small remainder of variation that is of theological importance. At many points the refinement of interpretation depends upon a meticulous reconstruction of the original text which can be derived only through a critical analysis of the surviving manuscripts.

Again, because Christians recorded the Word in books it became subject to certain other limitations which affected it in important ways. Whether they employed roll or codex, it was not possible at first to gather all documents of the Word into a single book. Each prophecy was an independent unit, like the Dead Sea roll of Isaiah, or of Habakkuk. Each Gospel first circulated separately and locally. The first collections gathered were comparatively small, like the five books of Moses, or the four Gospels, or the letters of Paul. All these small collections appeared by the third century, and the first collection of the whole Bible appeared in the fourth century, written in Greek, and in Egypt. When first the Christians sought to decide upon a canon they did not accomplish this by copying the selected documents in one book. The first canon of scripture was merely a list, and its component parts were still separate rolls or codices in circulation. If one wished to collect canonical scripture, he must gather a big armful of scrolls. Whereas with us a one-volume Bible is a strong psychological argument for a fixed canon of authoritative documents, in the early centuries the opposite condition made all the easier the varieties of opinion on the canon. As long as man relied upon the hand-written book it was rare to find in a single volume a complete Bible, or even a complete Testament. The Torah, the Prophets, the Gospels, and Pauline letters, each group continued to circulate separately. Especially the Psalter and the Apocalypse of John were usually copied alone. This bibliographical condition had its effect upon the usage and textual preservation of all the documents. It meant that not all the parts of the Bible were subjected to the same experience, to the same circulation, to the same textual influences, or to the same scribal interpretations.

Such are the vicissitudes to which the divine Word is subject when it assumes written form, as a book. All the human conditions here briefly described are relevant to the general human-divine relationship, and a true conception of the Bible must take all this into account. God's Word is revealed through the prophet, transmitted by the scribe, recovered and refined by the textual critic, interpreted by the theologian, and proclaimed by the preacher, for the life of the people.

II

Against this background let us observe how the Christian Scripture was transmitted before the Reformation. The Bible of the first Christians consisted only of the Torah (i.e., the Pentateuch) and the writings of the Prophets. When Jesus urges the "Golden Rule" (Matt. 7:12) he explains: "This is the Law and the Prophets." Paul also, in his letter to the Romans (3:21), points out that "the Law and the Prophets bear witness" to the righteousness of God. These constituted the Scripture of the Jews at that time, for the Pentateuch had reached its final form about 400 B.C. (shortly before the Samaritan schism), and the selected writings of the Prophets had

[27]

formally been canonized about 200 B.C. But the classical Hebrew language had given place to the colloquial Aramaic and Greek before the turn of the era. In Palestinian synagogues the Hebrew Scriptures were translated into colloquial Aramaic, although this remained an oral form for several generations, until about 100 B.C. (cf. Neh. 8:1-8). However, for Greek-speaking Jews the Law and the Prophets were gradually turned into formal Greek translation by 100 B.C., and this is the form that later dominated in the Christian churches also. Old Testament quotations that were utilized in the first Christian writings clearly show their derivation from this Greek translation, or Septuagint. When Jewish authorities extended the canon about A.D. 90 to include their final group, called simply the Writings, Christians accepted these as well. But it was not until the fourth century that Christians settled upon the contents of a New Testament canon to be added to the inherited Jewish Bible.[7]

The preservation of the Hebrew Old Testament was long the function of Jewish scholars exclusively. A highly important factor bearing upon the authoritative text is the circumstance that Hebrew words were spelled with consonants only and the vowel qualities omitted. This gave rise to many points of ambiguous sense and of variant interpretation. About A.D. 600-900 the Old Testament text was subjected to a complete revision which has since been authoritative for both Jews and Christians. We refer especially to the school of Palestinian Jewish scholars known as the Masoretes. At this time the vowel qualities were written in, by a system of "pointing"; though medieval Jews were assured that the ancient prophet Ezra had conferred this interpretation of the original Mosaic revelation. So thorough and influential was the work of the Masoretes that they instituted a new era for the Old Testament text, with the result that copies of the pre-Masoretic form were completely lost—until 1947. It is true that the Masorete scholars used such earlier information as was available to them. They knew the Babylonian Targums, or Aramaic translations, which had grown up and had assumed literary form before the turn of the era. They had access to the vast library of Talmudic commentary and are credited with scholarly judgment in its use. It is nevertheless true that they cut the Hebrew Old Testament away from its literary roots and thereby magnified the difficulties of the textual critic who would seek to recover an original text. The Old Testament today in the hands of Jews and Christians is substantially that of the medieval Masoretic scholars.

To this day handwritten copies on parchment rolls are produced for use in the synagogues. No document known to literature has been copied with more meticulous fidelity, with the result that for all the large number of manuscripts in existence relatively few differences have been found.[8] But it is the Masoretic text which all these manuscripts uniformly attest. This Masoretic text was influential upon all the European translations in the medieval period, and later upon the English King James Version. Its basic text has been subject only to eclectic emendation, in the minute attention of Jewish scholars through the centuries.[9] The results of their studies were crystallized in the first Hebrew Old Testament ever to be printed, the famous Soncino Bible of 1488 (whose 1494 edition was translated into the German by Luther). The earliest Hebrew Old Testament printed by Christians appeared in the 1522 Complutensian Polyglot.[10]

It is important to note that the Eastern Orthodox Church of the Byzantine Empire did not find the Word of God in the Hebrew text. Its speech continued, of course, to be Greek and there was available to it the ancient Greek version. Indeed, we may call this Greek translation the first modern-speech Bible inasmuch as it was made for the large and important Greek-speaking Jewish population in Egypt during the period between 250 and 100 B.C. When this Greek version was adopted by the early Christians (whose primary language was Greek) there followed a series of rival revisions, alternately Jewish and Christian. About A.D. 130 a converted Jew from Pontus by the name of Aquila produced a quite literal translation which was officially adopted by Jews and used in synagogues. A long generation later (about 180-192), the Christians countered with a fresh translation by Theodotion, and because of its excellence in the text of Daniel it there displaced the traditional Greek of the Septuagint in Christian usage.

But the best Greek translation was made by another Jewish proselyte, Symmachus, about A.D. 200.[11] Two centuries later the Latin scholar, Jerome, compared these Greek versions as follows: "Aquila translates word for word, Theodotion differs slightly from the Septuagint, and Symmachus follows the sense." In this comparison one observes the critical factors that require decision, in producing a good translation: shall it be literal, or traditional, or interpretative? As long as the great Byzantine Empire lasted, until the brilliant culture of Constantinople fell before the Saracens in 1453, the authoritative Word of God throughout Eastern Christendom was found in the Greek text, and to this day it remains the official Bible of the Greek Orthodox Church. In the West, both Hebrew and Greek were eclipsed by the official Latin Vulgate, with the result that the Old Testament was consulted neither in its original Hebrew nor in its ancient Greek translation. Only the Reformation was to change this.

III

In the remainder of this presentation we shall speak exclusively of Christianity and the preservation of its unique Scripture. At the outset we must recognize the fact that we know nothing clearly about the text of the New Testament documents earlier than the third century, since we have in hand no earlier text.[12] All of the earliest papyrus or parchment witnesses extant date only from the third and fourth centuries, and furthermore they come exclusively from the Egyptian Christian communities. It is a paradox that while we know least about primitive Christianity in Egypt (as compared with Palestine, Syria, Asia Minor, Greece, or Italy), we know more about the Egyptian text of the New Testament than any other. This earliest text, which we know from manuscripts in hand, was a regional text some distance removed from the activities of Paul and the Evangelists, and from the earliest Asia Minor churches we know. Not a single document in the New Testament canon was written originally in Egypt, unless we accept a minority opinion on the Gospel of John. Yet no extant copy of the Greek New Testament has come into our hands from any other region, prior to A.D. 400. Our third-century papyri from Egypt contain substantial portions of the Gospels and Acts, the Pauline letters, and the Apocalypse of John. From Egyptian Christianity have come also the oldest copies of complete Greek Bibles. But the New Testament canon is not the same in any two of them. Fourth-century Codex Vaticanus has lost its final leaves and therefore we cannot know whether it contained the twenty-seven books we have, which were at that time approved by the influential Athanasius, the Bishop of Alexandria. The contemporary Codex Sinaiticus added at least two more books: the pseudonymous Epistle of Barnabas and the apocalypse known as the Shepherd of Hermas. The slightly later Codex Alexandrinus added a different two: the Epistles of Clement. But as for the text in these three most ancient Bibles we find them standing together in mutual support. Although they do differ somewhat from one another, they unite in witness of a basic form which not unnaturally has been called "Egyptian." But they do differ from third-century texts in papyri more recently discovered, and as yet we cannot say which textual form is the more authentic.

Our problem has become still more complicated, with the further recent discovery that another distinctively different recension was in use in Palestine as early as the third century (the "Caesarean" text). This recension appears in the quotations of Origen of Alexandria—later of Caesarea— about A.D. 200, and it is further attested in numerous manuscripts of scattered origin. Furthermore, from the fifth century there comes a manuscript witness from the West with still another textual type. This manuscript, containing the Four Gospels and the Acts, reveals its general milieu by the fact that it contains in opposite columns both the Greek and a pre-Vulgate Latin. It was probably produced in the bilingual region of

Southern Italy or Sicily. Although its text has been called "Western," it is supported by manuscript witnesses which range all the way from Egypt to Spain.

At the time of the Renaissance all the major biblical texts had settled down into traditional though corrupted forms. The Hebrew Old Testament had assumed the form produced by the Masoretic revisers in the early Middle Ages (600-900). Jewish scholars primarily, rather than Christian, took the initiative for the preservation of the Semitic original, and controlled the dominant form. As for the Greek Septuagint, it had eclipsed all other translations of the Old Testament into Greek, and indeed in the eastern Mediterranean it stood as the authentic text (as it still does in the Greek Orthodox Church today). In the West, the Latin Vulgate Bible derived from Jerome had displaced all earlier recensions, both in the Latin and in all other early versions. This Vulgate text had been repeatedly revised critically until the sixteenth-century Council of Trent (1545-1563) and the subsequent edict by Pope Clement VIII in 1592 which established its unique and final supremacy.[13] The conservative character of the Clementine Vulgate has been described by the late Cardinal Bea: "In the case of a text of a certain doctrinal importance, the translators preferred the safer way, i.e., preserving substantially that meaning which had been accepted in the Church for centuries." The contents of the Vulgate were expanded beyond the Hebrew canon, because the Latin followed rather the Greek Septuagint in including as canonical the books which are otherwise known as "apocryphal"; and therefore Western Christianity used this larger Bible. It was this Vulgate translation which in turn became the basis for all the first translations in the European languages, including the English of Wyclif.

The Greek New Testament also became stereotyped by A.D. 600, obscuring all the primitive recensions. Its Byzantine ecclesiastical text was repeated by countless scribes, for use throughout the Orthodox Church. It was employed also by Western scholars, as well as sixteenth-century printers who gave it the widest dissemination. The initial translation of the New

Testament into Syriac in the second century was displaced by a popular traditional form known as the "peshitta" (meaning "vulgate"). Even the Coptic translation that was first produced in Christian communities of upper Egypt about A.D. 200 came to be dominated by the later Bohairic dialect of the northern Delta. Such was the general state of the biblical text as late as mid-Renaissance, about A.D. 1500.

This textual situation which developed and prevailed down to the Renaissance is delineated more sharply when we draw the contrast with our own day. Only twenty years ago, caves by the Dead Sea yielded Hebrew Old Testament texts pre-Christian in date (as early as 250 B.C.). These texts were even pre-Septuagint, and for the first time offered to us a Hebrew attestation that is prior to the earliest Greek witnesses. Furthermore, they were pre-Masoretic, thus exposing an original Hebrew before the Masoretic process of revision. Quite sensational is the recovery of a copy of the Book of Daniel from the second century B.C., approximately fifty years after its composition!

As for the Greek Old Testament, our times are favored by the discovery of papyrus copies of the Septuagint version from the third century, which now may be compared with three well-known codices of the fourth and fifth centuries hitherto available in the Vatican and the British Museum. Even from the B.C. period there are several small fragments, including a bit of Deuteronomy now in the John Rylands Library which was recovered from mummy wrappings of about 150 B.C. Also of the other rival Greek translations which we have earlier mentioned, fragments were newly discovered about the beginning of this century.

For the New Testament, we are now in possession of a number of pre-Vulgate Latin texts which cut back beyond Jerome's editorial product and reveal the characteristic text of the Latin version during its first two centuries. Likewise, we have become possessed only in the last generations of copies of the pre-Peshitta Syriac which antedate the traditional recension continuing in use even today in the Syrian Church. These primitive texts were produced about A.D. 400 and are now the sole witness to the original Syriac translation of about A.D. 200.

Far up the Nile River, near Assiout, copies of the Coptic text of the Gospel of John have been unearthed in recent decades, which were produced as early as the fourth century, about two hundred years after that translation was first made from the original Greek. All three of these versions—Latin, Syriac, Coptic—originated no later than A.D. 200; therefore they offer today persuasive testimony as to the primitive Greek text on which they were based.

Nevertheless, it remains true that Greek manuscripts will always bear the primary witness in the recovery and the reconstruction of the original text of the Greek New Testament. Fortunately, in this very generation sensational acquisitions have occurred. In a private library in Dublin (A. Chester Beatty) are to be seen three papyrus codices (P45, P46, P47), all from the third century, with the text of the Gospels, the Book of Acts, the Apocalypse of John, and the earliest extant corpus of the Epistles of Paul.[14] When these were edited and made accessible to all, thirty years ago, they were then our first and only textual witnesses as early as the third century. Another private library, in Geneva (Martin Bodmer), in recent years revealed and published sensational finds. First, in 1956 there was edited a papyrus copy containing only the Gospel of John separately (P66), judged according to the handwriting to have been written about A.D. 200, approximately a century after the original composition. Yet again, in 1961 there appeared a papyrus copy of the Gospels of Luke and John (P75), possibly produced in the last years of the second century in Egypt. Still another third-century papyrus has come from the Bodmer Library, with the text of the Epistles of Peter and Jude. The earliest surviving text of any part of the Greek New Testament is a tiny papyrus fragment containing John 18:30-38, judged palaeographically to have been copied about A.D. 125 in Egypt, nearly contemporary with the autograph itself.

This summary of textual opportunity today, both realized and potential, is in sharp contrast with the situation of a bright

Renaissance five hundred years ago. The transmission of the biblical text through the first fifteen centuries of the Christian era served only to bring it to a precritical traditional form, in all the variety of the ancient languages. Uncritical texts therefore were basic to the first modern-speech translations which appeared throughout Europe in the thirteenth and fourteenth centuries. When the printing press in its first century produced vernacular Bibles in all the languages of Europe (including English), these were all translated from the current traditional uncritical bases.

The critical period of textual research as applied to the biblical text has taken place subsequent to the Renaissance, and most effectively in the last two centuries. The scholar of the Middle Ages and the Renaissance lacked the initiative and the motivation to consult the old texts, although we are now aware that some ancient copies even then existed in monastic isolation. He could not have distinguished the various recensions of the text, nor could he have known the course of transmission through which the text had passed. In our time there continue to be fresh discoveries of ever older sources which by far antedate that age of tradition, and these have spurred textual scholarship to the recovery of more critical and more trustworthy texts in original Hebrew and Greek, as well as in the primitive translations into Latin, Syriac, and Coptic. In turn, this has resulted in a spate of superior vernacular versions, including an ever lengthening series of modern translations in English reflecting the critical qualities of an improved base. These translations set off in contrast the first efforts of the Medieval Age, when monks and scholars produced conservative commentaries based on static texts, honoring above all the authority of tradition.

Notes

1. The oldest extant manuscript copies of the Hebrew Old Testament are: Cairo, Karaite Synagogue, A.D. 895, containing the Prophets, written in Tiberias (Palestine) by Moshe ben Asher; and Aleppo, Synagogue of the Sephardim, the oldest copy we possess of the entire Old Testament, from about A.D. 900. In the British Museum, Or. 4445 contains the Torah (or Pentateuch) and also is judged to date about A.D. 900. The Leningrad Public Library possesses (MS B 3) the Later Prophets, copied in A.D. 916; and (B 19a) the entire Old Testament, copied in A.D. 1008. With the discovery after 1947 of the Qumran library certain Old Testament books (Isa., Hab., Pss., Lev.) and portions of books, in the Hebrew, derive from a thousand years earlier.

2. This Greek translation, known as the Septuagint, survives in largely complete text in the parchment Codices Vaticanus and Sinaiticus (since 1933 in the British Museum). A few fragments survive from the pre-Christian period.

3. The major sources heretofore have been the Codices Vaticanus and Sinaiticus (complete Greek Bibles). In this very generation substantial portions of the Greek New Testament (e.g. John, Luke, Paul) have been acquired from Egypt, written there by third-century scribes.

4. The length of a papyrus roll necessary for any "book" would vary with its width and the scribal style, and yet the typical scribe was economical of costly space. An original New Testament roll would extend between thirty feet (Matt. or Luke or Acts) and fifteen feet (General Epistles or the Apocalypse)—the usual limits for Greek literary rolls.

5. Discoveries in Egypt through the past century attest the use of papyrus rolls for a thousand years (300 B.C.–A.D. 700), with the highest incidence of modern survival about A.D. 300. The earliest codex or leaf-book consisted of papyrus sheets, and is illustrated today by Christian books as early as A.D. 200.

6. Irish monks produced Codex Sangallensis, a Greek text of the Gospels with Latin interlinear readings, which still remains in the Stiftsbibliothek of St. Gallen. Another portion of the same manuscript is Codex Boernerianus of the Pauline Epistles, which is now in the Landesbibliothek in Dresden. To this text, Codex Augiensis now at Reichenau bears close resemblance, thus pointing to a common exemplar; and all three copies may be attributed to St. Gallen monks. Boernerianus (folio 23) has eight lines of Irish in the margin. Also at St. Gallen today are a Lectionary of the Gospels and a fragment of a Four Gospels manuscript. All of these codices derive from the ninth century and apparently from the activity of Irish monks on the Continent, especially in the school of Hartmut.

7. The earliest extant selection of canonical books including both Old Testament and New Testament is that in the Codex Claramontanus; Harnack attributes this list to Egypt about A.D. 300. The Festal Letter of Athanasius in A.D. 367 is the first to settle upon the same content we now possess in the New Testament.

8. Benjamin Kennicott and Giovanni de Rossi, between them, collated the Masoretic text in 1,346 manuscript copies, and reported finding only 1,688 variants.

9. William A. Irwin observes that "we are still very far from the autographs of the Biblical authors (Ira Price, *Ancestry of Our English Bible*, ed. William A. Irwin and Allen P. Wikgren, New York, 1937, p. 32).

10. The first printing of Biblical Hebrew was the Bologna Psalter of 1477 (August 29), an edition of three hundred copies.

11. A portion of this version was discovered in 1897, in a *genizah* (storage room) of a Cairo synagogue.

12. The single exception to this is a tiny Greek papyrus fragment from a mummy wrapping, now preserved in the John Rylands Library (Gr. 457) which papyrologists have dated about A.D. 125. See C. H. Roberts, *An Unpublished Fragment of the Fourth Gospel* (Manchester, 1935).

13. Continual corruption of the Vulgate text caused repeated efforts at revision throughout the medieval period: Cassiodorus in a South Italian monastery (540), Alcuin of York at the Aachen court of Charlemagne (801), Theodulph of Orleans (early 9th c.), Archbishop Lanfranc of Canterbury (11th c.), the Cistercians Abbot Stephen Harding (1109) and Cardinal Nicholas of Manjacoria (1150), and the Victorines of Paris in 1226. A high degree of textual mixture and variance is the characteristic of the eight thousand Vulgate manuscripts surviving from the Middle Ages. Even today, a new "Benedictine edition" of the Vulgate is currently in preparation.

14. Of the Pauline papyrus (P46), thirty of the eighty-six surviving leaves are possessed by the University of Michigan; but the definitive publication in 1936 by Sir Frederic Kenyon included the whole.

Imaginative Authority in Spanish Literature

Otis H. Green
University of Pennsylvania

When we meditate upon the German proverb *Der Mensch ist was er isst*, we find that the second verb—*isst*—has a different meaning according as it is spelled with a double, or with a single *s*. If with a double *s*, the adage falls into the realm of the dieticians: a man is what he *eats*. If, on the other hand, we alter the proverb and give its final verb merely a single *s*, we obtain a Gertrude Steinean "rose-is-a-rose-is-a-rose": a man is what he *is*. Applying this Steinean conception to Spanish literature, we find that it expresses an "accepted idea," an *idée reçue*: Spanish literature *ist was sie ist*. According to the *opinio communis*, the literature of Spain is a secondary literature, credited with having given to the world *Don Quixote* and the picaresque novel, plus some plots transmitted to the rest of Europe by Corneille, Molière, Lesage, Alexandre Dumas, Camus, and Montherlant.

These ideas are especially false in the ordinary critical appraisals of the picaresque novel and of *Don Quixote*. A 1962 example of such inherited critical appraisals is found in a book issued by one of our best university presses, Gilbert Highet's *The Anatomy of Satire*,[1] which groups *Don Quixote* with eight other works (the *Pickwick Papers*, Evelyn Waugh's *Scott-King's Modern Europe*, and six others) in a section entitled "Tales of Travel and Adventure." Furthermore, in his chapter on parody Highet describes *Don Quixote* as a mock-heroic parody intended to ridicule the fantastic romances of chivalry. In both respects Cervantes' intention and achievement were immensely greater. Travel and adventure are but a means to an end, and his condemnations of the romances of derring-do are subservient to a positive aim: to utilize the framework of the old-style novels as a bottle for new wine—as a new *form* which should enable the novelist to plumb and expound, through the speech and the acts of a madman blest with intervals of amazing lucidity, the gist of human experience in a difficult, but also in a moral—and therefore a beautiful—universe.

So we state as our proposition: Spanish literature during its century of greatness is not a secondary literature, but a literature that produced an impressive number of new literary forms—the all-important new forms that Jacques Barzun has called the mark of decisive cultural change: Spanish forms that were admired, copied, and naturalized—some of them—in the rest of Europe. Ernest Martinenche, reviewing many years ago Gustave Reynier's *Le roman réaliste au XVII* siècle,[2] declared that at all times the Spanish leaven was necessary for the renewal of the French imagination. Using several of these newly created forms as building blocks, I hope to structure an argument that will lead us, together, to conclude that the older literature of Spain is a literature of imaginative power. The works chosen are these: Rojas' *La Celestina*; Torres Naharro's *Comedia Serafina*; the anonymous *Lazarillo de Tormes*; Tirso de Molina's *El condenado por desconfiado*; *Don Quixote*; and Gracián's *El Criticón*. These range in date from about 1500 to 1657. From them we shall gather examples of what I have chosen to call "imaginative authority." But I must make more clear just what I mean by these words. I shall define largely by means of examples. First of all, a negative one.

Imaginative authority is a quality found wanting, by reviewers, in Thornton Wilder's *The Eighth Day*—denied to this work because Wilder's dramatic characters are abstractions that do not follow you out of the theater. Wilder, in other words, does not speak with compelling authority. His imagination does not impose itself on ours.

My next example is a positive one, taken from the field of religion. By imaginative authority I mean a power that simply *has* to be recognized, a power akin to the social authority of the saint, the claim of the saint even upon men of genius. Douglas V. Steere has written in a book entitled *On Beginning from Within*:

When the brilliant desert explorer Charles Foucauld, a hero of all France by the age of twenty-seven, came to the Abbé Huvelin's little church and, finding the Abbé in the confessional, asked him to step out for a visit about the condition of his soul, the Abbé quietly told him to enter the confessional, to get down on his knees like the humblest peasant, and to make his confession. The great man obeyed, and out of what broke through there, came one of the most moving religious spirits of the century.[3]

This is not simply the authority of the Roman Catholic Church; it is the authority of an apostle who does not act simply of himself. The authority of the truly creative writer is not dissimilar; he too is the mouthpiece of a reality greater than himself.

This human and literary reality is possessed by Don Quixote in an eminent degree—and here I speak of the Knight of La Mancha as a personage, as a man, reserving for farther on our consideration of the *book* called *Don Quixote*. Of Don Quixote the man William J. Entwistle has written:

He is not defeated, though often cast down. He addresses wantons as ladies, and they act as ladies for the nonce; an innkeeper, a barber, a priest, a peasant are forced into chivalrous roles by his enthusiasm. He compels country gentlemen, nobles, clergymen to reflect seriously upon great themes: public service, the function of culture, the principles of the arts, the duties of government; yet he never states what truth is; in the dialogues between the Knight and Sancho Panza, the problem arises in multifold forms, but the solution is never revealed.[4]

This is imaginative authority, that imposes itself on the great— a duke and duchess, a canon of Toledo—no less than on the lowly and the vile—shepherds, galley slaves.

Behind this mad and lovable character stands his creator, the conceiver of what J. B. Priestley has called "the best idea an author ever had";[5] back of the literary character stands the man of flesh and bone, Miguel de Cervantes. "Let us not be mistaken," Leo Spitzer has written,

the real protagonist of this novel is not Quixote, with his continual misrepresentations of reality; the hero is Cervantes, the artist himself, who combines a critical and illusionist art according to his own free will. From the moment we open the book to the moment we put it down, we are given to understand that an almighty power is directing us, who leads us WHERE HE PLEASES. This narrative is simply one exaltation of the independent mind of man—and of a particularly powerful type of man: the artist.[6]

This Spanish artist, Miguel de Cervantes, exerted from his deathbed, and across two hundred and sixteen years, an authority so strong that it caused Sir Walter Scott, when he lay dying, to ask John Gibson Lockhart to read aloud to him Cervantes' noble farewell to life, to friends, and to the Muses—brave words that we all may read in the prefatory matter of Cervantes' posthumous romance, *Los trabajos de Persiles y Segismunda.*

All of this amounts to imaginative authority. At this point I shall assume that my definition and illustration of this power have become clear; in the remainder of my discourse I shall examine the special literary works already listed, in an endeavor to show in what way their authors possessed this power and used it to achieve their purposes.

Cervantes had antecedents. Numerous examples are present in a work which surely played a part in Cervantes' apprenticeship in the art of writing: *La Celestina,* by Fernando de Rojas, printed a century before *Don Quixote.* Its protagonist, the infamous hag Celestina, lives her own life, both in and out of the pages of Rojas' book. We hear the swish of her dusty skirts across the centuries, just as we hear the winding of Roland's horn in Dante's *Inferno.* Celestina is a bawd, the best in her profession, and more than worthy of the fees she collects and the general esteem in which her city holds her. She, too, has been given *life* by a writer of genius. When she is at last sure that her most recent customer, the wealthy Calisto, is caught in her net, she replies to one who has just remarked that

Calisto is dying of lovesickness: "Yes, he is ill, as we all can see; but he can recover. Whether or not he does so, rests in the hand of this frail old woman: *está en la mano desta flaca vieja.*" The author has given to this infamous but fascinating hag a connection with the dark agents of man's Universal Adversary, but such connection is not needed. The destructive, and the restorative, powers of Celestina are presented in strictly human terms. She accomplishes her ends by overpowering force of character. She has, in other words, convincing poetic authority.

We shall take yet another example of authoritative imagination from this book of Fernando de Rojas. The old bawd is at last dead, dead because she overreached herself in her cunning and excessive greed; dead, because even her force of character cannot accomplish everything. Elicia, her understudy and almost-daughter, is demoralized by the catastrophe, but this state too must end, and her reaction comes at length. The girl expresses her inner and outward recovery in these words that still have power to move us: "I'm going to make a bleach for this hair of mine—its blonde lustre is all faded; and when I've done *that*, I'm going to count my hens; I'm going to make my bed, sweep the street in front of my door, and sprinkle down the dust, as a sign that my grieving is over." Américo Castro observes[7] that the girl's figure here acquires the consistency of life by reason of something *incarnated* into herself, into her street, into her neighborhood. Even to this day, this critic adds, in remote Andalusian towns, at nightfall, women sprinkle water in front of their doorways and, bent over, sweep away the dust, counting their chickens as they sweep. For the year 1500 this re-creation of reality in such a way as to move the emotions is sheer genius.

Bartolomé de Torres Naharro, like Fernando de Rojas, seems a man born before his time. Prior to the recovery of Aristotle's *Poetics* this Spaniard, who died about 1520, anticipated much of that vindication of the power of the imagination which, after the Aristotelian restoration, came to be taken for granted. He divided comedy into two grand divisions: romantic

[42]

comedy, full of *imagined* happenings; and realistic comedy *avant la lettre*—dramatic realism before the term had been thought of. In this latter department, his plays on the recruiting procedures of the Spanish army in Italy, and on the corruption that went on in the management of the houses of the princes of the Church, are remarkable, at this early date. But my concrete example of imaginative authority is taken from Torres Naharro's imaginative and semitragic play called *Comedia Serafina*, based on the folkloric account of a nobleman who puts his wife to death in order that he may contract a more advantageous marriage in accordance with the king's wishes. Torres Naharro replaces the king by a mere father, perhaps because his sense of decorum required that a king should not appear except in a genuine tragedy; but he causes the would-be bigamist to fall into impotent despair at the thought of the contemplated murder: though he kill his wife and join himself to the object of his love, he will not be able to live with the latter, nor with himself: *que conmigo ni con ella no podré tener amor.*

This is the climax of the play, writes Joseph E. Gillet.[8] There has been no actual death, but there need not be. The substitute for death (the doomed lady is saved by a *deus ex machina*) is, for the bigamist, spiritual as against physical punishment, utter confusion, complete loss of reality:

> I am like a fancied thought,
> Like a wind-driven cloud,
> Like the shadow of the rooftops,
> Like a statue carved in salt,
> Like an animal, wild and fierce
> Painted on a whitewashed wall.

This replacing of death by confusion and loss of identity will have a fruitful development in Spain's classic drama of the seventeenth century. Its appearance here, before 1520, constitutes a noteworthy landmark. The poet has made a convincing psychological analysis, and has found authoritative words with which to express it.

The anonymous protopicaresque novel, *The Life of Laza-rillo de Tormes: His Good Fortune and His Adversities,*[9] was composed before 1550, perhaps a fair number of years before. Its title, with its reference to two types of Fortune, is ironical: the only *good* fortune is the financial success achieved, dis-honorably, by the protagonist at the end. This book is as out-standing as *La Celestina* in its ability to strike the reader's sense of reality with genuine poetic shock. Only in recent years have critics penetrated beneath the surface of this story of the dead-ening of a boy's soul by sordid surroundings and social shams.[10] There is an infinitely subtle—and progressive—inversion of values, until the antihero finds what he calls his Fortune as the hanger-on of a certain archpriest in Toledo. The boy, now grown to manhood, marries the priest's concubine, serving as a protective screen, at the same time that he is profitably em-ployed in the priest's commercial ventures.

There is also an infinite subtlety in the anonymous author's use of traditional, folkloristic, and literary motifs to point up a painful social, religious, economic, and psychological reality.

The most poignant feature of this work is that the picaro begins life as a lad essentially of good stuff, worthy of a better fate. Evidently conceived by an author who sympathized with the spirit of the religious reform initiated by Erasmus, this boy is not only Spain's protopicaro; he is the *only* picaro who shows pity.[11] The episode in which he shows it is famous.

Attracted by the impressive appearance of an hidalgo whom he sees, bright and early one happy morning (happy, as the lad interprets the supposedly good omens), Lázaro enters the man's service as a boy-of-all-work, only to make two devastating discoveries: first, the hidalgo is completely impoverished, living as an exile in a strange city because of a supposed affront to his honor; second, even that honor, like the hidalgo himself, is phony: honor is dishonor. One needs his shams to cover the hollowness of his ideas and of his life.

I am leading up to the lad's manifestation of pity, so un-expected in a novel of roguery. You must know, therefore, that the hidalgo has an empty house that he has somehow man-

[44]

aged to rent, that he has a reasonably good suit of clothes and a fair cape, and, also, a most durable toothpick. To his new servant he explains his manner of life, and his abstinence from anything resembling dinner, with a series of lies and pseudo-dietary considerations, after which the boy—having sized up the situation—falls back on his own resources: the social security consisting of some tripe, some bovine knucklebones, and some nubbins of crusty bread that he has received as alms and has been carrying between his shirt and the unwashed skin of his belly.

This treasure he takes out, silently, and begins to eat. The hidalgo, famished, looks on and finally breaks his silence: "How neatly you eat, Lázaro. It makes one want to join you." I continue, utilizing Dámaso Alonso's paraphrase:[12] The ice is broken when the man learns that it is cows' knucklebones that the boy is gnawing. It so happens the cows' feet are the hidalgo's favorite viand. Lázaro, now fully aware of the truth—a shattering truth, but not irremediable, so long as the scraps hold out and others may be had in the street—feels within him a stirring of pity, even of tenderness for this master as hungry as he is—the only master, be it said in his justification, who has treated the boy like a human being. The two at last have found a common bond—their hunger; and each throws up a smoke screen of defense, the one to hide his humiliation in the eyes of a creature infinitely low, the other, in his moment of moral greatness, endeavoring to reduce that humiliation to minimal terms.

But the tale as a whole is not conceived in terms of moral greatness. Lázaro will soon slip to a lower level, and a time will come when the hidalgo will leave the boy in the lurch, disappearing for good and allowing his ex-servant to struggle with his creditors.

Everything in this tale leads up to a pseudojustification—almost a justification—of Lázaro's descent and consent to his own degradation. The subtlety of the foreshadowings has only recently been fully perceived. Yet from the sixteenth century the work has had a remarkable success. The reason is that this is *literature of power,* of a power so great that one knows he is dealing with a classic, even though he lacks an adequate interpretation of the ironies, the turning of white into black. This book is powerful because the author has a compelling imagination—one that speaks in authentic terms to ours.

Let us now look for authoritative imagination in Spain's classical drama. Some thirty years after *Lazarillo de Tormes,* Lope de Vega began his conquest of the Spanish stage, which by the year 1600 was completely his—so completely, indeed, that for two centuries there were few attempts to cast anything into dramatic form except along the lines of his *comedia nueva.* I say *his,* because it was he and not his brilliant predecessor Torres Naharro who imposed this typical form on the Spanish nation.

There is something paradoxical in my use of the word *form* in this connection, for one of the charges leveled against the *comedia nueva* is precisely its formlessness. Yet it was—most certainly—a form, the form *chosen* by Spanish dramatists, and *expected* by generations of theatergoers as the only one acceptable. In one of Lope's plays a character expresses this preference:

> Give me a plot that shows
> Invention, though it sin against "Art,"
> For in this my taste is Spanish . . .

"If we look at the Spanish drama," wrote Joseph E. Gillet, "with an abstracting and subdividing mind, we shall get a logical, but unreal concept of a drama which is, at bottom, primitive and magical."

Lope was fond of quoting Cicero's dictum that comedy is a mirror which reflects "our customs." That is a misstatement if it is thought to mean that the *comedia* is a sort of genre painting, that it is concerned with human doings as against human dreams of the possible and the desirable. But the comedia *is* a mirror, and a remarkable one, if we think of it as a collective enterprise built and resting upon the two great collective ideals of the Spaniards: in the secular sphere, *honor;*

in the religious, *faith*, the Catholic faith. Or rather, the *comedia* represents a technique that uses *many* mirrors. The sense of formlessness that one may get from it derives from the practice of illuminating the central theme of a play by setting up numerous lanterns, each with its intensifying mirror behind it, all of them focused on the play's theme, all of them cooperating in making it effectively understandable.

I shall take as our example a drama by a disciple of Lope who was the most eloquent defender of the master's anti-Aristotelian dramaturgy—the Mercedarian friar Tirso de Molina. I have chosen his great but imperfect play *The Doubter Damned* precisely because it is so far removed from what, today, we consider drama to be. It is, in fact, a dramatic representation, a reduction to visible and auditory form, of the awe-inspiring theological concept of free will as against predestination. It is ideally suited to the theme of the present discourse inasmuch as it shows how the creative imagination can convert *anything* into literature,[13] in exactly the same way that Carlyle said of the true poetic soul that it has only to be struck, and the sound it yields will be music.

The theme of *The Doubter Damned* is the completely sufficient power of God's grace, no matter how mysteriously, how inscrutably, this power works in heaven and on earth.

To achieve his purpose the dramatist has chosen as underpinning two traditional folk tales: one is the story of a sinner who is saved through Divine Grace; the other tells of a supposedly holy hermit who renounces faith when he beholds the salvation of a thief and plunges into despair, determined to enjoy the sin he is predestined to be punished for.

Tirso's main character, Paulo, is more than an argument personified. He is a figure born of Buddhism and adapted by three other religions. His drama possesses human significance apart from its theology: Paulo is a victim of moral ambitions unsanctified by charity which carry him to perversity and crime; he would penetrate the secrets of Heaven, and by Heaven he is crushed. But the main interest of *The Doubter Damned* is theological and cannot be understood apart from Augustinian teaching.

In the opening scene we behold Paulo, who for ten years has mortified his flesh in the desert and who "tempts" God by insisting that he be shown his future destiny (supposedly glorious). Punishing this temerity, God allows the Devil to deceive Paulo, just as Job was tempted by the same enemy of mankind. The Devil (revealed to the audience as such, but adequately disguised as an angel) tells the hermit that he must go to Naples where he will encounter a certain Enrico. Whatever Enrico's fate is, that shall be the fate of Paulo also. (Of course this prophecy, being diabolical, is not carried out: Enrico is saved while Paulo in his despair goes to eternal damnation.)

The poet presents the position of God in all fairness. In order to offset the effects of the diabolical vision, a *genuine* angel is sent disguised as a humble shepherd who descends the mountain weaving a crown intended for the just man, singing, as he goes, of the mercy of God and of the ease with which God pardons repentant sinners. The angel chides Paulo—now a bandit—for his distrust, and proves with arguments that one should never despair of salvation. Paulo hesitates for a moment, wonders whether he has made a terrible mistake, but again falls into his temptation: "Surely both of us must go / To eternal punishment." God has thus extended His hand to the sinner, and the sinner has rejected it by an act of that free will which God gave to all those whom He created in His image.

St. Augustine, in his sermons and his commentaries on the Psalms, has given an exposition of the mental processes of the sinner in the clutches of despair. Once a desperate sinner makes up his mind that nothing can save him, he commits whatever sin appeals to him at the moment; he loses self-control and acts without constraint of anything save his own despair. Believing himself doomed to Hell, he decides to grasp what the world has to offer. Recognizing the evil of his course, he yet wilfully follows it, knowing that he does so freely. (In our play, the robber becomes a murderer.) On the other hand, the sinner who turns his back on despair and heeds God's voice may be regenerated and returned to God's friendship: "When once that voice is heard and believed," wrote St. Augustine, "those who were submerged in that profound abyss emerge therefrom." (In our play, the sinner Enrico hears, understands, and emerges.)

Thus Enrico, for all his wickedness, is never guilty of the sin of presumption which Augustine discusses in his *Tractatus*. Enrico does not assume that God is too merciful to punish the sinner who flouts God's justice. Enrico is humble: God knows him, he says; God knows his end; and whatever that end is to be, God is good. When Enrico is first accosted by Paulo with the greeting "God's name be praised," the malefactor replies: "May His name be praised forever." Enrico, however, is so hardened in crime that he will require the extra gift of *effective* grace:

> May just Heaven punish me,
> For although I *would* repent,
> The power to do so is not in me.

This effective grace is the *extra* gift that saved St. Paul with the violence of a fulmination on the road to Damascus. Enrico's spiritual condition is exactly the same as that of the witch in Cervantes' *Dialogue of the Dogs*: sin has become so ingrained that the witch cannot lift up her hand to God's, though God is extending His hand downward in mercy: yet the witch insists that God is good, and knows what end is reserved for her.

Over and over again, Enrico repeats his confidence in God's goodness and mercy; he even preaches to Paulo, warning him of his guilt of despair. Finally Enrico succeeds in repenting fully and—as the light of understanding and of reason at last dawns for him—he asks the Virgin to tell her Son that he would prefer a thousand deaths to the memory of having offended his Lord; and he cries out: "Oh Lord, have mercy upon me! / More than this I cannot say." Paulo, on the other hand, rejects all thought of salvation: "There's no mercy for such men." As the eternal destiny of the two is made clear, the Judge exclaims: "These are God's mysteries."

It is time to bring this analysis back to its starting point, which was its connection with the theme of the creative, the authoritative imagination. It is that psychological power, and that alone, that has succeeded—in this drama—in converting into *poetry* the aridities of theological abstraction so that even an unbeliever becomes aware that—within the Christian framework—the soul's eternal health or eternal ruin constitutes the mightiest drama of all. To me, much of the power of *The Doubter Damned* stems from the fairness with which the Divine position is set forth. Paulo's soul is infinitely precious to God, and God sends his angel in the tattered robes of an unlearned shepherd to try to convince his erring sheep, while hidden musicians sing:

> God in his infinite mercy
> Cries out to the sinning soul
> That it should beg of His mercy
> What His mercy to none has denied.

There is, therefore, in God's plan for His universe, no such thing as predamnation.

If one asks what has happened, in this drama of souls, to the much vaunted Spanish realism, the answer is simply that Spanish writers employ what we can call realism when it suits their literary purpose to do so, while over all there reigns a higher decorum. Alonso López, the great Aristotelian theoretician, confesses in his *Philosophía antigua poética* of 1596 that when in a dramatic representation he hears slaves or shepherds or other folk of lowly station deliver themselves of lofty and well-reasoned speeches, he takes delight therein, *provided the medium be verse, not prose.*[14] This last requirement has to do with *art as illusion*: the verse is like the frame that sets off a painting from the wall space which it adorns; it provides evidence that the world of the authentically poetic imagination obeys laws unknown to the everyday genre painting composed of the repetitions and wearying comings and goings of our quite ordinary mundane existence, whose language is unmeasured and uncadenced prose.

Cervantes has given us a personal estimate of his literary achievement in a long poem entitled *Journey to Parnassus,* published one year before his death. It is a true estimate: "I am he who in inventive power / Exceeds most others. . . ." He has also left, in *Don Quixote* and in his minor works, statements of his ideas in the field of literary theory—statements which have been gathered up and analyzed with great perception and subtlety by E. C. Riley in his book *Cervantes's Theory of the Novel.*[15]

In his masterwork Cervantes says that the doings of Don Quixote, his adventures and his mishaps as a madman with lucid intervals, should be read and enjoyed either with laughter (*risa*) or with a sense of wonder (*admiración*). In the *Journey to Parnassus,* and elsewhere, he gives various hints as to how we should interpret *laughter* and *wonder.* He does not mean by *laughter* that he, Cervantes, is a comic author and his *Don Quixote* a joke book. In the *Parnassus* he wrote:

> *Yo he dado en el Quijote pasatiempo*
> *Al pecho melancólico y mohino—*
>
> In my *Quixote* I offer kind nepenthe
> To every man of melancholy mind.

To every man of melancholy mind. . . . That is to say that literature, in one of its aspects, is *release from tension*—that it has a therapeutic action which modern aesthetics recognizes as an important part of the function of the arts. And what of *wonder?* This is the Aristotelian and Renaissance doctrine of *admiratio.* The poet should get his poem off the ground, and with it the hearts of his readers: *Sursum corda!* The whole idea is expressed in concentrated form in two lines from an Italian contemporary of Cervantes:

> *È del poeta il far la meraviglia;*
> *Chi non sa far stupir vada alla striglia—*
>
> The poet's only task is to create wonder;
> Who can't, or won't, should go and curry mules.

Cervantes' masterwork, and most of his minor ones, reveal his particularly original method of producing wonder. It consists of reporting, with all the details of modern magical realism, a most extraordinary, even an incredible happening, and then relating the strange event to perfectly natural causes.

The outstanding example is Don Quixote himself, Don Quixote and all his works. His story is one long succession of poetic shocks. As was shown in 1905 by Rafael Salillas (in a book that fell into oblivion);[16] and again in 1939 and 1948 by Father Mauricio Iriarte in his studies on Huarte de San Juan and his book on differential psychology (1575);[17] and by myself in articles published in 1957, 1961, and 1964, as well as in Volume IV of *Spain and the Western Tradition*; and, most recently of all, about 1966 by Nora Kirchner in a doctoral dissertation on Cervantes' psychopathology;[18] as shown by all these researchers, Cervantes entrusted his illuminating ideas on the nature of fiction, and indeed on practically all the subjects beneath the moon, to the mind and to the eloquent lips of his deep-seeing madman, and he did this in the wisest of all possible manners, determining the nature of each *disparate*, of each rash, impulsive, or crazy act, as well as its outcome and its yielding to saner impulses as the hero's overheated brain cooled down—determining all of this by what to him in that century was simple psychological and medical reality.

The result is that we have in *Don Quixote* the first modern critical novel. In one of the chapters of Part II, Cervantes, speaking for himself, tells of his need for self-restraint in this critical activity. Too many episodes, too numerous digressions spoil the tale, and so, though he feels competent to hold forth on any and every subject, and feels a tremendous urge to do so, he has taken discretion as his guide and unity as his goal—for which decision he asks praise both for the things included, and the critical discussions painfully omitted. Many of the latter remain, however, integrated into the narrative with consummate art. "This man can say anything," writes Mark Van Doren in *Don Quixote's Profession*,

short or long; he knows his way, as a genius does, through lab-
yrinths of intellect and language; and there is endless learning at
his command. The slightest object can remind him of vast subjects for discourse: an acorn of the Golden Age, a millpond of the
seven seas. And the final memory may be of a voice, magnificent
not merely for itself but for the mind that inspires it, which one
will not expect to hear again in any book.[19]

So it is that we have the marvelous book that Cervantes has
left us—a romance of chivalry that is really not fabulous, though
full of the craziest events; a book that is wise, intellectually
mature, as exquisite in its golden mellowness as the autumn's
finest apple. So it is that we see incarnated into the lives of
the two protagonists, into their very substance, the things, the
ideas, the problems, the doubts that these two extraordinary
human beings encounter on the dusty roads and in the wretched
inns of La Mancha and Aragon and Catalonia—which is to say,
in their journey through life, theirs and ours.

The moments of poetic shock are legion. Most poignant of
all, it seems to me, is the ending. To Don Quixote himself the
vision from his deathbed—as he sees a brighter world beyond—
is so wonderful that it causes him to cry out with a great shout.

Many have been troubled by this death, with its renuncia-
tion, and by the series of humiliations to which Cervantes subjects his hero in Part II—by the hero's return to his home to die,
supposedly full of hard realism and complete disillusion with
the dreams of worldly glory so long, and so recently, entertained.
This is simply to fail to understand. The humiliations are not a
sign that Cervantes has lost all love for his creature, all faith in
his own life. The humiliations are necessary—according to the
current theories of psychology and medicine—to produce the
cooling emotion of melancholy which, together with brain-re-
frigerating sleep, will restore Don Quixote to his sanity, and thus
end his career as a fame-seeking do-gooder. The author could not
allow his creature to die in his error. Instead, he brings him back
—with perfect naturalness—from his centrifugal and fame-seeking outward journey, along a centripetal path of deep perception
into the nature of another kind of glory, a glory "that fadeth

not away." He brings him, also, to the brink of the silent river beyond which wait the saints. All this I have shown in an article entitled "Reality, Will and Grace in Cervantes," and in the final volume of *Spain and the Western Tradition*. In short, Don Quixote's death is his greatest achievement. It is presented with supreme artistry, with the utmost imaginative authority.

Completeness would require that I include in this lecture an equally detailed interpretation of the last great prose work of Spain's Golden Age, Gracián's *El Criticón*, wherein the author makes the keenest analyses of this mundane world. It tells the life-story of two men who, having patiently and painfully achieved, each of them, his true status as a "person," arrive at the Court of Queen Artemia, who is none other than Knowledge. This is a wondrous journey; I can merely suggest it. In another place I have written:

But not everything is farce in this world of farces. In Chapter X the pilgrims ask the Queen of Equity how they may arrive at the dwelling of her ladyship Happiness. By way of answer the Queen calls her four handmaids (the cardinal virtues), points to the first of them, and says: "This one, who is Justice, will tell you where and how to look; this second one, Prudence, will reveal her to you; with the third, who is Fortitude, you shall reach her; and with the fourth, whose name is Temperance, you will make her yours." At this point there is a harmonious blast of trumpets as a fragrant zephyr begins to stir. The upward magnetic pull of the stars becomes actually perceptible, and the wind, growing stronger, lifts them toward heaven. "He who wishes to know where they stopped must seek them farther on . . ."[20]

He must seek them farther on. . . . Here is another indication, among so many that seem to have been overlooked in the writings of Gracián, that his "essays"—in the sense of *experiments* in the manner of Montaigne—have to do with this mundane, this lowly world, though the great beyond is ever present in the author's mind as the haven where life's little bark comes to rest, where—to revert to abstract language—the confusion gives way to meaning. The play of

Gracián's imagination, in this allegory, is outstanding and authentic.

Thus we have them lined up—the great monuments of Spain's older literature, though with notable omissions. I have surveyed them, obviously, in a religious context. I might feel apologetic about this: What right has the critic to choose a vantage point—like Archimedes' imaginary fulcrum in the sky—from which to view the object of his studies? But in reality the choice is not mine—it was made by the Spaniards themselves, by the authors of these works, who wrote in a religious context. J. Hillis Miller, in an essay entitled "Literature and Religion" in a 1967 book called *The Relations of Literary Study*,[21] points up the methodological problems faced by the critic when the connections of religion and literature are in question. Though there is no golden rule for a happy steering between extremes, there is an attitude toward literary study which will enable one to escape some of the dangers. The critic must be as learned as possible in other disciplines: history, philosophy, theology, the arts, and so on. Nevertheless, the end of literary study is still elucidation of the intrinsic meanings of poems, plays, novels. The proper model for the relation of the elucidator to the work he studies is not that of the scientist to physical objects, but that of one man to another in charity. If the critic approaches the poem with this kind of reverence for its integrity, it will respond to questioning and take its part in that dialogue between reader and work which is the life of literary study.

Notes

1. Princeton, N. J., 1962.
2. Paris, 1914; reviewed by Ernest Martinenche in *Revista de filología española*, II (1915), 82-86.
3. New York, 1943.
4. "The Search for the Heroic Poem," in University of Pennsylvania Bicentennial Conference, *Studies in Civilization* (Philadelphia, 1941), pp. 89-103.
5. *Literature and Western Man* (New York, 1960), p. 49.
6. "Linguistic Perspectivism in the *Don Quijote*," in *Linguistics and Literary History: Essays in Stylistics* (Princeton, N. J., 1948).
7. *"La Celestina" como contienda literaria (Castas y casticismos)* (Madrid, 1965).
8. *"Propalladia" and Other Works of Bartolomé de Torres Naharro*, Vol. IV: *Torres Naharro and the Drama of the Renaissance*, transcribed, edited, and completed by Otis H. Green (Philadelphia, 1961), pp. 484-485, *et alibi*.
9. *La novela picaresca española*, edited with important introduction by Francisco Rico, Vol. I (Barcelona, 1967).
10. Alexander A. Parker, *Literature and the Delinquent: A Study of the Picaresque Novel* (Edinburgh, 1967).
11. Rico, p. lxv.
12. *De los siglos oscuros al de oro* (Madrid, 1958), pp. 227 f.; cited by Rico p. lxv.
13. Otis H. Green, *Spain and the Western Tradition: The Castilian Mind in Literature from "El Cid" to Calderón* (Madison, Wis., 1963-1966), II, 271-276; IV, 51, 253; "Realidad, voluntad y gracia en Cervantes," *Ibérida: Revista de filología*, III (1961), 113-128 (see below); "A Hispanist's Thoughts on *The Anatomy of Satire* (by Gilbert Highet)," *Romance Philology*, XVII (1963), 123-133; "El Licenciado Vidriera: Its Relation to the *Viaje del Parnaso* and the *Examen de ingenios* of Huarte," in *Linguistic and Literary Studies in Honor of Helmut A. Hatzfeld* (Washington, 1964).
14. (3 vols.; Madrid, 1953), II, 183-184.
15. E. C. Riley, *Cervantes's Theory of the Novel* (Oxford, 1962).
16. *Un gran inspirador de Cervantes: Juan Huarte* (Madrid, 1905).
17. Mauricio de Iriarte, *El doctor Huarte de San Juan y su "Examen de ingenios"* (Madrid, 1939, 1948).
18. Nora I. Kirchner, "Don Quijote de la Mancha: A Study in Classical Paranoia" (unpublished dissertation, Illinois State University, Normal, Ill., c. 1966).
19. New York, 1958.
20. Green, *Spain* . . . , IV, 51.
21. James Thorpe, ed., *The Relations of Literary Study: Essays on Interdisciplinary Contributions* (New York, 1967), 125-126.

IV

The Place of Averroes' Commentary on the Poetics in the History of Medieval Criticism

O. B. Hardison
University of North Carolina

Aristotle's *Poetics* was written between 347 and 322 B.C. In view of the prestige which the treatise now enjoys, it often comes as a surprise to the contemporary student of criticism to learn that after Aristotle's death the *Poetics* disappeared almost without trace from the ancient literary scene. Obviously the text must have been copied during the classical and Byzantine periods; otherwise we would have no manuscripts at all. The influence on all later manuscripts of a single source, the eleventh-century manuscript designated Paris 1741, indicates, however, that the stemma of the *Poetics* is relatively uncomplicated. Evidently there was little demand for the work in antiquity. Efforts to reconstruct the history of the text before the eleventh century have produced tenuous, often contradictory results. The same may be said for efforts to trace the influence of the *Poetics* on post-Aristotelian criticism, such as those made by McMahon, Rostagni, and (most recently) C. O. Brink.[1] If Aristotle's *Poetics* had any influence, it was via two or three intermediaries, which, by warping its thought to fit the prevailing assumptions of rhetorical criticism, obliterated just those qualities that are today considered characteristically Aristotelian. The fragmentary essay *On the Poets* appears to have been far more widely known than the *Poetics*, and Theophrastus, Aristotle's pupil and popularizer, had far more influence on later critical thought than his master.

According to the widely accepted view offered by Joel Spingarn in his *History of Literary Criticism in the Renaissance*,[2] the *Poetics* remained almost unknown from the time of its composition until the early sixteenth century. An abortive effort at translation was made by Giorgio Valla in 1498. Ten years later, in 1508, the Greek text, edited by John Lascaris, was issued by Aldus. The volume in which it appeared was entitled *Rhetores Graeci*, a title which indicates that neither Lascaris nor Aldus sensed the fundamental difference between Aristotle's theory of rhetoric and his theory of poetry. The first passable Latin translation of the *Poetics* was made by Alessandro de' Pazzi (Paccius) and published posthumously in 1536. This translation made the *Poetics* available as a subject for university lectures. Thus during the early 1540's we find Bartolomeo Lombardi and later (after Lombardi's death) Vincenzo Maggi lecturing on the *Poetics* at Padua and Ferrara. Finally, in 1548 Francesco Robortello's *Explicationes* was published, and the *Poetics* gradually came to be considered a prescriptive document. "Laws" of art were discovered in it which became the basis of neoclassical criticism. Lodovico Castelvetro's *Poetica d'Aristotele Vulgarizzata*, published in 1570, is the first commentary to offer something like the famous "law" of the three unities. Adulation of the *Poetics* reached its climax in seventeenth-century France—the notorious "quarrel" over Corneille's *Cid* is a case in point—and continued, though with more moderation, in the eighteenth century. Not until the romantic period was the preeminence of the *Poetics* challenged.

This is a useful preliminary view of the history of the *Poetics*. It is still, perhaps, correct in outline; but as more specialized studies have appeared, the need for revision in details has become increasingly apparent. One of the most important errors made by Spingarn is his failure to do justice to the history of the *Poetics* in the Middle Ages. Although he knew that a work purporting to represent Aristotle's theory of poetry was extant as early as the thirteenth century, he apparently did not have firsthand knowledge of this work and had only a vague notion of its background and content. Thanks to the work of David Margoliouth, Jaroslav Tkatsch, Georges Lacombe, and

Bernard Weinberg,[3] we are now in a much better position than Spingarn to trace the history of the *Poetics* and appreciate its significance. The remainder of this paper will concentrate on these two subjects.

I

The version of the *Poetics* that influenced the Middle Ages was not Greek but Arabic. According to the best guesses of Margoliouth and Tkatsch, the source of the Arabic tradition is a Greek manuscript dating before the year 700 and independent of the archetype that is the source of Paris 1741 and its descendents. This manuscript, for example, preserved the word *anonumos* in Chapter I (1474^b9), which is missing in the Greek manuscripts. Around the year 900 the Greek manuscript was translated into Syriac by Isac ibn-Hunain. Fragments of Hunain's translation are preserved in the *Butyrum sapientiae*, a thirteenth-century miscellany of philosophic and other lore compiled by Bishop Gregory Barhebraeus, and in the *Dialogues* of Jacob bar Sakko (d. 1241), and are reprinted by Margoliouth in his *Analecta orientalia ad Poeticam Aristoteleam*.[4] The Syriac translation was, in turn, converted into Arabic around 920 by Abu Bishr. It is available in an edition prepared by Fausto Lasinio (Pisa, 1872) and in a Latin translation forming the appendix of Margoliouth's *Poetics of Aristotle*, published in 1911. It has some significance for the reconstruction of the Greek text, although Margoliouth's extravagant claims almost succeeded in discrediting it entirely. Its interest for the historian of criticism, however, is that its vocabulary departs widely from the Greek. It thus initiated the process of assimilating Aristotle by misinterpretation that continued throughout the Middle Ages.

The next phase in the history of the medieval *Poetics* is the result of the adoption by Arab philosophers of a scheme originally formulated by Alexander of Aphrodisias and other late Greek commentators on Aristotle. According to this scheme, Aristotle divided human knowledge (*scientia*, often translated as "science") into four main branches. First come

[59]

the instrumental sciences of the *Organon*. These are sciences of technique or "faculties," and they have no "content" in the Aristotelian sense of that term. The other three branches, which *do* have content, are the theoretic (including metaphysics, mathematics, astronomy, and physics), the practical (including politics, economics, and ethics), and the productive (including most professions and crafts). It is the *Organon* that is important for present purposes. Today, scholars agree that the *Organon* is made up of six works; namely, *Categories, On Interpretation, Prior* and *Posterior Analytics, Topics,* and *Sophistic Refutations.* To these six books the late Greek commentators and their Arab disciples added the *Rhetoric* and the *Poetics.* The most influential Arab expression of this theory is the *Catalogue of the Sciences* written by Al-farabi in the tenth century. This work was twice translated into Latin during the twelfth century, first by Gerard of Cremona and second by John of Seville.[5] The theory which it proposes may be called the "context theory" of the *Poetics*, since it arises from the context within which Aristotle was thought to have placed his treatise. To include the *Poetics* in the *Organon* is to assert that it is an essay on method, and that the method itself is a "faculty" without "content." Furthermore, since each of the logical faculties was supposed to be distinguished from the others by its use of a unique logical device, the inclusion of *Poetics* in the *Organon* shifted emphasis from "imitation," the key term in the Greek *Poetics*, to the "device" which differentiates poetry from its sister faculties. The result is clearly illustrated in the twelfth-century treatise "On the Division of the Sciences" by Dominicus Gundissalinus,[6] where the parts of the *Organon* are tabulated as follows:

PART	PURPOSE	DEVICE
Categories, On Interpretation, Prior and *Posterior Analytics*	Demonstration	Demonstrative syllogism
Topics	Probable demonstration	Probable (dialectical) syllogism

[60]

Sophistic	Error made to seem truth	False (*errativa*) syllogism
Rhetoric	Persuasion	Enthymeme
Poetic	Imaginative representation	Imaginative (*ymaginativa*) syllogism

This interpretation ignores imitation, plot, characterization, catharsis, and most of the other subjects stressed by Aristotle in favor of an element—the imaginative syllogism—for which the reader of the Greek text will search in vain. It also ignores the moral "purpose" usually attributed to poetry in the Middle Ages, because to bring in moral questions would be to assign a "content" to poetry—in Aristotelian terms, to treat it as a subdivision of "practical science" rather than of the *Organon*. Poetry is "imaginative representation" and its device is "the imaginative syllogism." Gundissalinus does not explain exactly what these terms mean, but their general import is clear enough. "Imaginative representation" is the creation of illusion by means of images, a concept almost antithetical to "imitation." The "imaginative syllogism" is a technique of manipulating language so as to produce the illusion. The term "imaginative" does not mean "of or related to the imagination," but something like "using the figures (or images) of rhetoric." A few scattered comments suggest that Gundissalinus had in mind the figures of exaggeration and understatement, but he leaves the matter somewhat ambiguous.

To return to the Arabic *Poetics*, the next contribution to the tradition after Al-farabi was made by Avicenna (980-1037). Avicenna accepted the idea that the *Poetica* is a logical work and part of the *Organon*. His most important innovation was to divide the *Poetics* into seven sections. This division represents a theory concerning the organization and content of the *Poetics*, and, of course, gives an impression somewhat different from that given by the modern division of the text into twenty-six chapters.

The third and most important Arab student of the *Poetics*

was Averroes (Ibn Roshd, 1120-1198). Averroes is considered the greatest of the Arab philosophers of the Middle Ages, and he is also the Arab philosopher who most deeply influenced the Latin West.[7] During his long and active career he wrote commentaries on all of Aristotle's major works, and all but two of these were translated into Latin during the scholastic renaissance of the thirteenth century. Medieval interest in the *Poetics* must therefore be understood as a by-product of scholasticism, and in particular, that phase of scholasticism which was a self-conscious revolt against the earlier, Platonizing tradition of medieval thought.

Averroes wrote his commentaries in three forms. First there is the "great" commentary, in which he quotes a short passage (lemma) from the source, then discusses it, and then proceeds to the next passage. This, incidentally, is why Dante calls him "Averrois che 'l gran commento feo" in the *Divine Comedy* (*Inf.*, IV, 144). Next, there is the "middle" commentary, in which Averroes cites a passage from Aristotle by a brief identifying phrase or sentence, and then proceeds to discuss the whole section associated with the quotation. Finally, there is the "paraphrase" or "analysis," in which Averroes speaks in his own person, explaining, quoting, and interjecting new ideas, so that a "paraphrase" often amounts to an original essay on an Aristotelian topic.

Averroes treated several of Aristotle's works in more than one form. Commentaries in all three forms exist, for example, for the *Posterior Analytics*, the *Physics*, the *de Caelo*, and the *Metaphysics*. The *Poetics*, however, is treated only once and in the form of the "middle" commentary. This should be kept in mind, because the Latin translation is sometimes misleadingly called a "paraphrase."

The absence of a "great" commentary on the *Poetics* is significant. Averroes remarks frequently that much of what Aristotle says applies to Greek poetry and is irrelevant to the Arabs. In fact, large sections of the *Poetics* were unintelligible to him. He had never read Homer, nor had he seen anything remotely resembling a Greek drama. To make sense of the

Poetics he was forced to interpolate material alien to it, to transpose passages from one section to another, and to omit many passages which the modern reader would consider central. Moreover, he freely substituted references to Arab poetry for the Greek examples provided by Aristotle. His references show a surprising knowledge of Arab poetry from pre-Islamic times to the popular Hispano-Arabic forms of his own day, but they obscure rather than clarify the sense of the original. The product of all this effort is a work which its most loving modern student, Jaroslav Tkatsch, has called "a medley of monstrous misunderstandings and wild fantasies,"[8] but which, for all its limitations, had a significant influence on European criticism.

Two key ideas, both of them foreign to Aristotle, run through Averroes' commentary. The first is the notion derived from Al-farabi and Avicenna that poetry is a branch of logic. The second also owes something to earlier Arab commentaries, but its basic source would seem to be the vocabulary of the Arab translation. This is the idea that poetry can be defined as the art of praise and blame. Praise and blame are rhetorical techniques, explained at length in Books I and III of Aristotle's *Rhetoric*. They are brought into the *Poetics* in Chapter IV, where Aristotle asserts the first two forms of poetry were "lampooning verses" and "praises of famous men." Averroes could understand this theory much better than the complex theory of imitation developed in the first three chapters of the *Poetics*. Better still, it seemed consistent with what he knew of the history of Arab poetry, whose early forms tend heavily to invective and ecomiastic verse. From this apparent point of contact between the *Poetics* and Arab literary tradition, Averroes moved outward to the genres and function of poetry. Not only did poetry originate in praise and blame, its major forms fall into one or the other category. Epic and tragedy are poems of praise; comedy (by which Averroes means satire) is a form of blame; and ode is a mixed form that employs both techniques. Good poets praise good men in order to lead their readers to virtue, while base poets satirize and vituperate evil men and thus warn against vice. This approach, it should be noted, assigns poetry an ethical function and is incompatible (or, at least, hard to reconcile) with the theory that poetry is a branch of logic. Averroes either failed to perceive the conflict or was indifferent to it, for the two theories exist side-by-side in his commentary, and no effort is made to harmonize them.

Whatever the deficiencies of Averroes' interpretation, his commentary began a long European career in 1256, when it was translated into Latin. The translator was a German monk, Hermannus Alemannus, living in Toledo under the patronage of John, Bishop of Burgos.[9] Hermannus had previously translated the middle commentary on the *Nicomachean Ethics* (1240), and his translation of the commentary on the *Poetics* forms a kind of appendix to his translation of the commentary on the *Rhetoric*. He was one of a number of scholars involved in the first phase of the scholastic recovery of Aristotle, which depended on translations from Arabic rather than the Greek originals. In his preface to the commentary on the *Poetics* Hermannus says that he planned to translate the *Poetics* itself into Latin but had to give up because of the difficulty of the vocabulary. His admission shows that the original was just as obscure to a thirteenth-century European as it was to Averroes.

If the *Poetics* was unintelligible to Hermannus and his contemporaries, Averroes was not. Twenty-three manuscripts of the Hermannus translation survive, and it was printed in 1481, thus becoming the first version of Aristotle's literary theory published during the Renaissance.[10] Its compatibility with medieval critical ideas is attested by the fact that in 1278 William of Moerbeke, Bishop of Corinth, made a remarkably accurate translation from the Greek, which was, however, ignored; William's translation exists in only two manuscripts, both dating from the thirteenth century, and it was not printed until 1953.[11] The obvious moral of this tale is that the late Middle Ages was not prepared to assimilate the *Poetics*. On the other hand, Averroes' commentary was easy to assimilate. The distortions which disconcert the modern reader are the very features which made the work intelligible and attractive to the medieval audience. In effect, it enlisted Aristotle in support of the most characteristic (and most un-Aristotelian) features of medieval poetic theory.

A few quotations from the Hermannus translation will illustrate this point. In a preface referring to both the *Rhetoric* and the *Poetics* Hermannus discusses the placing of these works in Aristotle's system of the sciences:

That these two books are part of logic no one will doubt who has read the books of Al-farabi, Avicenna, and Averroes, and various others. Indeed, this is quite obvious from this text itself. Nor can one be excused (as some may think) because of the *Rhetoric* of Marcus Tullius Cicero and the *Ars poetica* of Horace. Tully made rhetoric a part of "civil philosophy" and thoroughly treated it from this point of view. Horace, on the other hand, treated poetry as a part of grammar.[12]

This quite explicitly locates the *Poetics* in the *Organon*. To avoid possible confusion, Hermannus cites the two common rival theories of poetry—first, the theory that considered rhetoric and poetry a part of "civil" philosophy, by which he means "practical" or "moral" philosophy; and second, the theory associating poetry with grammar. The first theory, attributed justifiably to Cicero, is the didactic theory, which considers poetry a device of ethical instruction.[13] It is commonplace in medieval criticism, and both Averroes and Hermannus subscribed to it in practice. In his preface, however, Hermannus takes pains to call attention to the difference between it and the allegedly Aristotelian theory, which emphasizes technique rather than content. The second theory, which Hermannus attributes to Horace, leads to emphasis on the prosodic element of poetry. Classical grammar included the study of syllables and quantity, and hence the study of the various poetic meters. According to the grammarians, the difference between poetry and nonpoetry is the use of meter; and the differences between the various poetic genres are the meters themselves. This inverts the normal relation between form and content. Poetry becomes "heroic," for example, by using dactylic hexameter, and only secondarily by narrating the deeds of noble heroes. In the same way, the essence of elegy is the elegaic distich, of satire and comedy, iambic meter, of the ode, lyric strophes, and so forth. The authors collected by Heinrich Keil in the sixth volume of his *Grammatici Latini*, entitled simply *Scriptores de Arte Metrica*, amply illustrate the grammatical theory.[14] Again, Hermannus explicitly rejects the *ars metrica* in favor of the logical theory attributed to Aristotle and justified by "Al-farabi, Avicenna, Averroes, and various others."

The appropriateness of Hermannus' emphasis on the logical "placement" of poetry is apparent from the first section of the commentary.[15] In Chapter I of the *Poetics* Aristotle discusses imitation and then moves on to consider the differentiation of poetic genres according to means of imitation. The word *imitatio* appears very infrequently in Hermannus. It is replaced by the phrase *sermo imaginativus*, to which *assimilatio* and *representatio* are often added as synonyms. In the following passage, I have translated *imaginativus* as "figurative" and *assimilatio* as "resemblance," although there are no really adequate English equivalents:

Aristotle says. . . . Poetic expression is figurative (*imaginativus*). There are three kinds of figuration and resemblance (*assimilatio*), two simple and the third composed of the first two. One of these simple forms consists of the comparison of one thing to another and its use to exemplify the thing, and this occurs in any language through the expressions proper to it, like *quasi* or *sicut* and similar words, called particles of comparison. . . . And in this art this is called "exchange" [*concambium*]. . . . The second type occurs when the comparison is reversed, as when you say "the sun is like this woman" rather than "this woman is like the sun." And the third kind is compounded from these two.[16]

The definition (here somewhat condensed) is entirely foreign to Aristotle. The justification for it is that the identification of poetry and logic requires "imitation" to be interpreted as the use of a technical device. Gundissalinus called this device the "imaginative syllogism." Averroes and Hermannus are much more explicit. The poetic device is comparison, which is subdivided, with the help of hints in *Poetics*, Chapter XX, into three parts: (1) simile and metaphor, (2) inverted simile and metaphor, and (3) a "mixed" form which should probably be understood as the proportional analogy. The Aristotelian concept of poetry as an imitation of action, human character, and/ or nature is replaced by the concept of poetry as the skillful manipulation of figures of comparison.

This surprising interpretation of imitation had some traceable influence. St. Thomas Aquinas, for example, remarks at the beginning of his commentary on the *Posterior Analytics* that *similitudo*—poetic comparison—is the basic device of poetry.[17] Two centuries later, Savonarola wrote that "without logic no one can be called a poet," and added, "clearly, the syllogism which the Philosopher calls Example is the object of poetic art, just as the enthymeme is the object of rhetoric, induction and the probable syllogism of dialectic, and the syllogism proper the object of the *Prior analytics*."[18] More generally, the notion that poetry is essentially the clever use of figures is certainly compatible with late medieval aureate diction, although it is impossible, so far as I know, to show direct influence.

The relation of poetry to logic continued to be debated until late in the sixteenth century. On the other hand, the theory destined to have the greatest influence on later critics is the one which is dominant in the Averroes commentary. This is the theory of praise and blame. Returning to Averroes' discussion of Chapter I of the *Poetics*, we find that the initial definition of poetry, offered as a quotation from Aristotle himself, is as follows: "Aristotle says: Every poem and all poetic speech are either blame or praise (*aut vituperatio aut laudatio*). And this is evident from examination of poems themselves, especially the poems which are concerned with matters of choice, either honest or base."[19] The passage is, of course, not in the *Poetics*. Like the definition of imitation, it is an interpolation required to reconcile the text with the presuppositions of the commentator. Unlike that definition, however, it has some Aristotelian precedent. Averroes has transposed the notion that the original poetic forms were encomia and lampooning verses from Chapter IV to Chapter I and converted it from an observation about primitive poems to a categorical assertion about poetry in general.

The praise-blame theory was attractive to Averroes for two reasons. First of all, it furnished a point of contact between Arab and Greek poetry. Second, it justified poetry by making it an instrument of moral instruction. These ideas are combined in a comment on Chapter II of the *Poetics,* where, after remarking that the Greeks had many excellent poems of praise, Averroes adds, "Children should be brought up to read those poems which incite and incline one to acts of fortitude and magnificence. In their poems the Arabs treat only these two virtues, although they do not incite to these virtues because they are good in themselves but because they are a means of attaining honor and glory."[20] Averroes is probably thinking of the *quasidah* and is certainly hinting that the native form can be made even more moral than it has traditionally been. Incidentally, this criticism of Arab poets for failing to live up to Aristotle's standards accounts, as we will see, for the last echo of the Averroes commentary in European criticism.

The didactic motive extends throughout the commentary. Consider, for example, the following expansion of Aristotle's discussion of "object of imitation":

Aristotle says: Those who represent and emulate do so in order to induce others to perform certain voluntary acts and to refrain from certain others. Thus the objects of the representation were necessarily virtues or vices. For all action and all character is concerned with one or the other of these two; namely, virtue or vice. Necessarily, then, good and virtuous men represented good and virtuous characters; and base men, vices and depraved characters. And since all resemblance and representation is for the presentation of the proper and improper or base, it is clear that its object is to encourage goodness and refute vice. . . . And from these kinds of men came praise and blame; that is, praise of good men and rebuke of bad ones.[21]

What Aristotle says, of course, is that the object of imitation is action (*praxis*), not virtue or vice. He then adds that actions are performed by agents (*prattontas*) who are of necessity better than, similar to, or worse than ourselves. This is not a moral exhortation but an analytic statement based on the fact that "practical philosophy" is the division of philosophy devoted to the study of human actions, and within this division, the categories of evaluation are goodness and badness. The commentary distorts Aristotle's position in two ways. First, it makes character rather than action the object of imitation and intensifies the moral overtones of this revision by making virtue and vice the specific qualities of character to be imitated. Second, it again transposes the remarks made by Aristotle concerning the earliest poets from Chapter IV to another context.

The exotic combination of additions, transposed passages, and warped interpretations continues in the later sections of the commentary. According to Aristotle, the *Iliad* anticipates tragedy in its seriousness, its sustained plot, and its emphasis on dialogue, while the *Margites* anticipates comedy by dramatizing "the ludicrous" rather than continuing the earlier Greek tradition of personal satire. Because he knew neither Homer nor Greek drama, Averroes failed completely to understand these distinctions. Homer, he says, "established the first principles of these arts, and there was no one before him whose achievement either in praise or blame had anything worth mentioning."[22] Tragedy is defined simply as the *"ars laudandi,"* while comedy is *"ars vituperandi"*—the art of rebuking "not only everything that is bad, but what is despicable and almost beyond cure; that is, what is base and almost worthless."[23] If this not only misses but inverts Aristotle's thoughts about the geniality that Homer introduced into comic tradition, it also wholly ignores the distinction between dramatic and narrative form. We are reminded here of the medieval habit, illustrated in the work of Dante, Lydgate, and Chaucer among others, of referring to narrative poems as "comedies" or "tragedies." Averroes' commentary did not create this misconception but may well have encouraged it. Benvenuto da Imola, for example, found that the Averroes commentary provided just the theory needed to explain the organization of Dante's *Comedy*.

Needless to say, the confusion of the commentary concerning poetic form produces a woefully distorted interpretation of the six "parts" of tragedy listed by Aristotle in *Poetics* VI. Plot becomes *sermo fabularis*; character *consuetudines*, a category that includes both actions and morals; thought becomes *credulitas*; diction *metrum*; song *tonus*; and spectacle something called *consideratio*, by which Averroes seems to mean the gestures and facial expressions used by orators to emphasize their arguments.[24] Equally characteristic, the concepts of probability and necessity are interpreted morally, with the surprising result that the poet is denied the right to create fictions:

And it is evident from what has been said about poetic speeches that representations that are based on lies are not proper to the poet's work. These are called proverbial tales and exempla like those found in the book by Aesop and similar fabulous writings. It is therefore proper for the poet to speak only of things that either are or can be; such things, moreover, as should be desired or spurned. . . . The poet gives names only to things that exist and at times speaks in universals; and therefore the art of poetry is closer to philosophy than the art of proverbial tales.[25]

Again, reversal is treated not as a sudden change in the action of a work but as a shift in poetic technique from praise to blame or vice versa. It is

the representation of the reverse of what is proposed in praise, so that the soul first rejects and despises the thing imitated, and then is changed from this attitude by imitation of what is praiseworthy. Thus, for example, if one should desire to depict good fortune and fortunate men, he should begin by depicting ill fortune and unfortunate men and then suddenly change to depiction of good fortune and men who have it.[26]

An intriguing problem emerges here. If tragedy is "the art of praise" and is intended to incite men to virtue, should it not avoid the disasters that usually overtake the tragic protagonist? Averroes appears to waver. He recognizes the importance of pity and fear, but his example of an ideal tragedy is the story of Abraham, which ends happily. A little later he adds that "certain poets introduce into their tragedies representation of things through which only *admiratio* is intended rather than fear or sorrow."[27] This is the earliest use that I have found of the term *admiratio* in relation to tragedy. In Averroes it is a positive emotion aroused by the moral excellence of those being praised. In the Renaissance it became a key critical term, but was used in two rather different senses. On the one hand, it can mean "admiration" in Averroes' sense. This usage preserves the tradition that tragedy is based on praise and that its figures should be literally admirable. On the other, it can mean something like awe or wonder at the tragic events and is used by didactic critics like Sir Philip Sidney who teach that tragedy shows the awesome fall of great men because of their moral failings.

As a final example of Averroes' misinterpretation of Aristotle, we can turn to his comments on *Poetics* XII, which deals with the Greek terms used to designate the structure of tragedy—parode, episode, stasimon, and the like. Averroes solves the problem by substituting terms from rhetoric:

[Aristotle] mentions in this discussion the parts that are proper to Greek poems. Of these, the parts that are found in Arab poems are three. First comes the part that resembles the exordium of rhetoric. It is the part where the Arabs speak of houses and noble buildings and of ruins and remains. . . . And the second is the praise proper; and the third is the part that is like the rhetorical conclusion. And this third part is usually either an invocation or petition to the man being praised, or a commendatory section praising the valuable poem itself.[28]

This is an outline of the contents of the classic Arabic ode form, the *quasidah*. Its chief significance, however, is its suggestion that the formulas of rhetoric for organizing speeches are equally applicable to literature. This would doubtless have seemed a gratifying confirmation of what many Latin readers of the commentary already believed. The original passage in the

Poetics, conversely, would have been as unintelligible to them as to Averroes.

II

Let us now turn from the Averroes-Hermannus commentary to its influence on subsequent criticism. Two kinds of evidence are available. The first is the history of the manuscripts and editions, and the second, references to the commentary by significant critics.

The bibliographical history of the commentary is complex, but this very complexity testifies to its enduring interest. The twenty-three surviving manuscripts range in time from the thirteenth to the fifteenth century, and in location from Spain and France to England, Italy, and even Poland. The manuscripts[29] fall into two distinct families. The first family is by far the larger. Manuscripts of this family usually contain, in addition to the Averroes-Hermannus commentary, translations of Aristotle's *Politics* and *Rhetoric,* and either the *Ethics* or the *Magna Moralia.* Evidently this family stems from an anthology of Aristotelian works on "practical philosophy" compiled toward the end of the thirteenth century. The inclusion of the commentary on the *Poetics* indicates that the users of the manuscript regarded the work as an exposition of the didactic view of poetry—i.e., that they read it in terms of the praise-blame theory rather than the logical theory.

The second family of manuscripts has in common the fact that the commentary on the *Poetics* is included with works on science and logic. It thus reflects the "context theory" according to which the *Poetics* is a part of the *Organon.* The fact that the manuscripts of this family are in the minority does not mean that the "context theory" is insignificant, but it shows that the didactic view was more attractive to medieval writers. This conclusion is confirmed by the way in which medieval and early renaissance critics used the commentary.

The Hermannus translation was not the only translation of the commentary that circulated during the Middle Ages. In 1337 Todros Todrosi, a Jewish philosopher living near Arles

[72]

in France, translated the Averroes commentary into Hebrew. Several manuscripts of this work are extant, and it became the source for two sixteenth-century Latin translations. That Todrosi also translated Averroes' commentaries on the *Sophistical Refutations* and the *Rhetoric* suggests that he considered the *Poetics* part of the *Organon*.

By the fifteenth century, most of the manuscripts are Italian. This doubtless reflects the migration of Averroists from Paris to Padua and Venice following bitter denunciations of them by St. Thomas Aquinas and his followers. It was at Venice that the Hermannus version was first printed. It appeared in 1481 together with the *Rhetoric* in an edition published by Philipus Venetus. Although not reprinted again in the fifteenth century, it was issued at least five times in the sixteenth, in 1515, 1525, 1556, 1572, and 1600.[30] In addition, two other translations, both from the Hebrew of Todrosi, were issued. The first was made by Abraham de Balmes, a Neapolitan physician. It appeared in 1523, and later as part of the Giunta "Aristotle with Averroes" edition of 1574. The other was made by Jacob Mantinus, physician to Pope Paul III, and appeared in the Giunta "Aristotle" of 1552 and 1562.

The large number of manuscripts, editions, and translations of the Averroes commentary shows that it was read and "in demand" from 1300 to the end of the sixteenth century. Perhaps the most remarkable observation that emerges from this brief review of its history is that Averroes continued to be popular long after the Greek *Poetics* had been edited, translated into Latin and Italian, and minutely analyzed by humanist commentators. We may conclude tentatively that in spite of his failings, Averroes offered a view of poetry that conservative humanists of the sixteenth century were reluctant to abandon.

References to the Averroes commentary begin almost immediately after its translation into Latin. Roger Bacon referred to the translation of "master Hermannus" with qualified approval,[31] and a fourteenth-century manuscript of what appear to be lecture notes on the commentary has recently been discovered by Professor William Boggess of the University of Georgia. So far as I know, however, the first critic to make extensive use of the commentary is Benvenuto da Imola, one of the fourteenth-century commentators on Dante. Benvenuto knew the Hermannus translation well. Confidently claiming "Aristotle's authority" for his definition, he asserts that "it is manifest to whoever contemplates the forces of poetry . . . that all poetic discourse is either praise or blame."[32] Later he cites Averroes rather than Aristotle to support the idea that poetry is morally edifying. Evidently, he considered both writers equally authoritative and did not differentiate between them.

Benvenuto's general acknowledgment is complemented by his analysis of the structure of the *Divine Comedy*. It is, he believes, a poem fully in accord with Aristotle's rules. The *Inferno* is a work based on "blame." It consists of a series of vignettes showing the ugliness of vice and its terrible consequences. It thus warns the reader to reform. After the *Inferno* comes the first of two "reversals" of the sort advocated by Averroes. The *Inferno* stresses unhappiness, the despair of the damned. In the *Purgatory* the tone abruptly changes to hope. The *Purgatory* contains some "blame"; but however wicked, the characters in this section have redeeming qualities which are "praised" by Dante. The second reversal comes at the beginning of the *Paradiso*. Here the tone changes from hope to joyful fulfillment, and the technique from a mixture of blame and praise to unqualified praise of men of preeminent virtue whom the reader is encouraged to emulate. As Benvenuto remarks, "no other poet ever knew how to praise or blame with more excellence. . . . [Dante] honored virtue with encomia and lacerated vice and vicious men."[33]

Although Benvenuto's commentary was known in the sixteenth century, he remains primarily a medieval figure. It is significant that the next critic to be influenced by the Averroes commentary is Coluccio Salutati. Salutati is the most famous of Petrarch's disciples and was regarded during the sixteenth century as a full-fledged humanist. Among his many works, his allegorical interpretation of the life of Hercules, *De laboribus*

Herculis, is especially significant. It stands midway between Boccaccio's *Genealogy of the Gods* and the allegorized mythologies
of such sixteenth-century writers as Comes (or Conti) and
Cartari. The first book of the *De laboribus* is a little "art of
poetry," in which Salutati offers a theory that in parts may be
accurately described as Averroes expanded and ornamented
by examples from the Latin classics. In Chapter II Salutati attempts to differentiate between rhetoric and poetic. This is
difficult because, following Averroes, he believes that the two
disciplines share the same "matter"—that is, praise and blame.
They are eventually distinguished by the assertion that poetry
is (1) in meter (an echo of the *ars metrica*) and (2) employs
"imaginative and figurative discourse," an idea derived from
Averroes' definition of imitation. Later, the tired classical definition of the orator as *vir bonus dicendi peritus* is reworked
to apply to the poet, who is called a *vir optimus laudandi
vituperandique peritus*—a perfect man skilled in praise and
blame. Even Horace is assimilated into the system. The "delight and instruct" formula from the *Ars Poetica* is explained
in the following way: "The reprehension of vice may profit
right away, but does not immediately please; praise pleases but
does not immediately profit. Therefore blame is primarily for
utility, praise for pleasure; although in a secondary way the
former may please and the latter profit."[34] As is appropriate
for a forward-looking humanist, Salutati compliments modern
poets on their ability to "celebrate virtue and criticize vice"
in the way prescribed in "[Aristotle's] little book."[35]

Averroistic ideas remained attractive during the sixteenth
century, although they were occasionally attacked and more
frequently disguised by an increasingly heavy overlay of erudi-
tion. Savonarola, Robortello, Segni, Maggi and Lombardi, and
Mazzoni all debate the "placing" of poetry among the sciences
and all decide that poetic is at least in part a branch of logic.
Pietro Vettori was not only aware of Averroes, he edited the
commentary for the Giunta "Aristotle" of 1552, eight years before composing his own analysis of the *Poetics.*[36] Almost every
one of these writers cites the Averroes commentary directly

and with respect, often to buttress his own position. As late as 1575, in fact, Alessandro Piccolomini appealed to "the authority of Averroes which has always had great force with me" to refute Robortello's theory of the origin of poetry.[37] Throughout the sixteenth century, it may be added, the didactic theory of poetry existed side-by-side in rather uncomfortable proximity with more precisely Aristotelian doctrines. The fact is that the *Poetics* was difficult to accommodate to the moralistic attitudes of the humanists, whereas Aristotle as interpreted by Averroes is not only moral but oppressively so. In the early part of the century, before the publication of the great commentaries on the *Poetics*, the problem was not fully understood. Aulo Parrasio, for example, was responsible for the first of many efforts to harmonize Horace with Aristotle. His "Commentary on the *Ars Poetica*" appeared posthumously in 1531. Although one reference in the commentary seems to be to the Greek *Poetics*, the remainder of his allegedly Aristotelian principles are evidently quotations or paraphrases from Hermannus Alemannus.[38] Obviously, such an approach became increasingly difficult as time went by. The tension between didacticism and Aristotelian criticism finally became an open break in Lodovico Castelvetro's *Poetica d'Aristotele Vulgarizzata*, published in 1570. Although Castelvetro himself radically distorted the *Poetics*, his interpretation is free of the influence of Averroes. For this reason, he was viewed with suspicion by his great humanistic contemporary Torquato Tasso. In the *Discorsi del Poema Eroico*, published in 1594, Tasso attacked Castelvetro's rather hardheaded view that praise is irrelevant to heroic poetry. "Without doubt," Tasso wrote,

Castelvetro erred when he said that praise is not appropriate to the heroic poem, because if the heroic poet were to celebrate virtue, he would have to exalt it clear up to the heavens with his praises. On the other side, St. Basil says that Homer's *Iliad* is nothing but a praise of virtue, and Averroes has the same opinion in his commentary on poetry, and Plutarch too. . . . Therefore, leaving aside the followers of Castelvetro in their ignorance, let us follow the opinions of . . . St. Basil, of Averroes, of Plutarch, and of Aristotle himself.[39]

In the last decade of the sixteenth century, in other words, the most eloquent spokesman of Italian humanism found Averroes not only worthy of citing, but in some respects more truly Aristotelian than the most influential student of the *Poetics* that the age produced.

Tasso was, however, already an anachronism in his own age. The canons of neoclassicism were beginning to harden around the freer poetic of the Renaissance. These canons had little place for the barbarous Latin and benighted scholarship of the Averroes commentary. *Concettismo*, which briefly rivaled neoclassicism in Italy, revived the notion that poetry is a matter of cleverly manipulating figurative language, but its sources are Aristotle himself, not his Arabian commentator. The last unambiguous echo of the Averroes commentary that I have been able to discover is in Thomas Rymer's 1674 preface to his translation of Rapin's *Reflections*. Rymer remembers Averroes not for his theory of poetry, but for his rebuke of Arab poets. "The *Arabians*," says Rymer, "observe but little these laws of Aristotle: yet Averroes rather chooses to blame the practice of his countrymen as vicious than to allow any imputation on the doctrine of his *Philosopher* as imperfect."[40] If this makes Averroes a predecessor of Corneille, Boileau, and Alexander Pope, it also writes finis to the story of his influence on European criticism.

Notes

1. A. P. McMahon, *Seven Questions on Aristotelian Definitions of Tragedy and Comedy*, Harvard Studies in Classical Philology, XI (1929), 99-108; Augusto Rostagni, "Aristotele e l'Aristotelianismo nella Storia dell'Estetica Antica," in *Scritti Minori* (Turin, 1955), I, 76-254; C. O. Brink, *Horace on Poetry: Prolegomena to the Literary Epistles* (Cambridge, 1963).

2. New York, 1899.

3. David Margoliouth, *The Poetics of Aristotle Translated from Greek into English and from Arabic into Latin* (London, 1911); Jaroslav Tkatsch, *Die Arabische Ubersetzung der Poetik des Aristoteles* (2 vols.; Vienna and Leipzig, 1928, 1932); Georges Lacombe, *Aristoteles Latinus, pars prior* (Rome, 1939) and *Pars posterior* (Oxford, 1955); Bernard Weinberg, *A History of Literary Criticism in the Italian Renaissance* (2 vols.; Chicago, 1961).

4. London, 1887.

5. See Angel Gonzalez Palencia, *Catálogo de las Ciencias* (Madrid,, 1953). This work includes the translation of the *Catalogue* by Gerard of Cremona.

6. Text and extensive discussion in Ludwig Baur, *Dominici Gundissalini De Divisione Philosophiae, Beiträge zur Geschichte der Philosophie des Mittelalters* (Münster, 1903), Vol. IV, Nos. 2-3. See also Richard McKeon, "Rhetoric in the Middle Ages," in *Critics and Criticism*, ed. R. S. Crane (Chicago, 1952), 260-296.

7. Still basic to the subject is Ernst Renan, *Averroës et l'Averroisme* (Paris, 1852). It is treated in the standard histories, as, for example, Etienne Gilson, *The Christian Philosophy of the Middle Ages* (New York, 1955), 181-255, 387-402. See also Fernand Van Steenberghen, *Aristotle in the West* (Louvain, 1955).

8. Jaroslav Tkatsch, "Ueber den Arabischen Kommentar des Averoes zum Poetik des Aristoteles," *Wiener Studien*, XXIV (1902), 76.

9. See G. H. Luquet, "Hermann l'Allemand," *Revue de l'Histoire des Religions*, XLIV (1901), 407-422.

10. MSS listed in Lacombe, *Aristoteles Latinus*. They are Nos. 323, 353, 426, 706, 707, 732, 871, 908, 941, 943, 963, 1191, 1196, 1211, 1247, 1466, 1494, 1630, 1661, 1753, 1814, 1821, 1935. The edition of 1481 was issued by Philipus Venetus under the title, *Aristotelis rhetorica ex arabico latine reddita Alemanno Todesco ecc. excerpta ex Aristotelis poetica per eundem Ermannum de Averrois textu.*

11. *De Arte Poetica Guillelmo de Moerbeke Interprete*, ed. E. Valgimigli, *Aristoteles Latinus*, Vol. XXXIII (Paris, 1953).

12. Quoted in Lacombe, *Aristoteles Latinus, pars prior*, p. 211: "Quod autem hi duo libri logicales sint, nemo dubitat qui libros perspexerit arabum famosorum, Alfaribi videlicet et Avicenne et Avenrosdi et quorundam aliorum. Imo ex ipso textu manifestius hoc patebit. Neque excusabiles sunt, ut fortassis alicui videbitur propter Marci Tullii rhetoricam et Oratii poetriam. Tullius namque rhetoricam partem civilis scientiae posuit et secundum hanc intentionem eam potissime tractavit. Oratius vero poetriam prout pertinet ad grammaticam expedivit."

13. Cf., for example, *Pro Archia Poeta*. But Hermannus is most probably thinking of passages in Cicero's rhetorical treatises like *De Oratore*, I, xv, where Cicero discusses the system of the sciences and emphatically "places" oratory—and hence, to a medieval reader, poetry as well—in the "practical" division.

14. *Grammatici Latini* (7 vols.; Leipzig, 1897-1923). The seventh volume supplements the *scriptores de arte metrica* collected in volume six by reprinting Bede's important treatise on meter.

15. Here and below I have used as my basic text of Hermannus the recent

edition by William F. Boggess, "Averrois Cordubensis Commentarium Medium in Aristotelis Poetriam" (unpublished dissertation, University of North Carolina, Department of Classics, 1965).

16. "Dixit [Aristoteles] . . . sermones poetici sermones sunt ymaginativi. Modi autem ymaginationis et assimilationis tres sunt: duo simplices et tertius compositus ex illis. Unus eorum simplicem est assimilatio rei ad rem et exemplatio eius ad ipsam. Et hoc fit in qualibet lingua aut per dictiones proprias illi linguae ut est haec dictio quasi vel sicut et quae istis similantur quae nominantur sinkategoreumata similitudinis. . . . Et istud nominatur in hac arte concambium. . . . secunda autem divisio est ut convertatur assimilatio ut si dicas: sol quasi est talis mulier aut sol est talis mulier, non talis mulier est quasi sol et non talis mulier est sol. et tertia species sermonum poeticorum composita est ex his duabus." (Boggess, pp. 3-5).

17. *Thomae Aquinatis praeclarissima commentaria in libra Aristotelis Peri hermenias et Posteriorum analyticorum* (Venice, 1553), p. 36ᵛ.

18. Fra Girolamo Savonarola, *De divisione omnium scientiarum* (Florence, 1496), p. 807: ". . . manifestum est syllogismum illum, qui a Philosopho vocatur Exemplum, objectum esse artis Poeticae, quemadmodum Enthymema objectum Rhetoricae, Inductio ac syllogismus probabilis topicae, Demonstratio libri poster. analyticorum." Also p. 810: "Sine Logica neminem posse poetam appellari manifestum est."

19. "Dixit: Omne itaque poema et omnis oratio poetica aut est vituperatio aut est laudatio. et hoc patet per inductionem poematum et proprie poematum ipsorum quae fiunt de rebus voluntariis id est honestis et turpis" (Boggess, p. 3).

20. ". . . filii instruantur et exerceantur in carminibus quae ad actus fortitudinis et largitatis sive liberalitatis incitant et inclinant. non enim instigant arabes in carminibus suis nisi ad has duas virtutibus a numero virtutum, neque simpliciter ad has in quantum virtutes sunt, sed in quantum per eas adquiritur altitudo honoris et gloriae" (Boggess, p. 10).

21. "Ex quo representatores et assimilatores per hoc intendunt instigare ad quasdam actiones quae circa voluntaria consistunt et retrahere a quibusdam, erunt necessario ea quae intendunt per suas representationes aut virtutes aut vicia. omnis enim actio et omnis mos non versatur nisi circa alterum istorum videlicet virtutum aut vicium. Necessario ergo opportet ut boni et virtuosi non representent nisi virtutes et virtuosos, mali autem malicias et malos. et quando quidem omnis assimilatio et representatio non fit nisi per ostentationem decentis aut indecentis sive turpis, patens est quoniam non intenditur per hoc nisi assecutio decentis et refutatio turpis . . . et ab his manieribus hominum prodiit laudatio et vituperatio, scilicet laus bonorum et vituperatio malorum" (Boggess, pp. 7-8).

22. ". . . dederit principia istarum artium, et . . . non fuerit ante ipsum quisquam cuius factum in arte laudandi aliquam habuit quae sit relatione digna . . . neque etiam in arte vituperandi. . . ." (Boggess, p. 14).

23. "non solum . . . omnis eius quod malum est, sed despicabile et quasi subsannabile, id est quod abiectum est et de quo quasi non curatur" (Boggess, p. 15). E.g., *consideratio* is explained in one place as "gesticulatio sive vultuum acceptio sicut utitur hiis rhetorica" (Boggess, p. 23).

24. E.g., *consideratio* is explained in one place as "gesticulatio sive vultuum acceptio sicut utitur hiis rhetorica" (Boggess, p. 23).

25. "Et patet enim ex hiis quae dicta sunt de intentione sermonum poeticorum quoniam representationes quae fiunt per figmenta mendosa adinventicia non sunt de opere poetae. et sunt ea quae nominantur proverbia et exempla, ut ea quae sunt in libro Hisopi et consimilibus fabulosis conscriptionibus. Ideoque poetae non pertinet loqui nisi in rebus quae sunt aut quas possibile

est esse. Talia quippe sunt quae appetenda sunt aut refutanda. . . . poeta vero non ponit nomina nisi rebus existantibus. Et fortassis loquuntur in universalibus. Ideoque ars poetriae propinquior est philosophiae quam sit ars adinventiva proverbiorum" (Boggess, pp. 29-30).

26. ". . . imitationem contrarii eius quod intenditur ad laudandum, primitus ut ipsum respuat aut abhorreat anima et ut deinde permutetur ab hoc ad imitationem ipsiusmet quod laudandum est. ut cum quis voluerit imitari seu representare felicitatem et ei pertinentes incipiat primo ab imitatione infelicitatis et ab illis qui ei pertinent, deinde permutetur ad imitationem felicitatis et ei pertinentibus. . . ." (Boggess, pp. 34-35).

27. ". . . quidem poetarum intromittunt in tragediam representationem rerum per quas intenditur admiratio tantum absque hoc quod sint timorose aut dolorose" (Boggess, p. 42).

28. "Partes autem quae in ipsis reperuntur in poematibus arabum sunt tres. Prima est quae se habet apud ipsos in poemate ad modum exordii in rethorica, et est ea in qua mentionem facunt mansionum sive edificiorum nobilium et ruinarum. . . . et pars secunda est ipsa laus. et tertia pars est quae habet se ad modum conclusionis in rethorica. et huius partis plurimum apud eos aut invocatio et deprecatio aliqua pro eo quem laudaverunt aut commendatio carminis impensi in laudem ipsius" (Boggess, p. 37).

29. See n. 10.

30. See Lane Cooper and Alfred Gudeman, *A Bibliography of the Poetics of Aristotle* (New Haven, 1928).

31. *Opus Tertium* in *Opera Inedita*, ed. J. S. Breuer (London, 1859), pp. 303-308.

32. *Benvenuto . . . illustrata nella vita e nelle opere e di lui commento Latino*, ed. and trans. Giovanni Tamburini (Imola, 1855), I, 10: "Si farà ciò agevolmente manifesto a chiunque contempli le forze poetiche, come fa testimonianza Aristotele, imperciochè ogni discorso, o poema, o è lode oppure vitupero. . . ."

33. *Ibid.*: ". . . niun altro poeta seppe mai laudare, o vituperare con più eccellenza ed efficacia maggiore di quella, che adoperò il perfettissimo poeta Dante: ornò di encomi le virtù, ed i virtuosi: saettò di punture i vizi, ed i viziosi. . . ."

34. *De Laboribus Herculis*, ed. B. L. Ullman (Zurich, 1951), I, 68: "'Aut prodesse volunt aut delectare poetae.' Prodest quidem reprehensor vitiis obvians sed non immediate delectat. Delectat vero commendans sed non statim et immediate prodest. Principaliter igitur utilitate vituperatio correspondet, delectationi laus, licit secondario prosit hoc, illa delectat."

35. *Ibid.*: "Carpent equidem nostri poetae vitiosos . . . celebrant . . . virtutes."

36. *Secundum Volumen Aristotelis Stagiritae de Rhetorica et Poetica cum Averrois Cordubensis in Easdem Paraphrasibus* (Venice, 1552).

37. ". . . l'autorità d'Averroe, ch'in me sempre ha potuto assai" (*Annotationi di M. Alessandro Piccolomini nel Libro della Poetica d'Aristotele*, Venice, 1575, p. 61).

38. *A. Iani Parrhasii . . . in Q. Horatii Flacci Artem Poeticam Commentaria* (Naples, 1531). Cf. Weinberg, *History*, I, 370-371.

39. "Discorsi del Poema Eroico," in *Prose Diverse*, ed. Cesare Guasti (Florence, 1875), I, 165-166: "errò senza dubbio il Castelvetro quando egli disse, che al poeta eroico non si conveniva il lodare; perciò che se il poeta eroico celebra la virtù eroica, dee inalzarla con le lodi sino al cielo. Pero san Basilio dice, che L'Iliade d'Omero altro non è che una lode della virtù; ed Averroe, sopra il comento della poesia, porta la medesima opinione; e Plutarco. . . .

Lasciando dunque i seguaci del Castelvetro nella loro opinione, or noi seguiam quella di . . . san Basilio, d'Averroe, di Plutarco e d'Aristotele medesimo."

40. Preface to "Rapin's Reflections on Aristotle's Treatise of Poesie," in *Critical Works of Thomas Rymer*, ed. Curt Zimansky (New Haven, 1956), p. 3. In his *Short View* Rymer refers to Averroes again and quotes him (*Critical Works*, p. 109).

V

On Tubs and Whales: From the Psalmist and Alexander the Great to Heinrich von Kleist

John G. Kunstmann
University of North Carolina

In Heinrich von Kleist's play *Die Hermannsschlacht*, lines 614-618 (Act II, Scene 8) read as follows:

> Du wirfst dem Walfisch, wie das Sprichwort sagt,
> Zum Spielen eine Tonne vor;
> Doch wenn du irgend dich auf offnem Meere noch
> Erhalten kannst, so bitt ich dich,
> Lass es was anders, als Thusnelden, sein.

You throw out to the whale, as the proverb puts it, a tun or a cask, for him, the whale, to play with. These words are spoken by Thusnelda, the wife of Hermann or Arminius, and with them she addresses her husband, the hero of the *Hermannsschlacht*, the battle in the Teutoburg forest, and the victor over the Roman general Quintilius Varus. And the whale to whom she refers—I nearly said the wolf to whom she refers—is a Roman gentleman, Ventidius Carbo.[1]

What Thusnelda means, amounts to this: You, Hermann, throw me, your wife, to the hated enemy, the Roman Ventidius, exactly as the proverb says that one throws a cask to a whale for him to play with—you are using me as bait!

The commentators, among them Adolf Lichtenheld and the formidable Erich Schmidt,[2] claim that the expression "to throw a tub to a whale" was imported into German by Lessing who, they say, got it from his reading of Jonathan Swift's *A Tale of a Tub*. Lessing, to be sure, uses the expression. He uses it twice. Once in his *Hamburgische Dramaturgie* ("A tub for our

[82]

critics, those whales!") and again in *Ernst und Falk: Talks for Freemasons*.³ It is, of course, *possible* for Lessing to have become acquainted with the expression "to throw a tub to a whale" during his reading of Swift and other English authors. It is also possible for Kleist to have learned the expression from his reading of Lessing. Possible. But the German commentators should have paid attention to Kleist's or Thusnelda's parenthetical remark *wie das Sprichwort sagt* (as the proverb says). Naturally, one need not take this remark at face value. On the other hand, Kleist's reference to a proverb, presumably a German proverb, should have been investigated. Had these commentators done so, they would have found ample evidence of the existence and use of the expression "to throw a tub to a whale" in German literature, especially in German literature of the eighteenth century and in writers earlier than Lessing. I shall not tire you by an enumeration of the authors and the reading of the pertinent passages. Suffice it to say that Goethe uses the expression, more than once, and that he is aware of the fact that he is using a proverb, although this fact seems to have escaped 'the American compiler of the proverbs in Goethe's works.⁴ And let it be enough to point out that Daniel Casper von Lohenstein in 1689–1690—note the date, 1689–1690, i.e., *before* Swift—uses the expression in his "Grossmütiger Feldherr Arminius" ("Magnanimous General Arminius") and that he employs it in such a manner that it is clear that he expects his readers to "get the point"; in other words, he is not introducing something neological.⁵ The aforementioned commentators and critics might have thought of the possibility of a connection between Kleist's Arminius *play* and Daniel Casper von Lohenstein's Arminius *novel*. But this is not all. I was fortunate in discovering for the first time, I believe, the earliest account in German of the fact of throwing out a tub to a whale in a sixteenth-century document, thus bringing the earliest German documentation of the custom or fact of throwing a tub to a whale or a sea monster pretty close to the earliest mention of such a thing in English. I found this reference—I stumbled upon it—in Ulrich Schmidel's account of his voyage to South America during the years 1534–1554. After his return to his native Germany Ulrich Schmidel sat down and wrote out the story of his adventures. One of them deals with some immense sea monsters: one of them is so powerful and mighty and big it can inflict most serious damage to ships. This happens especially when the ship is becalmed; then the ship must lie still; it cannot move, neither forward nor to the rear; then there approaches this gigantic marine animal, and it pushes so hard against the ship that a regular earthquake ensues and a general trembling of the vessel all over. Now, when such a thing happens, immediately and forthwith one must throw one or two big casks out of the ship, and when the above-mentioned giant of a marine animal bumps into them, then he forgets the ship and plays with the casks—the ship, of course, gets away.[6]

Ulrich Schmidel's account may be a report of something actually witnessed by him off the coast of South America between 1534 and 1554 or he may be telling a gigantic fish story, a whale of a tale, something he had picked up during his journey. At any rate, he or his informants knew about throwing a tub to a whale. But his or their knowledge was shared by at least one more German contemporary: by no less a person than Dr. Pomeranus, i.e., Dr. Johann Bugenhagen, the ecclesiastical organizer of the Reformation, the "Pastor" of the Reformation movement, the "Luther" of Low Germany, the Reformer of Denmark, Luther's intimate friend and assistant in the revision of Luther's Bible translation. According to the "Protocoll" (the minutes) for 1539–1541 and the "manuscript entries, Old Testament, dated 1539," Bugenhagen "said he had heard from mariners that sailors throw a tub [*vas*] into the water with which [the whale] plays, by tossing it up into the air, and then the whale devours it."[7]

I shall omit at this juncture the various accounts of the throwing out of a tub to a whale and the allusions to this custom as something well-known in the Scandinavian countries and in the Netherlands, where they turn up from the sixteenth century on. I shall return to them later. Right now, let me say something about the tub and the whale as they play a role or no role in Italy and in France. As for Italy, I shall confine myself to the testimony of Aldrovandi (d. 1605) as found in this eminent naturalist's *Vlyssis Aldrovandi Philosophi et Medici Bononiensis de piscibus libri quinque et de cetis liber unus . . .* (Bononiae, 1613; the colophon has the date 1612). Here we read, *de cetis*, pages 672-673: "They [the whales] are delighted with the aroma of recently pitch-smeared vessels, to such an extent that they come close up and rub themselves against the ship. The sailors, fearing the destruction of the ship, throw out to the whales large casks that have been smeared over with pitch, in order that the whales might leave the ship. The whales play with the casks and belch up high in the air the water which is hurled forth through a tube in the head."[8]

In France I have not met an allusion to the custom of throwing out a tub to a whale nor have I ever run across a French expression similar to the English-German expression "to throw a tub to a whale." It is, I believe, significant in this connection that Fischart in his German adaptation of Rabelais' *Gargantua* uses the expression *spilt wie der Walfisch mit den Tonnen* (plays, as does the whale, with the tubs), the equivalent of which does *not* occur in the French, even though Rabelais writes about the *monstreux physetere* who is frightened away by the blare of trumpets.[9] Likewise have I noted that Johann Joachim Christoph Bode, a well-known translator of the works of Montaigne—he did this toward the end of the eighteenth century—has the passage: "In brief, by throwing out this tub for the whale to play with, by means of which he dispersed their wrath and diverted it into idle debates, he succeeded in putting the common people to sleep. . . ." But there is *not* in the original French this proverbial phrase![10] It seems, then, that the French, although they or at least parts of their nation were a seafaring people familiar with whales and whaling, for one reason or another, did not borrow it from one of their neighbors or coin this or a similar phrase.

Much more astonishing to me than the fact that, so far, I have not been able to discover this locution in French is the

[85]

fact that I have not been able to discover it in American New England whaling lore. Herman Melville was, as he says, "picking up whatever random allusions to whales he could anyways find in any book whatsoever, sacred or profane" and I should be the happiest of mortals if somebody, now or at any time hereafter, would point out to me that I have overlooked in his writings or in the writings of other Americans the phrase "to throw out a tub to a whale." I confess I have not read through the hundreds and hundreds of small and large books and articles and casual items on whaling which have been written in the United States by the whalers of New England and the people who have written about them. But I had the most excellent cooperation of two persons in this matter: one, the son of the former president of Northwestern University, Mr. Sumner W. Scott, a Ph.D. of the English Department of the University of Chicago and the one man who, in my knowledge and experience, has read and excerpted more New England whaling literature than any other living human being (he had to—he did it for his Ph.D. dissertation) and, second, the great pharmaceutical scholar, Professor Geiling, who, because he needed certain innards of the whale for his investigations and because scientific foundation money and departmental funds were not forthcoming for the purchase of said innards, went out a-whaling himself and procured them *in loco et situ* and in that connection became a lover of whales and a devoted and assiduous reader and a veritable repository of whaling lore. These two have assured me that they never ran across this proverbial expression in American writings—as a matter of fact, they had not heard of the phrase until they learned about it from me.

There is one exception, but it does not even prove the rule. I found the expression about the tub that is thrown to the whale in H. H. Brackenridge, *Modern Chivalry: Containing the Adventures of a Captain*, etc., Volume II, published by Jacob Johnson, and for sale at his bookstores in Philadelphia and in Richmond, Virginia, 1807. In this book, familiar to students of American literature, I found this passage (pp. 17-18): "The advocates for a [presidential] levee say, that it is useful in order to avoid the interruptions of persons calling on the President at his private hours—and is like throwing a barrel to a whale, in order to preserve the ship." I have a second "American" quotation, from a more or less contemporary *B* or *B–* novel involving this proverbial phrase, but here as in the Brackenridge case the use of the expression is purely a literary one and has nothing to do with actual whaling lore.

I believe you will agree with me when I say that Kleist, in quoting the proverb or the proverbial phrase about throwing a tub to a whale, did not have to fall back upon Lessing who, in turn, was not obliged to fall back on Swift's *Tale of a Tub*. Had Kleist been obliged to fall back on any particular writer, then it could have been any one of a considerable number of German writers—Goethe, Rabener, Klinger, Rückert, Lohenstein, and others.[11] And it could have been any one of several Scandinavian, or Dutch, or Italian writers. And it could have been any one of quite a few English authors. It appears that these peoples, including the Germans, were familiar with the expression "to throw a tub to a whale" and that they all connected with it the same literal meaning and the same figurative meaning, after they had ceased to employ the saying in the literal sense. The literal meaning being: one throws a tub or a cask or a similar utensil to a whale, in order to create a diversion. The attention of the whale or of any other large marine animal which is attacking the ship is diverted away from the ship by this maneuver, and the ship escapes while the marine monster is playing with the newfound toy. In other words, the throwing out of the tub or the cask was intended to be a lifesaver. The whole procedure, then, belongs under the general heading of *Abwehrzauber*,[12] magic means to ward off sickness, evil spirits, the evil eye, etc., a procedure which is often spoken of as *servatoria* (means to save from danger) or as *apotropeia* (means to avert danger or disaster) or as *phylacteria* (means of protection, a kind of prophylaxis, like the prophylaxis provided by a watchdog) or as *baskania* or *probaskania*, which includes the means of fascination as, for example, when you bewitch or cast a spell by means of the eye, the evil eye; hence, to deprive of the power of resistance as through terror and, naturally, the means to prevent such fascination or to neutralize it, the overcoming of a whammy by means of a double whammy. We are dealing here with something which is familiar to people who are acquainted with such compilations as Stith Thompson's "Motif-Index" where one finds such entries as "escape by use of substituted object; the object is attacked rather than the intended victim; escape from death or danger by deception; or captive throws his hat to lions who fight over it while he escapes." This is, incidentally, one of the "anthropological" aspects of our proverbial expression: it is an exemplification of the general belief in the avertability of evil by means of certain performances—here, the substitution of something for the intended victim, or the general practice of deception or the application of the belief in the stupidity or gullibility of evil spirits—I am thinking here of Shakespeare's "a swallowed bait, / On purpose laid to make the taker mad" (Sonnet 129, ll. 7-8).

So much for the literal meaning of the expression "to throw a tub to a whale." And the figurative meaning? The meaning which has replaced almost completely the literal application of the saying? Nowadays we enlightened people who smile at our benighted ancestors who believed in the evil eye and the possibility to avert it and we who, instead, believe in scientific claims of toothpaste manufacturers and in opinion polls and in the infallibility of computers, we still throw tubs at whales, but only in a manner of speaking. We mean thereby, as the *New English Dictionary* or Farmer and Henley's *Slang and Its Analogues Past and Present* put it, that "we create a diversion" and that we "emphasize small matters so that attention is distracted from essentials" or that we cause an attacker who may be a critic or an ordinary enemy to forget about the original and primary issue and that we make him follow a false scent by dragging a herring, a red herring, across his path. I deplore in this connection the use of the latter phrase on a certain occasion by former President Truman. In my opinion, he missed

Plate I

Plate II

II.
HIS ARTIBUS.

Ut te ipsum & navim serves, comitesq; pericli,
In pontum cunctas abjice divitias.

Cete quædam, & quas vulgo balænas vocant, tantæ esse magnitudinis in comperto est, ut naves etiam, quamvis prægrandes, evertere ac pesfundare valeant, & Oppianus in ἀλιευτ. idem affirmat. Tradunt autem quasdam ex istis, cum naves recens picatæ sunt, sentire illum odorem, eoque attractas affricare se navibus, atque ita, ni præcaveatur periculum, illas evertere. Nautæ igitur Picata dolia illis objiciunt, cum quibus dum ludunt, illi

illi effugiunt. Ferunt hoc symbolo usum fuisse maximum heroem, Mauricium Saxoniæ Ducem, cujus excelsus animus, & inprimis illustres virtutes bellicæ ad omnem posteritatem erunt celebres. Fieri autem potest, ut prudentiss, princeps innuere voluerit, non temerè occurrendum, sed obludendum esse potentioribus, si illorum vim & insultus aliter vitare & frangere nequeas, Nam profectò, secundum Paccuvii illud.

Cum contendi nequitum est, etiam tendenda est
plaga.

Neque etiam illud Spartani Regis apud Plutarchum apophthegma, de leoninæ & vulpinæ pellis usu ignotum est. Referri denique huc possunt egregia illa belli furta & stratagemata, ab omni prorsus reprehensione, secundum Valer: Max. remota, per quæ, ut Thucydides loquitur, τὸν πολέμιον μάλις᾽ ἄν τις ἀπατήσας, τὸς φίλως μίγις᾽ ἂν ὠφελήσειν: hostes mox decipiuntur, & amici plurimum juvantur Verissimum igitur est Polybianum illud apud Suidam: μία ψυχὴ τῆς ἀπάσης πολυχειρίας ἐν ἰσίοις, ποικίλως ἐνεργικώτερα: Unius mentis solertia aliquando efficacior, quam mille manus. Docere etiam potest hoc symbolum, imminente gravi aliquo periculo omnem honestam esse rationem expendiendæ salutis, & vitæ servandæ caussa insuper habendas omnes divitias. Verè namq; Alcestis, ud Eurip. ait:

ψυχῆς γὰρ ὐδὲν ἐςι τιμιώτερον.
Nam nihil est vita pretiosius.

the chance of a lifetime to familiarize millions of American citizens with the phrase "to throw a tub to a whale," thus assuring the phrase of a longer life, and he missed the chance of injecting into the political atmosphere of the country a new and, perhaps, a healthier aroma!

In British writing you find more or less the same development from the literal meaning to the figurative meaning of the expression, except that in British writing there seem to have been originally the proverbial expression "a tale of a tub" *and* the proverbial expression "to throw a tub to a whale."

Any remarks concerning the British English aspects of the phrase "to throw a tub to a whale" really should begin with a quotation from Morris Palmer Tilley's *A Dictionary of the Proverbs of England in the Sixteenth and Seventeenth Centuries.* . . . I shall do so. The entry in question, found on page 688, reads as follows:

T 597 To throw out a Tub to a Whale [To create a diversion]

> 1651 Taylor *Holy Dying* I iii, p. 277: He is at first entertained with trifles . . . and little images of things are laid before him, like a cock-boat to a whale, only to play withal.

> 1704 Swift *Tale Tub*, Auth. Pref., p. 50: seamen have a custom, when they meet a whale, to fling him out an empty tub . . . to divert him from laying violent hands upon the ship. See William G. Smith, *The Oxford Dictionary of English Proverbs*, p. 548. Cf. T 45: A Tale of a Tub.

In the 1651 Jeremy Taylor *Holy Dying* passage a cock-boat, known to you from *King Lear* as meaning a small boat, especially one that is used as a tender, is laid before a whale, in the hope, it seems, that the whale play with it. The second passage, the one from Jonathan Swift's *A Tale of a Tub*, explains *why* it is hoped that the whale will play with the cock-boat or, in the case of Swift, with the empty tub which is flung out to him: to divert him, the whale, "from laying violent hands upon the ship." I should pause here a moment and ask you to conjure up before your mind's eye the picture of a whale (1) with hands, (2) with violent hands which he (3) lays upon the ship. In my opinion, this would be a whale of an accomplishment, one that could be surpassed only by the feat of the brother-whale who does all this with one hand tied behind his back. Somehow this Swiftian expression reminds me of the impassioned oration delivered by a German critic of the alleged inability of German universities to take criticism. In his diatribe he said that the German universities in their insistence on being coddled act like raw eggs which, when anybody dares to treat them rough, stand up on their hindfeet and are prepared to give battle.

Let me return to the Tilley entry. It distinguishes, correctly, between the proverbial phrase "to throw out a tub to a whale," for which it gives two references, and the other proverbial expression "a tale of a tub."

The latter expression, "a tale of a tub," best known from Jonathan Swift's *A Tale of a Tub* of 1704, was certainly current already in the sixteenth century. It turns up in Sir Thomas More's *Confutacyon of Tyndale* (1532): "Consider the places and his wordes together, and ye shal find al his processe therin a fayre tale of a Tub [quoted from the 1557 edition]."

The same expression is listed a number of times in a *Dictionarie of the French and English Tongues, Compiled by Randle Cotgrave* (1611).[13] Here we read in the entry "cicogne. contes de la cicogne" these translations: "idle histories; vaine relations; tales of a tub, or, of a roasted horse." And, again, under "fariboles" we find enumerated "trifles; nifles, flim-flams; why-whawes; idle discourses; fond tatling; tales of a tub, or of a roasted horse." There is a third entry, "mocquerie": ". . . a mock; flowt, frumpe, scoffe, gibe, ieast, gull, gudgeon, derision; a mockerie, tale of a tub, ridiculous discourse. . . ." "Tale of a tub" also turns up as one of several English equivalents, synonymous with "flimflam" and "idle discourse," of the French "riotte." And if we consult the English-French part of Cotgrave's *Dictionairie* we find, *sub verbo* "tale" "a tale of a tub," and then the translations "riotte, mocquerie, conte de cicogne, chanson de ricochet." In this connection I remind you of Ben Jonson's *A Tale of a Tub* (1633), of an anonymous

A Tale of a Tub which appeared in 1638, and of the fact that Defoe, in his pamphlet on the grievances of Irish Dissenters (1704), describes a certain bill as a "tale of a tub" in the same sense in which Swift uses the expression in his *A Tale of a Tub*.

A "tale of a tub" is, then, a flimflam, a tale of a roasted horse and idle discourse or, as we today might say, an idle fiction, a fantastic tale. Why such a tale should be called a tale of a *tub*—in other words, what the *tub* has to do with the idle or fantastic aspects of the tale in question—I do not know, unless "tub" in the expression "tale of a tub" originally meant "pulpit."[14] "Pulpit" is one of the documented meanings of the English word "tub," and "tale of a tub" meaning a fantastic, even a lying tale might go back to the kind of tale told to an audience from a platform or dais or rostrum or pulpit, promising all sorts of highly fantastic things or merely narrating them— tales of a roasted horse, of roast goose, of two chickens in the pot, two cars in the garage, no income tax. . . . German has an expression which seems to belong here: *eine aufgestellte Tonne*, i.e., a set-up tun or vat or tub which, according to the *Dictionary* of the Brothers Grimm, means *ein erhöhter Standpunkt* signifying a raised platform or dais or pulpit where a speaker stands. And there is the phrase *der Redner steht in der Tonne*: the speaker stands in the tun or tub, an expression which apparently goes back directly to *doleum* or *dolium*, the vat or tun, which occurs in some of the medieval ecclesiastical plays, particularly in connection with the so-called *Teufelsspiel*. This "devil play" usually takes place in the middle of the stage, close to the *dolium* or tun which serves as the showpiece-throne of his Satanic Majesty. This *dolium* serves other purposes, too. But the principal function seems to be to serve as the unholy see of Satan whence he addresses his fellow devils, as, for example in the *Alsfelder Passionsspiel*: Hoc factor Luciper ascendit doleum et dicit . . . et tunc omnes diaboli circueunt doleum corisando et cantando.[15]

So much for the proverbial expression "a tale of a tub."

The oldest documented occurrence of the British English

phrase "to throw a tub to a whale" is found in Henry Watson's *The Shyppe of Fooles*, translated out of French (London: Wynken de Worde, 1509). The pertinent passage reads as follows (incidentally, there is no corresponding passage in the German original from the French translation of which Henry Watson made his English rendering) :

give audience unto my words if thou have any volente for to go upon the sea. Look that thou be well ware of the ire of the sea swine the which will follow thy shippe doing thee great trouble and mischief by long continuance.

> By the mean whereof
> if that thou wilt have good remedy
> thou must look if that it be too sore laden
> for if that it be too sore charged
> thou must find the means for to cast out some tonne
> or barell that he may play with. . . .[16]

A second passage, a bit later in the sixteenth century, is from *The Troublesome Raigne of King John* (1591):

> . . . the mariner
> Spying the hugie Whale whose monstrous bulke
> Doth beare the waves like mountaines fore the wind,
> Throwes out an emptie vessel, so to stay
> His fury[17]

From now on the passages where the phrase "to throw a tub to a whale" is used—the English passages—employ the phrase figuratively:

Dekker, *Seven Deadly Sins* (1606): Be wise, therefore, . . . play with these Whales of the Sea, till you escape them that are devourers of your Merchants.[18]

The Rehearsal Transpros'd: The Second Part, Answered by Andrew Marvel (London, 1673): But whereas I only threw it out like empty Cask to amuze him, knowing that I had a Whale to deal with, and least he should overset me; he runs away with it as a very serious business, and so moyles himself with tumbling and tossing it, that he is in danger of melting his Sperma Ceti. . . . What adoe he makes with Tubs, Kinderkins, Hogsheads, and their dimensions! (p. 115).

Let me give you now, passing over a long quotation from Richardson's *Clarissa* and others from the eighteenth century,[19] a nineteenth-century passage: "He . . . expatiated on the honours I had gained in the schools . . . as if it was necessary for a prebendary's footman to be as learned as his master. However . . . it served as a tub to the whale" (1809).[20] And, finally, two more or less contemporary passages: "An old writer observes that 'an able statesman, out of work, like a huge whale, will endeavour to overturn the ship unless he has an empty cask to play with." This is from the preface of W. K. Marriott's translation of Machiavelli's *Prince*, first published in 1908. And the *New English Dictionary* gives, as its latest entry, a quotation from the British *Nation* from the year 1912, and the same quotation, I believe, is the latest one in Apperson's *English Proverbs and Proverbial Phrases* . . . (London, 1929). It reads: "He throws a tub to the High Church Whale."

It might have been better for an understanding of the vogue of the proverbial saying concerning the throwing of a tub to a whale and of the original firm belief of people in the efficacy of the tub-throwing to avert evil, and their belief that they were dealing with a common proverb—for this, I repeat, it might have been better, had I not distinguished so much between German and English and other passages and had I concentrated my efforts more on the sixteenth century. I have, of course, referred to a number of sixteenth-century instances. Let me now add a few others, in the hope to clinch the case of the correctness of Heinrich von Kleist's statement that he or Thusnelda was quoting a *proverb*, a proverb which evidently was well known for centuries in Western Europe, especially in Germany, the Lowlands, England, Scandinavia, and Italy.

Let me call your attention to a report written at the end of the sixties of the sixteenth century by Marcus van Vaernewyck, a patrician citizen of Ghent. The Belgian scholar George Marlier discovered in this man's *Flemish Chronicle* a reference to the mariner's practice of throwing a tub to a whale. Marcus van Vaernewyck's account is entitled *Of the Troublous Times in the Netherlands and chiefly in Ghent 1566-68*. It is a most accurate account of the turbulent times in his homeland. The chronicler relates how the iconoclasts shattered the stained-glass windows of the churches in Ghent and then marched across country to Courtray destroying church property everywhere. But the bishop let them rage hoping that Ghent might be spared if they cooled their fury outside the city walls. I quote: "Even so they throw a barrel to the whale to prevent him from toying with the ships that come his way."[21]

It was at this time that Pieter Breughel the Elder was nearing the end of his life. He died in 1569, only months after the events described in the *Flemish Chronicle* had taken place. To this celebrated Dutch painter is ascribed an unsigned painting, now in Vienna, which has been designated as the earliest example of Netherlandish marine painting, in other words, a seascape. For a long time it was assumed that the painter had meant to portray that moment in the life of the prophet Jonah when the mariners "took up Jonah and cast him forth into the sea, and the sea ceased from raging." An examination of the painting makes clear, however, beyond any doubt, that it depicts the proverb concerning throwing a tub to a whale— Breughel had painted other proverbs. And the whale in the seascape is not the whale who swallowed Jonah; rather is it the whale who attacks a ship during a storm and is diverted from shattering the vessel through being sidetracked by a barrel thrown out to it.[22]

Next I should like to call your attention to one sixteenth-century agency which, in my opinion, did much for the dissemination of the belief underlying the practice of throwing a tub to a whale, and more, consequently, for acquaintance over large sections of Western Europe—all the way from Germany to Scandinavia to England to Iceland to Italy—with the phrase "to throw a tub to a whale." This agency was a *book*. It was Sebastian Münster's *Cosmography* of 1544. Münster's *Cosmography*, written in Latin, then still the lingua franca of the Western world, especially the world of scholarship, contained woodcuts. One of them (see Plate I) is entitled "Monstra marina et terrestria, quae passim in partibus aquilonis inveniuntur." In the top left-hand corner of this woodcut sailors are shown throwing out barrels to a whale, a most ferocious monster, that is getting too close for comfort to the ship. And the accompanying text reads in translation: "Occasionally whales, as big as mountains, are sighted in the neighborhood of Iceland. These whales cause the ships to capsize, unless they are scared off by the sound of trumpets [you will see a person blowing on what is evidently a trumpet] or unless they are fooled by means of round and empty casks which have been thrown into the sea and which, while they play with them, afford them amusement." Münster's book was translated from Latin into German, French, Italian, and English, and the various translations contained illustrations made from the original woodcuts of the original Latin edition with the explanations given on the woodcuts which, for obvious reasons, were never changed into the new language. One of the earliest impacts of Münster's *Cosmography* on England and English information and thinking is indicated by the following passage taken from *A Briefe Collection and compendious extract of straunge and memorable things, gathered oute of the Cosmographye of Sebastian Munster* (London, 1572): "There be great Whales as big as hylles almost nighe unto Iselande which are sometimes openly seene and those will drowne and overthrowe shyps, except they be made afearde with the sound of trompets and drums, or except some round and empty vessels be caste vnto them, wherwith they may play and sporte theym, because they are delited in playing with such thinges."[23]

A similar role in the dissemination of whale lore of this sort was played by the *Historia de Gentibus Septentrionalibus* of Olaus Magnus Gothus (Rome, 1555). (See Plate II). Note that here the two whales—they look to me as if they were licking their chops—are to be kept from doing mischief by one means only, the throwing out of tubs.[24] Plate III illustrates the fact that the proverb concerning the tub and the whale by the beginning of the seventeenth century had become part and parcel of the then flourishing emblem literature. The particular illustration is taken from the very popular book on "symbols," i.e., emblems, put together by Joachim Camerarius (d. 1574) and called *Symbolorum et Emblematum ex Aquatilibus et Reptilibus Desumptorum Centuria Quarta* (1604). Here, once more, you see one sailor blowing his trumpet, in an attempt to stave off the evil day, and several sailors casting out tubs and other cargo in an endeavor to save themselves from the whale. Above the engraving appears the distich:

> Ut te ipsum et navim serves, comitesque pericli,
> In pontum cunctas abjice divitias.

(If you wish to save yourself and your ship and those who share the danger, then throw out into the ocean all your possessions!)

Notice the "moral twist!"[25]

This emblem tradition with its moralizing twist continues into the eighteenth century. Witness the entry in Zedler's *Universal-Lexicon*, which appeared between 1732 and (counting in the supplementary volumes) 1754 and represents the thinking of the older German enlightenment: "When the whale plays with a barrel the sailors have thrown to him and thus allows the ship time to escape, he is an emblem of the fool who, for the sake of empty nothings, neglects his true profit."[26] This is the encyclopedia which was used by scholars and poets and writers around the middle and during the second half of the eighteenth century. It is noteworthy that the encyclopedia does not smile at the stupidity of superstitious people who believe that by throwing a tub to the whale they can avert evil. Rather does the entry call attention to the foolishness of the whale! And it is also noteworthy that Kleist could have got his information about the whale from this standard reference work of his time, quite aside from the greater possibility that he became acquainted with the *proverb*, as he calls it, by hearing it used and by remembering it.

Let us return for a moment to the illustrations in Münster's *Cosmography* and the text accompanying them, to the statement in the *Brief Collection* . . . of London, 1573, and to the illustration in Camerarius' *Centuria Quarta*. There is mentioned and pictured in these places a sort of companion piece to the throwing out of a tub to a whale: I refer to the blowing of trumpets and the making of noise in order to frighten away the monster.

It is right here where may be found the explanation of the fact that so many countries and languages of Western Europe know about the *apotropaion*, the *Abwehrzauber*, the magical means of averting disaster from a ship when it is attacked by a sea monster. The explanation may be that we are face to face with something that can be and has been learned from a book, with something that was unearthed by an antiquarian or by a humanist or a Renaissance person who had been pondering over some quaint and curious volume of forgotten lore and who was passing his discovery on as something worthwhile to know and, perhaps, in the hope that what had "worked" in the olden times, might "work" once more. In addition, of course, there may have been actual practice and actual belief, derived from personal experiences during encounters with whales and similar marine giants. Or there may have been both, the actual experience somewhere off the coast of South America or off the coast of Iceland, *and* the rediscovery of ancient lore which would or could take on the nature of precedent. We may, then, in this case be dealing with a bit of revived antiquity, dating back to the times of Alexander the Great and his admiral Nearchus. Strabo in his *Geographica*, in Book XV, Chapter II, paragraphs 11 and 12, and Arrianus in his *Indike*, Chapter XXX, tell the story of Alexander's admiral Nearchus and the near misadventure he and his fleet suffered in the Persian Gulf. The fleet was threatened by a great number of sea monsters, giant whales, and it seemed as if the ships and the sailors and the marines were lost. Then some of the pilots, evidently persons from the neighborhood and familiar with the local fauna, advised the foreigners, who had never before met this sort of enemy, they should make noise, lots of it, by blowing trumpets, clanging their weapons together, and so on. Thereupon Nearchus ordered that this be done and he also ordered the ships to proceed as fast as possible, to the accompaniment of this hellish din, in the direction of the whales.

And it worked! The whales submerged! The noise was too much for them. There are several other accounts of this "battle" and accounts based on the fear whales have of noise.[27]

So far I have told you a bit about the German, English, Dutch, Scandinavian, Italian, and Greek ancestors of Heinrich von Kleist's whale. There is still another ancestor, the Hebrew ancestor. His story must be told by means of the medieval interpretation of Psalm 104:26b.

Psalm 104:26b reads: ". . . there is that leviathan, whom thou hast made to play therein." That is, there is the crocodile, the dragon, the water serpent, the whale, the sea monster—any marine monster—there is that Moby-Dick of the oceanic fauna, whom thou, O God, hast made, fashioned, created, to play in the sea, such an animal's natural habitat.[28]

The translation of the King James Version quoted a moment ago is a correct translation of the original Hebrew text. It is, furthermore, a translation which fits the context. For Psalm 104 is a paean composed in praise of *Deus omnipotens, creator caeli et terrae*, the Almighty Creator, and at the same time it magnifies his fatherly kindness toward his creatures, including man. God has created and he takes care of the wild asses, the storks, the wild goats, the conies, the beasts of the fields, the fowls of the heaven, the young lions. Verse 24: "O Lord, how manifold are thy works! In wisdom hast thou made them all: the earth is full of thy riches." And now, having exhausted the earth and the sky, the psalmist moves on to another realm, the sea, for additional examples of the greatness and the majesty of the Creator. Verses 25 and 26: "So is this great and wide sea, wherein are things creeping innumerable, both small and great beasts. There go the ships. *There is that leviathan whom thou hast made to play therein.*"

In other words, the ocean is the pool or, as it were, the playground of the mighty sea monsters, of whom leviathan is the representative, which display God's power and goodness as they disport themselves in the sea—as Coverdale (1535) translates: "there is that Leuiathan, whom thou hast made, to take his pastyme therin." One is reminded of Herman Melville's description of the playing whale: "Stealing unawares upon the whale in the fancied security of the middle of solitary seas, you find him unbent from the vast corpulence of his dignity, and kittenlike, he plays on the ocean as if it were a hearth. But still you see his power in his play." Or one thinks of Tennyson's "The Lotus-Eaters": "Where the wallowing monster spouted his foam-fountains in the sea."

All this, I submit, makes sense. But notice how this sense, which is based on the Hebrew text, is changed in the course of time, starting, close to the beginning of the Christian era, with the translation of the Seventy, the Greek Septuaginta, and continuing that mistranslation into the Latin Vulgata of St. Jerome and, based on the wording of the Vulgata, embalming the mistranslation in the medieval commentaries, one author copying the interpretation of his predecessor or predecessors and passing it on to his successor—young Luther belongs to this group as long as he worked with the Vulgata text only—and thus establishing what amounts to a hallowed exegesis of our passage which now makes out this marine monster, this whale, this leviathan, to be a stupid beast, a gullible creature, created by God, not in order to show forth his almighty power and boundless goodness, but to be laughed at, to be ridiculed, to be mocked, and dealing ultimately not with *a* or *the* whale, but with *him* who is represented by the whale or leviathan, that is the Devil, *der dumme Teufel*, the stupid devil, as he is called so often in German—and all this, in order to explain the role, the utterly stupid role, played by the Devil or Satan in connection with the redemption of mankind through the death of the Savior on the cross.

All this became possible because one did *not* translate, correctly, "the leviathan whom thou hast made to play therein," i.e., in the ocean. Instead, one translated "the leviathan whom thou hast made, in order to play with it or with him," i.e., with leviathan; or one translated "in order to play with leviathan," i.e., to "ridicule leviathan, to hold him or it up to ridicule."

This mistranslation or these mistranslations resulted in two separate interpretations of Psalm 104:26b. One is the haggadic and rabbinical interpretation to which Heine alludes and which he reduces *ad absurdum* in his irreverent poem, "Disputation." Reluctantly, very reluctantly, I shall pass over this interpretation. The other one is the Christian interpretation of Psalm 104:26b. This interpretation I shall briefly summarize, because in it we have an application of all that is contained in the phrase "to throw a tub to a whale," emphasizing, however, the stupidity of the animal which permits itself to be sidetracked from its primary purpose by lack of understanding or, putting it positively, by its own stupidity.

These, then, are the principal features of the medieval Christian interpretation of Psalm 104:26b. The comments are based on the accepted rendering of the Vulgate. The context is disregarded. The *draco* is no longer a sea monster. The *draco* is *diabolus*, the devil. The passage means: "Thou, O God, hast created the devil." Originally, of course, God being incapable of creating something bad, the devil was a good angel. Through the fall of the angels he became a bad angel and an enemy of God and man, seeking to destroy man and to keep him out of God's kingdom. He should have known that he could not succeed. But he was too stupid to realize that he could not overcome God and God's plan of saving humanity. God, when he created the angel who later became the devil, foreknew what would happen, and so he took precautionary measures: he created the devil *ad illudendum ei*, for the express purpose that he, the devil, should be mocked; that he should be put to shame, and that he be neutralized. Result: the devil is no longer to be feared; man, i.e., Christian man, can laugh at the devil. As a matter of fact, all creation, to the extent that it is on the side of God, can laugh at the devil—can really have a good time at the devil's expense. The devil has become a tragico-comical figure, mainly because he is ignorant of what is going on: he does not know that he is foreordained to defeat through Christ's death; he does not realize that Christ's death will free man from the dominion and fear of the devil—that man, and others, as a result of it can *illudere ei*, poke fun at him, the "stupid devil," *der dumme Teufel,* this familiar figure of German-Germanic tradition. God himself is the first one to mock the devil, according to Albert the Great. Then, *a majore ad minus,* the good angels, the saints, *ecclesia,* and finally men (where "men" occasionally, at least by implication, means male human beings, and sometimes men and women). Yes, women also may and should, and do, deride the devil: if they have been prostitutes and later have become decent women through repentance and faith, they thereby have escaped from the jaws of the hellish monster which were ready to clamp down on them; faith in Christ has snatched them out of the mouth, out of the *gula* of the monstrous whale or dragon; they find refuge and eternal safety on the ship of the Church— "there go the ships," says the psalmist—and they literally thumb their noses at the gullible, stupid beast. The devil may not know; he does not realize that he is powerless; but God, the angels, and Christian men and women know it, and this knowledge coupled with the lack of knowledge on the part of the devil, as frequently in the devil scenes of the medieval religious plays, makes the devil's acts antics and him a comical figure.[29]

The source of this Western medieval Christian interpretation of Psalm 104:26b is, in all likelihood, the view taken of the redemption of mankind by several of the early Eastern Fathers, a view differing significantly from other, orthodox and more conventional views of this topic. It is, without going into details, the view according to which the redemption of mankind, achieved through the atoning death of Christ, really amounts to a sleight-of-hand performance on the part of God the Father who puts something over on the (stupid) devil. God, in other words, deceives the devil. The devil, when he contrived the death of Christ, did not know what he was letting himself in for. St. Paul's words in 1 Cor. 2:7-8 seem to have started this train of thought: "We speak the wisdom of God in mystery, even the hidden wisdom, which God ordained before the world unto our glory: which none of the princes of this world knew"—the chief prince is the devil—"for had they known it, they would not have crucified the Lord of glory."

According to this view, God, as it were, used the human nature or flesh of the Savior as a bait to lure the devil into thinking he could kill this human being, this Jesus of Nazareth; and so Leviathan, often represented as a monstrous whale, swallows the man Jesus, he kills him, unaware that thereby he brings about his own undoing, being caught on the hook of the divinity of Christ which God the Father, the divine fisherman, had cleverly disguised with the human flesh of God the Son. This view, in one form or another, is found in writings, genuine or merely ascribed, of Ignatius, bishop of Antioch (beginning of the second century) and, perhaps, also in writings of Origen. It certainly appears in the writings of Gregory of Nazianzus, Gregory of Nyssa, of Basil, the bishop of Caesarea, and of Cyrill, the bishop of Jerusalem. If St. Augustine (d. 430) was not the first of the Western Fathers to familiarize himself with this view and to accept it, then it was presumably his prestige in the West which brought about acquaintance with and use of this explanation of the economy of the redemption in theology and in art (especially in painting). The bishop of Hippo refers several times to the bait-hook trick by means of which the dragon-whale-devil is caught, just as he refers to the *muscipula*, the mousetrap, into which the devil-mouse is lured by the smell and the sight of the cheese which is, of course, the human nature of Christ.[30]

I have taken you far afield. Our starting point was, depending upon how you look at it, Dresden in the Saxony of Heinrich von Kleist at the beginning of the nineteenth century or it was that part of Northern Germania where Arminius, the chief of the Cherusci, on the ninth day of the ninth month of the ninth year of our era defeated the Roman general Quintilius Varus. And then we roamed over land and sea and watched Alexander the Great's fleet in the Persian Gulf have an encounter with a school of whales; we heard of a German who threw a tub to a whale somewhere off the coast of South America during the first half of the sixteenth century; and we were told how Englishmen, and Dutchmen, and Scandinavians, and Italians, and a Flemish painter, and a German theologian and a German humanist, each one, added here a mite and there a bit to our knowledge or at least to the lore of tubs and whales; and eventually even God Himself was made to contribute in the words of His commentators to the understanding of the saying "to throw a tub to a whale."

It may seem extravagant to go to such lengths, to bring in Church Fathers and even the creator of the Leviathan-Whale, God Himself. But let me ask: "Canst thou draw out leviathan with a hook? or his tongue with a cord which thou lettest down? Canst thou put an hook into his nose? or bore his jaw through with a thorn? Upon earth there is not his like, who is made without fear. He beholdeth all high things: he is a king over all the children of pride." Melville was right: "Applied to any other creature, than the Leviathan—to an ant or a flea—such portly terms might justly be deemed unwarrantably grandiloquent. But when Leviathan, the Whale, is the text, the case is altered."

Notes

1. Heinrich von Kleist composed his drama *Die Hermannsschlacht (The Battle of Hermann or Arminius)* in the city of Dresden in Saxony during the second half of the year 1808. It was published for the first time in 1821 by the Shakespeare translator Ludwig Tieck. The members of the Detmold Court Theatre, under the direction of August Pichler, presented the play for the first time on August 29, 1839 in Pyrmont, a small town in the former principality of Waldeck, celebrated to this day for its mineral springs.

2. Adolf Lichtenheld, ed., *Die Hermannsschlacht: Mit Einleitung und Anmerkungen* (Vienna, n.d., [1885?]), p. 80. *Heinrich von Kleists Werke: Im Verein mit Georg Minde-Pouet und Reinhold Steig hg. von Erich Schmidt, Kritisch durchgesehene und erläuterte Gesamtausgabe*, Bibliographisches Institut (Leipzig, n.d.), II. Band, bearbeitet von Erich Schmidt, p. 463 n.

3. *Sämtliche Schriften*, hg. von Lachmann-Muncker, X³, p. 216: "Eine Tonne, für unsere kritische Wallfische! Ich freue mich im voraus, wie trefflich sie damit spielen werden. Sie ist einzig und allein für sie ausgeworfen; besonders für den kleinen Wallfisch in dem Salzwasser zu Halle!" (*Hamburgische Dramaturgie*, II. Band, 101–104. Stück); also XIII, p. 396: "Tonnen, dachte ich, den jungen Wallfischen ausgeworfen!" "Ernst und Falk. Gespräche für Freymäurer. Fortsetzung. 1780. Viertes Gespräch").

4. Weimar edition, 38, 367.

5. Daniel Caspers von Lohenstein, *Grossmüthiger Feld-Herr Arminius oder Herrmann, Nebst seiner Durchlauchtigsten Thusnelda in einer sinn-reichen Staats- Liebes- und Helden-Geschichte* . . . (2nd ed.; Leipzig, 1731), I, 84a: "Die gerechtesten Herrscher, zu geschweigen die, welche sich mit Gewalt oder Arglist auf den Thron gespielt, müsten . . . den Pöfel mit Schau-Spielen und andern unnützen Zeit-Vertreib von der Bekümmerung umb die Herrschaft abziehen, und diesem so wie dem sonst erschrecklichen Wallfische eine Tonne zum Spielen fürwerffen. . . ." The reference in *Deutsches Wörterbuch* is, presumably, to the first edition (1689–1690).

6. Valentin Langmantel, ed., *Ulrich Schmidels Reise nach Süd-Amerika in den Jahren 1534-1554: Nach der Münchener Handschrift*, BLVS, CLXXXIV, (Tübingen, 1889), 110, ll. 18-30; cf. p. 162: "Item es hat auch vil annder selzamer vischs unnd möhrwunder, die nit genug sindt zu schreibenn oder darvonn auch nit woll aigentlich zu reden. Es ist ein ander grosser vischs, haist auff sein spanischs sumere, das ist teuschs ein schaubhuetvischs; das ist ein vischs darvonn mann nit genug sagen khan noch schreibenn, so ein gewaltiger unnd mechtiger grosser vischs ist es, thuet ann etlichen orten den schieffenn grossen schaden, denn so kein windt verhannden, derowegen die schieff stiel liegenn unnd khunen weder hindersich, noch fürsich, so komptt dieser fischs mit solchem gewaltigenn stoss anns schieff, das es alles erpitmet unnd erzittert, so mus man alsdann vonn stund an eins oder 2 grosse fas hin aus dem schieff werffenn unnd so gemelter vischs die vesser überkumptt, so lest er das schieff unnd spielt mit den vessern." See also pp. 21, 25. The oldest printed edition is from 1567 (Frankfurt a. M.); other editions came out in 1597 (*s.l.*) and in 1599 (Nuremberg). Schmidel's German account was translated into Latin (1599), Dutch (1706), Spanish (1731, 1836), and French (1837).

7. Weimar edition, *Die Deutsche Bibel*, III, 516, ll. 28-33; "Pomeranus dicebat se audisse a nautis, quod navigantes proiiciunt vas in aquam, cum quo ludit, wirfft auff in die lufft et iterum devorat."

8. "Nauium recens picatarum odore adeo oblectantur, vt proxime accedentes sese naui affricent. Nautae de nauis subuersione timidi, picata dolia eis obijciunt; vt nauim relinquant. Ludunt ceti cum dolijs, & aquam per fistulam capitis

emissam in sublime eructant." See also Fletcher S. Bassett, *Sea Phantoms or Legends and Superstitions of the Sea and of Sailors in All Lands and at All Times* (rev. ed.; Chicago, 1892), p. 237 (reproduction of woodcut, entitled "Whales Following Ship. Aldrovandus." Two spouting whales attacking a ship. A trumpeter standing on platform blowing trumpet. Two tubs in water between whales and ship. A third tub being lowered into water. The original of this woodcut is undoubtedly to be found in Sebastian Münster's *Cosmography* (see Plate I, following p. 88).

9. *Johann Fischarts Geschichtklitterung (Gargantua)*, ed. A. Alsleben. "Neudrucke deutscher Litteraturwerke des xvi. und xvii. Jahrhunderts," Nos. 65-71, p. 282. So already in the first edition of 1575. Compare Rabelais' *Gargantua*, chap. 23, "Comment Gargantua feut institué par Ponocrates en telle discipline qu' il ne perdoit heure du jour," and chap. 33, "Comment . . . feut un monstreux physetere apperceu. . . . Par le conseil du pilot feurent sonnées les trompettes . . . "; and see Gottlob Regis, ed., *Meister Franz Rabelais der Arzeney Doctoren Gargantua und Pantagruel* . . . (Leipzig, 1832), I, 684-686, and II, i, 665.

10. Johann Joachim Christoph Bode, trans., *Michael Montaigne's Gedanken und Meinungen über allerley Gegenstände. Ins Deutsche übersetzt* (Berlin, 1794), V, 117-118: ". . . Kurz, durch Auswerfung dieser Spieltonnen für den Wallfisch, wodurch er ihre Wuth zerstreute, und auf eitele Berathschlagungen ablenkte, schläferte er das Volk endlich ein." The original reads: "Somme que, par telle dispensation d'amusemens, divertissant leur furie et la dissipant en vaines consultations, il l' endormit en fin . . ." (*Michel de Montaigne, Essais, Livre Troisième, Chapitres I à VIII* . . . , par Jean Plattard, Paris, 1932, p. 67).

11. See *Deutsches Wörterbuch*, XI, 1, 1, *s.v.* "Tonne": Goethe—"Wie will man Kinder stillen ohne Puppen; oder Wallfische fangen ohne Tonnen" (Weimar edition, 38, 367); Rückert— "Zum Spielwerk werf' ich ihrer Meuterei / Wie einem Walfisch leere Tonnen hin" (10, 394); Klinger—"Der Bürgermeister, der ein heimlicher Feind des Schöppen war, warf ihm schnell eine Tonne hin" (3, 67); "das märchen von der tonne wurde schon von den Schweizern und von Gottsched den deutschen lesern empfohlen; vgl. auch Herder 3, 312, J. G. Forster 6, 142." In addition, *Deutsches Wörterbuch* mentions Lohenstein, Kleist, Lessing, and Swift. In XIII, col. 1223, *s.v.* "Walfisch," is mentioned, in addition to Bode, Kleist, and Lessing (only one quotation) Gottlieb Wilhelm Rabener. Rabener's *Schriften*, 2 (1751), 82, cited in *Deutsches Wörterbuch*, was not available to me. The following Rabener quotation is from "Abhandlung von Buchdruckerstöcken" (S. Neue Beiträge zum Vergnügen des Verstandes und Witzes, 1ster Band, 5tes Stück. 1745): "Ich dürfte nur erdichten, dass ein gewisser berühmter Mann, den ich nicht kenne, und den auch sonst niemand kennt, sich habe verlauten lassen: dergleichen Buchdruckerstöcke wären nichts anderes, als was die Tonnen bey den Wallfischen sind, welche man ihnen vorwirft, damit sie das Schiff in Ruhe lassen. Man gäbe nämlich dem geneigten Leser ein Bildchen in die Hand, dass er damit spielen, und die Schrift selbst verschonen sollte." Cf. Rabener's *Satiren* (5th ed.; Leipzig, 1759), p. 280, and *Gottlieb Wilhelm Rabeners Sämmtliche Werke*, ed. Ernst Ortlepp (Stuttgart, 1839), I, 353-354. In the case of the proverbial phrase, "dem Wallfisch eine Tonne zuwerfen," *Deutsches Wörterbuch*, which is not a thesaurus of proverbs nor a collection of proverbial sayings, has much more material than can be found in Karl Friedrich Wilhelm Wander's *Deutsches Sprichwörter-Lexikon: Ein Hausschatz für das deutsche Volk* (5 vols.; Leipzig, 1867-1880). *S.v.* "Walfisch," Wander lists the proverbial phrase "dem Walfisch die rothe Tonne hinwerfen" and explains the phrase as meaning "Jemand einen Gegenstand der Beschäftigung bieten, um seine Aufmerksamkeit und Kraft von Dingen abzulenken,

durch deren Angriff er gefährlich werden kann." No documentation! And *s.v.*
"Tonne" only the entry "Er hat eine Tonne in die See geworfen (dem Schiffer
ein Warnungszeichen gegeben)" comes close to our proverbial phrase. Again
no documentation! On the other hand, the collection of material in English is
plentiful and its documentation is adequate or good. Here are a few titles:
Notes & Queries, VIII (1853), 220, 304-305, 328; John S. Farmer and W. E.
Henley, eds., *Slang and Its Analogues Past and Present* (1904), VII, 220;
Temple Scott, ed., *Prose Works of Jonathan Swift, D.D.* (London, 1905), I, 39;
John Bartlett, *Familiar Quotations* (Boston, 1914), p. 291; *Swift's A Tale of a
Tub*, ed. A. C. Guthkelch and D. Nichol Smith (Oxford, 1920), pp. xxvi-
xxviii; G. L. Apperson, *English Proverbs and Proverbial Phrases: A Historical
Dictionary* (London-Toronto, 1929), p. 651; Morris Palmer Tilley, *A Dictionary
of the Proverbs of England in the Sixteenth and Seventeenth Centuries . . .*
(1950), p. 688; David P. French, "The Title of 'A Tale of a Tub,'" *Notes &
Queries*, CXCVI (1951), 473-474.

12. Cf. *Handwörterbuch des deutschen Aberglaubens*, I, 129-150.

13. I quote from the 1632 edition (London, printed by Adam Islip) and a
copy once owned and autographed by Robert Southey.

14. "Tub" meaning "pulpit" documented from ca. 1640. See *NED* and Eric
Partridge, *A Dictionary of Slang and Unconventional English* (New York,
1961), p. 913.

15. See *Alsfelder Passionsspiel*, ed. C. W. M. Grein (Cassel, 1874), ll. 133 ff.
Ibid., l. 139: "Lucifer in dem throne." Cf. R. Froning, *Das Drama des Mittel-
alters*, Zweiter Teil, p. 571; Friedberg *Passionsspiel* (*Haupts Zs. 7*, 547); Künzl.
Fronleichnamsspiel, v. 205: Lucifer in trone . . . ; Frankfurter Dirigierrolle in
Froning, p. 343: Deinde Sathanas ducat Jesum super dolium, quod positum
sit in medio ludi representans pinnaculum templi. . . . Item Sathanas ducat
Jhesum ad alium locum ludi super dolium representans montem excelsum,
ubi ostendat ei thesaurum et omnia regna mundi dicens . . . ; Froning, p. 581:
Sic Lucifer descendit de doleo; Haller Passion 98, 14 f.; Erlau IV, 132, etc.;
Spiel von Frau Jutten, l. 35: Luciper in deim throne. E. Wilken, *Geschichte
der geistlichen Spiele in Deutschland* (Göttingen, 1872), pp. 219 (with reference
to Redentiner Osterspiel), 224, 227; E. Hartl, *Das Drama des Mittelalters: Sein
Wesen und sein Werden . . .* (Leipzig, 1937), p. 64 with note.

16. "I Henry Watson . . . at the requeste of my worshypfull mayster
Wynkyn de Worde . . ." Of this translation by Henry Watson, the 1509 printing,
there exists today only one copy. It is a vellum copy, in the Bibliothèque Na-
tionale. Fortunately, there is available a facsimile of this one and only copy:
*Americana Series: Photostat Reproductions by the Massachusetts Historical
Society*, No. 163 (Boston, 1926). I have compared the pertinent passage in the
1509 printing with the corresponding passage in the 1517 Wynkyn de Worde
printing of *The shyppe of fooles*, now in the British Museum. Of this 1517
printing there is a film copy available, Edwards Brothers, No. 832. Cf. Fr.
Aurelius Pompen, O.F.M. *The English Versions of The Ship of Fools: A Contribution to the History of the Early French Renaissance in England* (London,
1925).

17. See A. J. Barnouw in "Monthly Letter, December 1939, of the Netherlands America Foundation," pp 1-3. In the 1611 printed version, the fourth
line reads, "That throwes out emptie vessels, so to stay," so quoted in *NED*.

18. Grosart, II, 27.

19. Richardson, *The History of Clarissa Harlowe* (1747-1748), III, 51:
"When a man talks to a woman upon such subjects, let her be ever so much in
Alt, 'tis strange, if he cannot throw out a tub to a whale;—that is to say, if he
cannot divert her from resenting one bold thing, by uttering two or three

full as bold; but for which more favourable interpretations will lie." See also Mrs. Brooke, *Lady J. Manderville* (1763), p. 148: "A wise writer . . . should throw in now and then an indiscretion in his conduct to play with, as seamen do a tub to the whale." Both quotes in Apperson.

20. Malkin, *Gil Blas* (Routledge), p. 41, quoted in Farmer and Henley, p. 220. See also Thomas Chandler Haliburton, *The Old Judge: Or, Life in a Colony* (London, 1849), I, 124, top. The quotation is from the copy owned by the University of Texas Library: ". . . your 'dashing Governor,' a regular politician, who believes that every man has his price . . . advocates a united legislature for all the colonies, the creation of a Viceroy, and the construction of a railroad to the Pacific, and other gigantic projects—tubs for the whale."

21. I owe this passage to Professor A. J. Barnouw (see n. 17).

22. See Gustav Glück, *Pieter Breughel The Elder*, trans. Eveline Byam Shaw (Paris, 1936), plate 63; description and discussion, p. 34.

23. "Cete grandia ad instar montium prope Islandiam aliquando conspiciuntur, quae naues euertunt nisi sono tubarum absterreantur, aut missis in mare rotundis & uacuis uasis, quorum lusu delectantur, ludificentur" (1554 ed., p. 850). See Guthkelch and Smith, pp. xxvii ff. and Gerald Strauss, *Sixteenth-Century Germany: Its Topography and Topographers* (Madison, Wis., 1959), pp. 127, 184.

24. The pertinent passage reads: "Verum malignitati eius remedio occurritur opportuno, tuba videlicit militari . . . ob asperum acutumque sonum, quem ferre haud potest: & magnis, ac immanibus vasis, seu doliis eiectis, cursum beluae impedientibus, siue pro lusu ei oppositis" (Book XXI, chap. vii, p. 736, of the 1555 Rome edition). The plate is reproduced from Olaus Magnus, *Historia om de Nordiska Folken*, Fjärde Delen (Uppsala-Stockholm, 1925), p. 246. The text indicates that Olaus Magnus knows about frightening whales away by means of noise. Compare what Erich Pontoppidan, Bishop of Bergen, who published his celebrated *Natural History of Norway* in 1755, has to say about a similar topic: "When they [the fishermen] are far from land it would be in vain to attempt to row away from them [the sea-snakes]; for these creatures shoot through the water like an arrow out of a bow, seeking constantly the coldest places. In this case they put the former method [this apparently refers to rowing against the highest part of the sea-snake, the part which is visible, and this makes the snake dive immediately (p. 203)] in execution, or lye upon their oars, and throw anything that comes to hand at them. If it be but a scuttle, or any light thing, so they be touch'd, they generally plunge into the water, or take another course," p. 203 of Part II, sec. viii (on the sea-snake) of *The Natural History of Norway . . . Interspersed with Physiological Notes from eminent Writers, and Transactions of Academies. In Two Parts. Translated from the Danish Original of the Right Rev^d. Erich Pontoppidan, Bishop of Bergen in Norway, and Member of the Royal Academy of Sciences at Copenhagen*, London, 1755. See Charles Gould, *Mythical Monsters* (London, 1886), p. 267.

25. The following passage seems to belong here. It is taken from *Mundus Symbolicus . . . conscriptus a . . . Philippo Picinello . . . traductus a . . . Augustino Erath* (Cologne, 1695), Book VI: "Pisces," chap. viii: Balaena, sec. 31 (p. 440a). "Miseri mortales, caducis rerum terrenarum bonis nimium quantum immersi, geminato damno, & coeli & terrae jacturam faciunt. Balaenae symbolo id demonstrat Aresius, quae dum vacuum dolium, a navigantibus objectum, inani labore, ac lusu prorsus inutili jactat, iisdem opportunam fugae ac salutis capessendae moram relinquit. Epigraphen addidit: FRUSTRA DECIPITUR. Verissime enim totam hominum mundanorum vitam nil nisi veram vanitatem, ac lusum continuum, inanissimumque dixeris. Inter Scriptores Sacros aperte id testatur

John G. Kunstmann

S. Gregorius Papa: Vana sunt gaudia saeculi: quasi manentia abblandiuntur, sed amatores suos cito transeundo decipiunt. Et inter prophanos Seneca: Cito nos omnis voluptas relinquit, quae fluit & transit, & pene, antequam veniat, aufertur."

26. Once more am I indebted to Prof. A. J. Barnouw who, in turn, is indebted to Ludwig Burchard.

27. I have used the edition of *Strabonis Geographica* prepared by Gustavus Kramer (Berlin, 1852), together with Abraham Jacob Penzel's *Des Strabo . . . allgemeine Erdbeschreibung*, Vol. IV (Lemgo, 1777), and for *Arriani Anabasis et Indica* the edition by Fr. Dübner (Paris, 1865). Concerning noise which frightens whales away cf. Philostratus: ". . . τὰς δὲ ναῦς ἔρυμα τούτου κωδωνοφορεῖν κατα πρύμναν τε καὶ πρῷραν, τὴν δ' ἠχὼ ἐκπλήττειν τὰ θηρία, καὶ μὴ ἐᾶν ἐμπελόϳειν ταῖς ναυσί (naves vero ad eos [= cetos] arcendos tintinnabula a puppi atque prora suspensa habere, quorum sonitum terrere beluas, nec navibus ut appropinquent permittere) (*Philostratorum et Callistrati Opera recognovit*, Antonius Westermann, Paris, 1878, p. 71). See also Otto Keller, *Die antike Tierwelt* (Leipzig, 1909), I, 411; C. Plinii Secundi *Naturalis Historiae* Liber Nonus, III: ". . . non voce, non sonitu, non ictu, sed fragore terrentur, nec nisi ruina turbantur." Perkmann, "Lärm," *Handwörterbuch des deutschen Aberglaubens*, V (Berlin-Leipzig, 1933), coll. 914-915.

28. John G. Kunstmann, "The Text is Leviathan," *University of North Carolina Lectures in the Humanities*, Fourteenth and Fifteenth Series, 1957-1958, 1958-1959 (Chapel Hill, N. C., 1960), pp. 39 55.

29. I have examined the following translations of Psalm 104:26 (Vulgata, Psalm 103:26) which are based on the Vulgata text, and the following commentaries of this passage. My list is woefully incomplete: I have confined myself, mainly, to the *Patrologia Latina* and to translations and commentaries in English and German up to Luther and Coverdale, and of these I shall offer only enough instances to establish the fact that the interpretation of Psalm 104:26 in the Christian West was based on the text of the Vulgate which, in turn, attempted to follow the LXX; that the interpretation was allegorical and consistently so, frequently merely repeating or paraphrasing what a predecessor had written; and that the interpretation of the passage in the Christian West exemplifies, in a nonprofane area, the belief in the possibility of directing the whale's attention away from his intended victim, in this case of directing the attention of the Devil away from Christ, so that the salvation of the world could take place. This is the selected list: *LXX* (δράκων οὗτος ὃν ἔπλασας ἐμπαίϳευν αὐτῷ); *Vulgata* (draco iste quem formasti ad illudendum ei); *Eusebius Hieronymus PL* XXVI, col. 1202: draco . . . datus est in hoc mundo ad illudendum nobis [ascribed to Jerome]; cf. coll. 833-835: an exthrahere poteris Leviathan hamo? Hami vero et sagenae differentiam hanc esse existimo ut hamum ipsum Salvatorem Filium Dei, carne vestitum intelligamus, sagena autem dici potest missa praedicatio Evangelii . . . ; also *PL*, XXIX, coll. 327-328 (Gallicanum Psalterium and Romanum Psalterium); *Tyrannius Rufinus* (d. 410; exerted great influence on Western theology through his translations of Eastern Fathers; *PL*, XXI, Coll. 354-355: . . . qui habebat mortis imperium, rapuit quidem in morte corpus Jesu, non sentiens in eo hamum divinitatis inclusum . . .); *Augustinus* (d. 430; *PL*, XXXVII, coll. 1381-1385: . . . Jam tu illude draconi: ad hoc enim hic factus est draco . . . sunt angeli qui illudant draconi; *PL*, XXXVIII, col. 726, Sermo CXXX: Incidimus enim in principem hujus saeculi, qui seduxit Adam et servum fecit, et coepit nos tamquam vernaculos possidere. Sed venit Redemptor et victus est deceptor. Et quid fecit Redemptor noster captivatori nostro? Ad pretium nostrum tetendit muscipulam crucem suam: posuit ibi quasi escam sanguinem suum. Ille autem potuit sanguinem

istum fundere, non meruit bibere . . . ; *PL,* XXXVIII, coll. 745-746, Sermo
CXXXIV: . . . Quid ergo ad horam exsultasti, quia invenisti in Christo carnem
mortalem? Muscipula tua erat: unde laetatus es, inde captus es. Ubi te exsultasti aliquid invenisse, inde nunc doles quod possederas perdidisse . . . ;
PL, XXXVIII, coll. 1209-1210, Sermo CCLXIII: . . . Exsultavit diabolus quando
mortuus est Christus, et ipsa morte Christi est diabolus victus: tanquam in
muscipula escam accepit. . . . Muscipula diaboli, crux Domini: esca qua capere-
tur, mors Domini . . .); ascribed to *Arnobius Junior* ("qui paulo post sanctum
Leonem papam vixisse videtur," *PL,* LIII, coll. 477-478); *Prosper Aquitanus* (a
younger contemporary of St. Augustine, *PL,* LI, col. 295: . . . ex angelo diabolus
factus est, ut malitiae et nequitiae ipsius a sanctis illuderetur . . .); *Cassiodorus
Senator* (d. 563; *PL,* LXX, coll. 737-738: . . . a Deo ita formatus est, ut ei
illuderetur ab angelis. . . . Illuditur etiam et a fidelibus viris . . .); *Gregorius
Magnus* (d. 604; *PL,* LXXVI, coll. 680-683; cf. also, because based on Gregory,
Odo Abbas Cluniacensis II in *PL,* CXXXIII, coll. 489-490); *Isidorus Hispalensis*
(d. 636; *PL,* LXXXII, col. 317; LXXXIII, coll. 567-577); *Beda Venerabilis* (d.
735; *Bedae presbyteri Commentarius in Psalmos,* Vol. VIII, Basileae, MDLXIII,
col. 966: . . . Quem tu in dignitate formasti, ipse ante se deformauit, & sic
formatus est ad illudendum eis, id est taliter ut illudatur ei a fidelibus . . .);
Walafridus Strabo Fuldensis (d. 849; *PL,* CXIII, coll. 840, 1017, 1265; the references are to his *Glossa Ordinaria*); *Haymon Halberstatensis* (d. 853; *PL,*
CXVI, coll. 549-550: . . . draco iste, id est, principalis diabolus, scilicet Beelzebub,
qui per Leviathan significatur, quem prima creatione creasti bonum, post casum
vero formasti ad illudendum, id est, illusibilem fecisti: illud enim ei etiam mere-
trices facient, quas in foedis vitiis illaqueatas cum [?] fortius tenere putat,
ipsae ab illius manibus elabuntur et per poenitentiam in Christi corpus tra-
ducuntur. . . . See also col. 843); *Notker Labeo Teutonicus* (d. 1022; Richard
Heinzel and Wilhelm Scherer, eds., *Notkers Psalmen nach der Wiener Handschrift,* Strassburg, 1876, p. 165 [he follows St. Augustine]; see Ernst Henrici,
Die Quellen von Notkers Psalmen, Strassburg, 1878, p. 267); *Bruno Herbi-
polenis* (bishop of Würzburg, 1034-1045; *PL,* CXLII, col. 375,—based on Cassiodorus); *Bruno Carthusianus* (d. 1101; *PL,* CLII, col. 1187); *Bruno Astensis
Signiensis Episcopus* (d. 1125; *PL,* CLXIV, col. 1097: . . . Postquam draco
iste per suam superbiam cecidit, talem eum Dominus formavit, et ad talem
suae minorationis formam redigit, ut non solum viri, sed ipsae quoque mulieres
ei illudere eumque decipere possint); *Oddo Astensis Monachus Benedictinus*
(contemporary of Bruno Astensis?; *PL,* CLXV, col. 1281); Fred Harsley, ed.,
Eadwine's Canterbury Psalter, Part II, London, 1889 (= *EETS,* 92, p. 179, from
ca. 1150); Karl D. Bülbring, ed., *The Earliest Complete English Prose Psalter* . . . , Part I, London, 1891 (= *EETS,* 97, p. 126); *Petrus Lombardus, Magister
Sententiarum* (d. 1164; *PL,* CXCI, coll. 940-941, refers to Augustine and Alcuin);
Cod. Pal. Vind. 2682 (last quarter of twelfth century; cf. Nils Törnquist, ed.,
*Cod. Pal. Vind. 2682. I. Eine frühmittelhochdeutsche Interlinearversion der
Psalmen aus dem ehemaligen Benediktinerstifte Millstatt in Kärnten . . . ,*
Lund-Kopenhagen, 1934, p. 168); *Gerhohus Praepositus Reicherspergensis*
(twelfth century; *PL,* CXCIV, coll. 629-630: . . . draco . . . decipitur, quia ab
angelis, vel a sanctis illuditur); (a statement similar to that in the *Gerhohus*
passage is found in *Le Bestiaire de Philippe de Thaün,* ed. E. Walberg, Lund-
Paris, 1900, pp. cix, 71-2); *Cgm. 341* (cf. Richard Ziehm, *Die mittelhochdeutsche
Übersetzung der Psalmen in der Handschrift Cgm. 341,* dissertation, Greifswald,
1911, p. 108: disen dracken hast beschaffen ze spotten in); *Windberg MS. and
Treves MS.* (see E. G. Graff, ed., *Deutsche Interlinearversionen der Psalmen.
Aus einer Windberger Handschrift zu München—XII. Jahrhundert—und einer
Handschrift zu Trier—XIII. Jahrhundert—zum ersten Male hg.,* Quedlinburg-

Leipzig, 1939, "Bibliothek der gesammten deutschen National-Literatur . . . , X," p. 482); *Alexander de Hales* (d. 1245; *Postilla irrefragabilis doctoris domini Alexandri de ales ordinis minorum super psalmos Aurea*, Venet., 1496, f. 291ᵛ a-b: . . . capitur hamo uel laqueo: sic diabolo illusit Christus praetendit ei escam humanitatis sub qua abscondit ferrum diuinitatis et dum voluit humanitatem captus est potentia diuinitatis . . .); *Albertus Magnus* (d. 1280; *Opera Omnia*, ed. Augustus Borgnet, XVII, Paris, 1893, 50–51: . . . ei, i.e., draconi, illuditur a Deo, quando aliquis quem jam tenebat, convertitur . . . ; cf. Albert on whales, *op. cit.*, XII, 515-517, 553: dracones etiam dicunt timere tonitrua . . .); *Wiclif's Bible* (Wiclif, d. 1384; J. Forshall and F. Madden, eds., *The Holy Bible . . . in the Earliest English Versions Made from the Latin Vulgate by John Wycliffe and His Followers*, Oxford, 1850, II, 843: . . . This dragoun that thou hast formed [which thou hast formyd] to begile to hym [for to scorne hym]); *Richard Rolle of Hampole* (d. 1349); H. R. Bramley, ed., *The Psalter or Psalms of David and Certain Canticles with a Translation and Exposition in English by Richard Rolle of Hampole*, Oxford, 1884, pp. 364-365: This dragun . . . he is here to suffire hethynge [scorn, contempt] of thaim that ouercumys temptaciouns . . . ; see C. Horstman, ed., *Yorkshire Writers: Richard Rolle of Hampole and His Followers*, London, 1896, II, 236; þis dragoun þou made biforn / For to plaie with him in skorn; cf. H. E. Allen, *Writings Ascribed to Richard Rolle, Hermit of Hampole, and Materials for His Biography*, New York, 1927, pp. 161-192); W. Kurrelmeyer, ed., *Die erste deutsche Bibel*, VII = *BLVS*, CCLIV, 396: "Dirr drack den du hast gebildet: in zeuerspotten." *Young Luther* (*Dictata super Psalterium. 1513-16*, Weimar edition, Weimar, 1886, IV, 191): *Draco iste quem formasti &. Illuditur ei, quando corpus fidelium ei obiicitur occidendum et puniendum ac devorandum. Sed quia animam herentem Christo occidere non potest, ideo impingit in aculeum et vincitur ab anima, dum vincit corpus sanctorum, et per hoc triumphant eum et in iudicio vindictam in illum sument.* Luther later translates: . . . Da sind Walfische, die du gemacht hast, das sie drinnen schertzen. See *Dr. Martin Luther's Bibelübersetzung nach der letzten Original-Ausgabe, kritisch bearbeitet von H. E. Bindseil und H. A. Niemeyer*, Dritter Theil (Halle, 1848), p. 241. Cf. Anselm Salzer, *Die Sinnbilder und Beiworte Mariens in der deutschen Literatur und lateinischen, Hymnenpoesie des Mittelalters*, Programm des k.k. Obergymnasiums der Benediktiner zu Seitenstetten (Linz, 1886-1894), pp. 508-512: "Angelschnur." Also Hans Schmidt, *Jona. Eine Untersuchung zur vergleichenden Religionsgeschichte* (Göttingen, 1907), pp. 175, 176-177, n. 1.

30. Without going into the problem (s) of authenticity and attribution which exist in connection with the writings of one or the other of the Fathers mentioned, I prefer to give several general references: Hastings Rashdall, *The Idea of Atonement in Christian Theology* (London, 1920), pp. 305-333; James A. Kleist, trans., *The Epistles of St. Clement of Rome and St. Ignatius of Antioch* (Westminster, Md., 1946), pp. 67, 124; J. H. Srawley, trans. *The Epistles of St. Ignatius, Bishop of Antioch* (London, 1919), p. 50; J. H. Srawley, trans. and ed., *The Catechetical Oration of St. Gregory of Nyssa*, "Early Church Classics" (London, 1917), pp. 75-78; *Gregorii Theologi vulgo Naziazeni, Archiepiscopi Constantinopolitani Opera . . .*, PG, XXXVII, coll. 460-461. On God, the divine fisherman, see, for a start, G. G. Coulton, *Art and the Reformation* (New York, 1928), pp. 296-298, and Reinhold Köhler, "Der Leviathan am Angel," *Germania* (Pfeiffer), XIII (1868), 158-159.

VI

The University in Spain and in the Indies: Point and Counterpoint*

John Tate Lanning
Duke University

The university is one of the uniquely diverse legacies of the Middle Ages to Spain. For four hundred years there, it was as fixed a thing as a refectory in a monastery. Prerequisite to all the professions, it was something so natural and so laudable as to require neither explanation nor apology. And the Castilian kings, upon whose heads so much defamation has fallen, deferred to the university and gave it an exalted place in the nation. They launched it with a royal *cédula* and the pontiff endorsed it with a papal bull—not vice versa. They sanctioned those cherished privileges and exemptions so natural to a medieval guild, not only as a right of ostentation but as a guarantee of protection and autonomy. Alfonso the Learned in 1256 was so tenderly solicitous of "the schools and general studies," as they dubbed the incipient universities, that in his code on universities, the very first in all Europe, he tenderly enjoined students to lead an honest life, and not to form gangs and fight the townspeople, but to remain peacefully in their lodgings at night and enjoy themselves when they had tired themselves from study. He allowed the professor access to the person of the king at all times—a rare and, sometimes, a profitable privilege. Judges he made to offer their seats on the bench when there appeared a law professor—that "Knight" and "Lord

---

* To document a lecture on so sweeping a subject as this from the archival sources, while nearly always possible, would be burdensome to me and pedantic to the reader. Though the points made here do generally rest upon documents found in the general and university archives of Spain and Spanish America, wherever I can I shall support them with monographic studies, which in turn cite sources with far more elaboration than would be feasible or necessary here.

[111]

of the Law."[1] This singular elevation of the university in the *Siete Partidas,* a reflection of the dominant ideas of the thirteenth century, is sustained by the literature of the Siglo de Oro. Imagine the king on a state tour, approaching Salamanca, the Mecca of Christian scholars, while the peasants trickle out to the highroad to gawk at this all-but-celestial scene. Then hear Gaspar Lucas de Hidalgo:

> El mundo todo al rey sale,
> Y viene con mano franca;
> Pero porque se señale
> Que Salamanca más vale,
> El rey viene a Salamanca.[2]

And, by doing to it what Lewis Mumford calls aesthetic violence, I shall pull this verse through the golden tapestry,[3] from the right to the wrong side:

> Out to see the king the whole world hath percolated,
> And comes with open hand so franka;
> But because as indicated,
> Salamanca's more estimated,
> The king comes to Salamanca.[4]

In Great Britain and the United States, an incisive stylist writes "the King's English"; in Spain to this day he writes "like a Salamancan professor." This last figure is inexportable. Once, a hapless American graduate student, just back from Spain, while strolling over the flagstones of a university with a famous iconoclastic editor of my youth, suffered a momentary aberration and ventured to shift the figure of speech thus: "Ah, the author of this book writes like a university professor!" Shot back the editor: "God forbid!" Then, turning away, the enraged man strode off fifteen paces when, his famous sense of ruthless truth surfacing, he wheeled around and called back: "Which department?"

This feeling that the University was a thing and a mood apart proved remarkably persistent. The King actually required owners of houses close to the university in Mexico City to sell or lease them to the professors, who needed to be nearby. In the eighteenth century, an outraged academic in the same city cried out: "These quacks practice medicine without fear of God our Lord and without the bachelor's degree."[5] To him there was no impiety in this juxtaposition of the divinity and the degree academic. Two years after his return from "Napoleonic captivity," Ferdinand VII visited the University of Alcalá de Henares, asked the graduates to sit down in his presence, and invited all the scholars to kiss his royal hand. As a climax, the eager administrators carried the king to the library to show him the manuscripts, rare books, and bibles from this famous collection.[6]

From the thirteenth to the nineteenth century, the Spaniards looked for the ideal location for a university. Alfonso wanted his university in a town of bracing breezes, ringed about with beautiful scenery, cheap in lodgings, bountiful in provisions, and free from the hubbub of commerce and the siren's call—heard not just at sea, but in seaports.[7] Still, in 1791, when the Spaniards, in a spirit of desperation, were establishing a school in Granada for Latin American youths to hold them to the metropolis in that age of revolution, they even then turned away from the court city as too distracting for students.[8] Yet, except for Salamanca, the great Spanish universities at home and in America—in "these" and "those" kingdoms—were placed in or close by the great cities. The proximity of Alcalá de Henares to the court at Madrid explains both its aristocratic and its scholarly distinction.

When the king authorized the universities of Mexico and San Marcos de Lima by royal *cédulas* in 1551, the University of Salamanca was at the apogee of its prestige in Spain. With an enrollment of 5,856 students, it boasted three times as many as Alcalá de Henares, and almost as many as there were people in the city itself. Famous professors, some of them celebrated abroad, took their peripatetic walks over its paving tiles. In the eighteenth century when officials in Madrid, after much sad experience at home, were pressing remorselessly for modernization overseas, the statesman Campomanes complained that the American universities, founded upon the model of Sal-amanca at its zenith, were frozen if not cast in its mold.⁹

Thus, in the New World, where the king owned the very earth personally, universities enjoyed only what the royal government wished to allow in their charters and statutes. So great, though, was the name of "university" that royal concessions to American institutions matched those won by the course of history in Spain. As the university governed itself at home, so it did in America. In Mexico, the cloister of the University took outraged exception when a judge of the royal *audiencia*, the supreme court, ventured to expedite police work by entering the University to facilitate the apprehension of a burglar. This separation from the power of the state explains why the Peruvian constabulary, in 1931—to give but one instance—stood before the gate of the sacrosanct University of San Marcos de Lima, shifting rifle butts from foot to foot, waiting for the word to break up a student sit-down strike inside—until the dictator issued a quiet command. The Prince of Wales was coming, and what was more incongruous than having students lolling in the halls, if not the groves, of academe while defacing and befouling a prime exhibit—the oldest university on the continent!

I. *Black Legend*

The greatest disaster ever to smite the Spanish reputation was that, as Spain reached an apogee in the sixteenth century, so did English literature.¹⁰ To Edmund Spenser, Philip II was a three-headed winged monster. Plays written to damn this trifurcated monarch were still being cheered in the eighteenth century by English audiences "to show that they got the point" when Walpole's opposition forced the country into the War of Jenkins' Ear—one of the cleanest triumphs of modern propaganda. Thomas Churchyard's lurid reporting from the Low Countries and John Foxe's *Book of Martyrs*, so convincing that it still makes the flesh ripple, sank so deep into English culture that Spain of the Inquisition became and remained the "dark Domdaniel." And who can ever know how many writers from

Washington Irving to Justin Winsor passed on the legend that Columbus confronted the professors of Salamanca who smiled him to scorn! And what gives the patriotic Spanish university historian apoplexy is the spectacle of a painting of this imaginary confrontation by the French artist Colin, exhibited in a Paris exposition, showing Columbus, his right hand on a book, his left pointing at a globe—a most unlikely stance. He is surrounded by supercilious professors, improperly vested, and friar after friar, all smiling and whispering, while one points his forefinger at his temple to say in the Latin way—"*Chiflado,* balmy."[11] If we cannot get rid of the false notion that Isabella pawned her jewels, what chance do we have with this story— it with all the elements of powerful and significant drama? Yet one historian demonstrates that no such confrontation took place and another, Konetzke, shows that Columbus' idea "floated in the very air," and that in their report to the crown, the professors were nearer right in their estimate of the distance and difficulties than was Columbus. But, as Von Ranke put it, never was greater error to lead to greater results.[12]

A second of innumerable fables has it that Copernicus' conception of the universe had no show in Salamanca or in the whole of Spain. When I read somewhere in Madariaga in 1947 that the Copernican system was defended in the University of Salamanca in the sixteenth century, I could not trust my eyes. A few hours in the archives at Salamanca are marvelously good for such congenitally limited sight.[13] In the same way, a statement made in Spain in 1760, and taken out of context, is distorted to show that the professors of Salamanca refused so late as 1770 to accept Newton's discoveries on the ground that, as their fathers had not done so, neither did they wish to introduce "a more exquisite taste" into the sciences. This statement, as George Addy says, stuck to Salamanca "like a burr."[14] Despite everything, astronomers in the overseas empire were always attuned to what was happening in Europe and proved valuable collaborators to scholars outside peninsular Spain. In fact, the strange heavens as seen from a new hemisphere were both monopoly of observation and a stimulant to the inquiring American. If, in America, there were no critical studies of Greek, Latin, and Hebrew, as in Alcalá de Henares, or in the Trilingual College of Salamanca, to give sixteenth-century America a Renaissance tinge, there were compensations: Baffled by the three hundred languages that confounded them on every hand, the Spaniards in the New World began to arrange vocabularies and write grammars that did more to preserve the world's languages than did all the grappling with ancient texts and tongues at home.[15] Optimistically, and in the same spirit, they launched chairs of living languages in the principal universities: Aztec and Otomí in Mexico, Quechua and Aimará in San Marcos de Lima, and Cakchiquel in San Carlos de Guatemala. If most of these, the first chairs of modern languages, fell into decline, it was because the students who needed them found that they could learn to speak an Indian tongue better with one vacation in a native village than they could with four years at the feet of the professor of Cakchiquel.[16]

In bloodletting, Spanish surgeons opened veins one time on the right wrist and the next on the left to avoid irritating and "inflaming" old incisions. Report of a famous English traveler in 1792: The Spaniards do not yet understand the circulation of the blood; they bleed first from one arm and then the other to avoid making the patient heavier on one side than on the other—a disaster for his equilibrium.[17] Spain was thus judged in the heat of war alone. But what were the causes? Samuel Johnson gives us a peep at one of the many of these:

> Has Heaven reserved, in pity to the poor,
> No pathless waste, or undiscovered shore?
> No secret island in the boundless main?
> No peaceful desert, yet unclaimed by Spain?
>
> *London* (1738)

II. *Organization and Practice*

The Spanish universities in the Indies came into being with at least three hundred years of Spanish experience to fall back upon. Hence, those who drafted the statutes of the universities of Mexico and of San Marcos de Lima, after which nearly all other American universities were modeled, transferred and codified the statutes of Salamanca. They eliminated, though, some of the dross that had accumulated in the life and administration of that illustrious academy. These "constitutions" followed so fearfully, so literally, and so long in America, carried a weight that the laws of nature are hardly entitled to. They entrusted the government of the typical American university to a cloister, composed of the holders of higher degrees, the licentiates and doctors in the city and within five leagues round about. This academic constituency elected eight councilors who served as an executive committee with many powers, including the right and obligation to elect a rector, or president, who assumed jurisdiction over the cloister and the students and administered justice to them short of "the drawing of blood and the mutilation of member." It did not follow the disastrous practice of Salamanca in electing some madcap student rector. A second officer, the *maestrescuela* from the Cathedral chapter, the *scholasticus* of the medieval "schools," oversaw the ceremonial awarding of higher degrees. In an everyday sense, the secretary of the university was the man who did most of the work of administration, and the bedels saw to the decency of the physical plant and maintained order among students and between professors.[18]

The major American universities had five faculties, or branches of knowledge: theology, canon law, civil law, medicine, and arts. They never established the humanities that did so much credit to Alcalá in the time of the Complutensian Polyglot, though Latin was the language of the classroom everywhere. Academic chairs were of two types, temporal or four-year and proprietary or lifetime. Both were won in a trial-lecture type of competition called opposition (*oposición*) in which each contestant took a text from a book opened with a knife and at random by a child. After twenty-four hours' preparation, he appeared, and recited a Latin lecture as the sand slowly slipped out of the hourglass standing ominously by his side.

Then he defended it. Happily, after student judges had forced the professors into demogogic and ruinous catering to them, the University of Mexico excluded the students and designated a board of mature judges composed of professors and officials.[19]

The proprietary chair was a valuable piece of property and its holder a man of prestige. In Salamanca, however, in the knowledge that he had this property tied up for life, the proprietary professor sometimes lost interest, collected his salary, and left his work to others. Moreover, at the end of twenty years, he might retire with his salary, making at best only a nominal payment to supplement the insignificant salary of a substitute—generally a young one. In fact, proprietary chairs were abolished at Alcalá de Henares in 1666 and, in the second half of the eighteenth century, Charles III decreed their extinction at Salamanca, but he did not put the decree in force; he merely threatened to do so to keep the professors from growing lax, not to mention growing rebellious.[20] In America, these chairs were not seriously challenged; but here and there, toward the end of the eighteenth century, education collapsed in some fields because young men, needing money for their work, would not enter the oppositions for the substitute interim professorship. In other instances, especially in medicine, not enough men graduated to form a proper slate of *opositores*, or contestants.[21]

Fighting over chairs, however, was a universal Spanish custom. Ferdinand and Isabella in 1494 and 1495 in vain forbade student judges to accept bribes and presents, charged them not to commit their votes in advance, and ruled against "'apportioning" money on the occasion of the trial-lectures.[22] Spaniards in all generations have watched the judges of these *oposiciones* with suspicion. In some places viceregal and academic authorities prohibited the noisy celebrations that followed them to prevent riots and clashes between the followers of the candidates. Indeed, in 1631, the University of San Marcos de Lima suspended the *oposiciones* themselves to avoid a chronic state of academic war.

III. *Student Life: Blood Purity*

What of the students? On the surface, at least, the Spaniards in both worlds were obsessed with blood purity and made it a prerequisite to the universities, to the professions, and even to the trades. But between Spain and America a curious transposition took place. In Spain, the university registrar never once asked, any more than did the Spanish law, whether a man was white, brown, or black. There blood purity had long meant that the aspirant was not "infamous," as were those who fought wild beasts for pay, those who threw down their arms in battle, those who sold their books after graduating, or those "Merry-andrews who went from place to place singing." Now it meant that the candidate was not only free from such archaic "infamy" but from heresy, Judaism, and Moslemism. After the expulsion of the Moors from Granada, the pragmatic of 1501 forbade the sons and grandsons of men sentenced by the Inquisition to come to America, or graduate as bachelor, licentiate, or doctor. Evasion was common in Spain and action was taken only when, say, a Jewish doctor from Portugal began to cut in on the local practice in some provincial town or, as they sometimes did, "when they boldly came to court." Indeed, "powerful houses" protected the family physician or the teacher of the children in them against the *corregidores* or even against the Royal Protomedicato, the Board of King's physicians itself. The business of forged documents of blood purity flourished.[23]

In America, other factors began to play. True, the statutes of the University of San Marcos de Lima merely repeated the Spanish prohibitions and said nothing of race.[24] To those "infamous" in Spain, the statutes of the University of Mexico added that neither Negroes, mulattoes, *chinos morenos* (mixture of Indian and Negro) nor any slaves or former slaves might matriculate or receive degrees.[25] The secretaries and rectors of universities, however, calmly ignored illegitimacy as a bar to the universities on the grounds that they had enrolled those "who could not select their own fathers" since the time "when the memory of man runneth not to the contrary." In the same way, they registered men of color except in the rare instances when some person, one suspects an interested person, challenged the student's registration, sometimes after he had reached the doctorate. In nearly all of these cases, the secretary of the University of Mexico, at the instance of the rector, investigated and then the rector ruled in the student's favor.[26] The king, in case of appeal, did the same thing for a price—the well-known *gracias al sacar*.[27] The colored castes became so numerous in the University of San Marcos de Lima that the viceroys after 1752 pressed the academic authorities to see to it that matriculants were not mulattoes, zambos, quadroons, or mestizos and, if any had registered through fraud, to expunge their degrees from the records. Every viceregal document on the question attributed the withdrawal of the whites and the decline of the University to the inundation of these "most vile types." The worth of a doctor's degree as property fell from twenty-five hundred to eight hundred pesos. So little availing was the counterattack, however, that Negro and mulatto surgeons, most of them trained under the apprentice system, dominated medical as well as surgical practice in Lima in the year 1800. In fact, a royal *cédula* erased the "infamy" of the Negro surgeon, Juan Manuel Valdés, and led to his doctoral investiture.[28] In the eighteenth century the white Americans, the creoles, with the support of the Peruvian viceroys, fought the admission of the Negro to the citizenship that permitted his entrance into the academies and into the professions. In 1810, however, they made an about-face because they wanted more citizens' heads to count in their struggle for proportional representation in the famous Cortes of 1810.[29] With the liberals dominant in Spain in the two years that followed, all those "who fetched their origins" from Africa were freely admitted to universities and seminaries.[30]

One characteristic of higher education in Spain and in the Indies was a fantastic respect for the memory. In the last edition of the statutes of the University of Mexico published in 1775, the editor cited, among the glories of the University, the case of Don Pedro de Paz Vasconcelos, a blind student who sold his books once he had read them, for he could then name the book and chapter and recite the passage by heart.[31] The excessive reliance upon memory, tending to elbow aside the understanding, was that, since the language of the Romans was the language of the schools, the student merely hit the passage in his textbook and stuck to it instead of falling back upon his own macaronic Latin. One suspects that the professor often did the same thing, except when, after class, he offered to clear up points in Castilian—but just outside the classroom door—not inside it. Indeed, Dr. Simeón Cañas, the antislavery advocate of Central America, giving a trial lecture in competition for the temporal chair of philosophy in 1800, after he had already won it two times, ran out of Latin or memory and had to sit down before the hourglass had trickled out sixty minutes of sand—a disgrace for which he contritely apologized to the cloister of the University of San Carlos.[32] Even as late as 1880 a distinguished historian of academic institutions in Spain proudly related that when Carlos Bovilla, early in the sixteenth century, cited St. Augustine in support of his argument, Gil González de Burgos replied that St. Augustine said no such thing, much less in that book. Whereupon, he declaimed the correct passage on the spot and by heart—crushing and humiliating his opponent.[33] In his *Commonwealth of Learning*, Diego Saavedra Fajardo—another Spaniard, be it said on behalf of that race—thought it perfectly proper that the Egyptians should select the grasshopper as the hieroglyphic for "the schools."[34]

IV. *Riots and Disorders*

True it is that the Spanish student in the old world and in the new, from the sixteenth to the twentieth century, has had the flair if not always the opportunity for rioting. Indeed, no bedel, no bulldog, and no dean has ever outwitted the undergraduate bent on mischief.

In Salamanca the nations were not clumps of Frenchmen, Flemings, Burgundians, Lombards, and Romans as at Paris, but Castilians, Andalusians, Biscayans, Catalans, Manchegans, Valencians, Estremadurans, Gallegans, and Portuguese, all from the Iberian peninsula and each classified by the other with some adverse cliché. The Biscayan was thus "slow-witted," and "not the most pacific," the Portuguese "mixed up in the head," and the Estremadurans had "a little of everything like an apothecary."[35]

Some of these nations, as it was said of the Basques and Andalusians, had only to stare at one another to set the very dogs abarking. In 1644, when some Biscayans stood looking at a fire, some of those of other nations began to shout "¡Cola! ¡Cola! ¡Cola! ("Tail! Tail! Tail!") as a tribute to their slow wits and academic standing. The fight was joined. Both sides brought up reinforcements. When the townspeople and police intervened, the students, like a loving husband and wife in a fight, stopped fighting each other and joined against the town. Counterattack followed attack, the battle raged through the town, into the fields, and surged back again. The desperate lieutenant *corregidor* even executed one student unshriven.[36] In the long run, though, any man so bold could expect to trudge through the streets barefooted, and repent, in church and on his knees, for violating the immunities of the University.

The University of Alcalá de Henares (1508) had all the ingredients for a beauty of a riot. The University was close to the court, many students were aristocratic, much indulged, and often idle. These were the lads who sallied out one Holy Week to divert themselves at a hanging in the town of Alcalá. The prisoner, a murderer who understood his students better than he controlled his temper, when brought under the gibbet, paused and turned to the students: "High-souled youths!" he began, "How can ye bear, in this holy season, to see my body dangling from this gibbet?" Even they had not thought of that. They took the culprit from the hangman and spirited him away to sanctuary. When the *alcalde* of the city took one student and beat him through the streets, he only afforded more excuse for rioting. Cardinal Ximénez, founder and patron, suggestive of university presidents today, chose to make light of this conduct as "the froth of academic fervor," mere boys' stuff. It got more serious, though, when the king paid a state visit and left his pages loitering at the university portals. These, as full of froth as the students, began to chide the "scholars." When the king emerged, he found that these sons of Castilian cavaliers had plastered his pages. It took all Ximénez' powers and some of his prestige to conciliate his Catholic Majesty.[37]

A shift to America will not afford relief. Wherever a few students are gathered together there the waggish trick, more often than the Lord, will be with them also. University students of San Carlos de Guatemala in 1681, amused at the sight of one Joseph Pérez mounted on a caparisoned mule, moved to mount him on his horse blanket instead and send him higher than e're rode Sancho. The Spanish captain, Jerónimo Paniagua, who ventured to intervene, got his house stoned. In a rage this proud officer pulled any student his men could seize upon into the bedel's quarters and, plying them with a cat-o'-nine-tails, forthwith got a confession—one that named the guiltless as well as the guilty.[38] This university, in fact, almost perished in its initial years because of the lethargy, the whims, and the brawls of its students.[39] In Mexico, as in other places in America, most lay students lived with their own families or guardians. Hence, they could only forgather for a moment after classes (in *corillos*) by the gates to whistle or, as they would have said, to pick the turkey with any passing female not patently snaggletoothed. Yet, the numerous parades and processions that marked university life throughout the empire gave opportunity for the letting off of what Cardinal Ximénez called "froth." In fact, in 1731, students in the parade on the day of St. Catherine, the patron saint of the University, taunted the police into an attack that killed a student and led to the suppression of the parade. Besides, the overemphasis upon athletics in those times was bullfighting. Accordingly, these seekers after knowledge and truth—more likely the moment of truth—planked up the plaza and staged bullfights in such numbers as seriously to interfere with class attendance. Eventually, after the University pulled down the planking to allow the viceroy's gold-leafed, many-horsed carriage to enter the central plaza, the crown prohibited these distracting fights.[40] Ar-chives in America throw up little evidence that such disorders often took the shape of articulate disrespect for professors, so much in vogue in Latin America today. One professor in Quito, though, did lament to the authorities: "I know I am an igno-ramus, but is it meet and right that my own students should give it to me in my very teeth?"[41]

Despite this jagged record, university students in the Span-ish Empire were really quiescent; but then the viceregal gov-ernments, without tyranny, had an effective control of every aspect of life that has not been matched in the national period except for the years of the great dictators, such as those of Juan Manuel de Rosas and Porfirio Díaz. The struggle of doctrinaire and immature students to run the contemporary Latin Amer-ican university, and the chaos resulting from it, led the rector of a Spanish university, Dr. Juan Manzano Manzano to say to me, not "What degenerates!" but wistfully, "Sons of ours they are."

v. *Rich and Poor*

A common assumption is that the Spaniards, both in Spain and in America, designed university education exclusively for the aristocracy. It is bound to be true, though fees were slight and tuition unheard of, that those who got academic degrees had to have or to find the means to live by their labor, by their wits, by their luck, or by their fathers. One type of medieval student, as one well-to-do parent lamented in that far-off day, sat in a window and strummed a guitar while wasting the fam-ily silver, but the classic one—in literature and in fact—was poor. One of them, in the "Order of the Wandering Students," declared his independence of wealth:

> This our order doth forbid;
>   Double clothes with loathing;
> He whose nakedness is hid
>   With one vest hath clothing.

Or

What I've said of upper clothes
To the nether reaches;
They who own a shirt, let those
Think no more of breeches.[42]

The Spanish university was at its zenith and coming into the full modern age, when the poor eleven-year-old lad that became Cervantes' *Licentiate Vidriera* set out for Salamanca. When, overcome with weariness, he lay down under a tree to refresh himself, two rich students returning to that "Spanish Minerva" with their servants and their equipage, roused and questioned him out of sheer curiosity. He was going to the awesome Salamanca. But why? "To make myself famous by my learning," he answered firmly. "I have even heard that men become bishops by study." Cervantes, who knew as well as any man has ever known what was in the bones of the Spaniard, had the two students take him up and patronize him at Salamanca and, indeed, he did become famous and wise—both when sane and when touched. Vicente Espinel, in his all-but-biographical *Life of Marcos Obregón*, in the reminiscent spirit of a returning Princeton graduate, remembered how a band of Salamancan students, too cold to stay in quarters, and too hungry to sleep, got an egg or so and began to forage for wood to cook it. They found an impressive piece, but when they plied it with the scarce kindling that the Castilian hills yield, they blew and blew but got only a nauseous yellow smoke. A piece of paper, more precious than wood, at last flickering into flame, revealed a great mule bone the dogs had stripped of the last shred of flesh.[43]

But the royal authorities, whenever they could, and in every century, continued to boost and finally to enforce the granting of bachelor's degrees to poverty-stricken students without any cost whatsoever. Twice in the reign of Charles III American universities got strict orders to graduate one man in ten without costs.[44] A close study of the surviving Degree Books reveals that the universities complied uncomplainingly with these humane orders. San Marcos never limited the number it graduated free. The costs of doctor's degrees, though, were

[125]

in many cases prohibitive; for the candidate had to fee his examiners, hire a band to herald his passing, pay for a great collation, stage a bullfight, and, sometimes, spend in the investiture alone enough to hire four professors *de prima* for a whole year. Men of the cloth, particularly in the religious orders, found other ways to avoid this payment, but the poor secular candidate could generally find a rich godfather who would bear these expenses for the honor of exhibiting the doctoral insignia under a canopy on the balcony of his house and for the prestige of riding to the investiture with this man of solid attainment and learning. In the eighteenth century, however, the crown limited the sums that might be lavished upon these ceremonies.[45]

VI. *The Old World and the New: Comparisons*

The surge of academic activity in the seventeenth century found Spain with thirty universities in 1645, a number that, with variations, remained standard for the next century and a half. The minor universities, more than half of the total, however, were so often in such a state of decline and neglect that the historian has trouble determining whether some of them were functioning at all at specific dates in the eighteenth century. Thus, the Spaniards grumbled: "The country has too many universities." The Americans, on the other hand, who had twenty-three—eight major and fifteen minor—complained that their institutions were too far apart. In proportion to the white population in America and in the metropolis, Americans were perhaps better served in higher education than were Spaniards. Their universities conferred 150,000 degrees of bachelor, licentiate, doctor, and master before independence.[46] The want of monograph, or synthesis, or, one fears, archives makes hazardous, though, even a guess at the number awarded in Spain.

In number of chairs and of students, the universities of Spain and America were not vastly different. Eighteen Spanish universities, the principal ones, had 457 chairs in 1785, Salamanca with the highest—fifty-five—and Valladolid second with forty-four. Sigüenza, at the bottom of the list, could show but nine.[47] The University of San Marcos de Lima, with forty chairs, ranked third in the whole Spanish world and, of course, first in the New.[48] In number of students, the Spanish universities, on the average, had more matriculants than did the American. No American institution ever approached the enrollment at Salamanca in 1551, but when Salamanca, with the passage of time, became more and more like any other major Spanish university, it fell within the range of the universities of Mexico and Lima at their peaks. Theology recruited more students than any other major faculty in all American universities and in most of those of Spain, ranking first at Salamanca and third at Alcalá de Henares,[49] but the ascendency of theology was a matter of culture, not of law or coercion. Medicine ranked last in every comparative classification on both sides of the Atlantic. Professors of the subject in America might not aspire to become rectors at universities, sat behind all others at doctoral investitures, and trudged along last in academic processions. Their students naturally were always scarce and always fewer than in any other field. Though medicine was of the Galenic variety as late as the eighteenth century, the want of Latin physicians consigned almost the entire Indian and Negro populations to the exclusive care of intruders and quacks.[50]

Professorial salaries in Spain and America were comparable, though the proprietary professors at Salamanca, at the end of the year, divided the surplus income from the University properties.[51] In the New World, salaries ranged in general, from one to 500 pesos and in Mexico, reached 700, while one chair in San Marcos de Lima yielded 1,350 a year.[52] These figures went unchanged for centuries. Individual raises never occurred. There is no need, though, to write this story with the eyes bathed in tears, for, in order to buy as much beef at one dollar a pound as a Guatemalan professor could buy in the seventeenth century for his 500 pesos, a professor in this country would need a salary of $108,000. "And even if it does make the president of Harvard wince, administrative and maintenance costs were only 29 per cent of instructional."[53]

VII. *Enlightenment and Change*

The Enlightenment and the changes coming with it ran a parallel course in the universities of Spain and in those of America. First of all, though, this movement was neither the work of Frenchified Spaniards nor of Frenchmen hovering at the court of the Spanish Bourbons. In fact, for the sake of fairness in Spanish intellectual history, it would be better to uproot Bourbon as a modifier for reform in Spain and confine it to Kentucky, where no semantic problem will arise. To Benito Feijóo, the idol of the universities, who began writing about 1726, it did not make any more sense to cling to things French, merely because they were French, than it does to you, for example, when Washington women with social ambitions cling to the skirts of a Perle Mesta. As a Spaniard, writing in Spanish, he remorselessly exposed all types of ridiculous notions, especially in medicine and science, and remained the country's leading spokesman for more than a generation. "My error," he began, "after so many years when experience has not been heeded, lies in believing that I may be."

One of the items he tried to combat was the notion fostered by undergraduates in all ages: that study shortens the span of life. For another, he contested the legend that the American white died early despite the plain fact that many Americans, Americans who studied at that, lived to be old men in sharp possession of their faculties. Indeed, the *Gazeta de México* joined him in countering this argument by publishing the story of a Mexican woman 146 years old with a son 95, and made nothing of it except to show some surprise that the son was a little hard of hearing.[54] He felt a special loathing for medical notions that rested upon nothing more than their hoary age. He knew that precious stones, the bezoar stone from the stomachs of certain Andean ruminants for syphilis, and the ground human craneum for mental disorders, clung like a leech to the *Pharmacopoea matritense*. He therefore cited kings and princes who had had their medicaments concocted of these ingredients who had shown no improvement. Some doctors and all apothecaries, he wryly concluded, favored costly medicines.[55]

The greatest handicap to academic reform among Salamancan professors was not an innate reluctance to accept anything that their fathers had not subscribed to, as the English reported; it was, instead, the fruit of a struggle between the Great Colleges—the *Colegios Mayores*—and the University on the one hand and, on the other, between the University and the Council of Castile over the continuation of the privileges and exemptions of the medieval academic guild. With philosophical and scientific change paced by universities in Valencia, Seville, and even Salamanca, by specialized colleges in Cádiz, Barcelona, and Madrid, the Spaniards strove through sweeping, yet detailed legislation in 1770, 1807, and 1820 to consolidate the academic gains under way for a century. In America, which was mere royal property, the university could hardly be so bold as to claim historical precedent against the king himself. Because ministerial intervention was invariably on the side of cleaning out the dross, discouraging quiddities, and advancing new scientific principles, such as the discoveries of Newton, Lavoisier, and Jenner, both Spain and America profited from it. In the course of a single generation the empire began to take to the new ideas as fast as they were accepted in Europe, showing at the end of the eighteenth century a lag no longer than it took a ship to sail from Cádiz to Vera Cruz.[56]

It was not likely, even in these circumstances, that universities could respond adequately, as critics have sometimes complained, to the demands of experiment, research, and engineering practices. The answer came in part by modernization within the American university, especially in philosophy; but the most complete response came in the establishment of independent colleges of surgery, of botanical research, of mining, and of the separate medical school with new subjects such as chemistry. This was a better and a more expeditious way to adapt to the new requirements than would have been the radical modification of the old university—financially hamstrung and under the weight of considerable useless tradition. Many universities weakened visibly at the end of the spurt the Enlightenment gave them. The plague of eighteenth-century wars—eight between England and Spain alone from 1702 to 1808—had a singularly frustrating effect upon both Spain and America. When you add the Napoleonic wars and the fourteen years of the wars of independence—and who knows how many in a chronic state of near bankruptcy—is it any shock that American universities could not find the means to respond as fast as they knew they should to the requirements of mathematics and the physical sciences? This tragic plight led, in many cases, to a decadence that ended in the total destruction of the old university. Spain, after curtailing them in 1774, abolished its minor universities altogether in 1807, and the Mexicans allowed their venerable colonial institution to fade away in 1833. Even so, it was the classic, even up-to-date education upon which the colonial university launched the first national leaders that so amazed the first European diplomats accredited to Hispanic America.

Notes

1. *Las Siete Partidas*, Part. II, tít. xxxi, leyes 2 y 8. See also C.Mª. Ajo G. y Sáinz de Zúñiga, *Historia de las universidades hispánicas: orígenes y desarrollo desde su aparición a nuestros días* (4 vols.; Avila, 1957-1960) I, 221-229.

2. Gaspar Lucas Hidalgo, "Diálogos de apacible entretenimiento," in *Biblioteca de Autores Españoles*, XXXVI, 285.

3. "Don Quixote believed that a book and its translation are like the two sides of a tapestry. The one is clear . . . ; the other blurred in outline, marred by thrums and knots" (Dale B. J. Randall, *The Golden Tapestry: A Critical Survey of the Non-chivalric Spanish Fiction in English Translation, 1543-1657,* Durham, N. C., 1963, p. 3).

4. "Unmetrical and strained though it be, . . . [this translation] may give some idea, not just of Salamanca's place in the Spanish consciousness, but of Hidalgo's tone . . ." (John Tate Lanning, "Old World Background of Latin American Culture," *The Kennecott Lecture Series, 1959-1960*, Tucson, 1960, p. 12 n.).

5. John Tate Lanning, "The Illicit Practice of Medicine in the Spanish Empire in America," *Homenaje a José María de la Peña y Cámara* (Madrid, 1969), p. 141.

6. Vicente de la Fuente, *Historia de las universidades, colegios y demás establecimientos de enseñanza en España* (4 vols.; Madrid, 1884–1889), IV, 344.

7. *Las Siete Partidas*, Part. II, tít. xxxi, ley 1.

8. Archivo General de Indias (Seville), Indiferente General, Legajo 1620. Expediente sobre fundación de un Colegio de Nobles Americanos en Granada, 1791-1799. See also John Tate Lanning, *The Eighteenth-Century Enlightenment in the University of San Carlos de Guatemala* (Ithaca, N. Y., 1956), pp. 333-335.

9. Joseph Skinner, ed. and trans., *The Present State of Peru* (London, 1805), p. 173.

10. See, for example, William Saunders Maltby, "The Origins of the Black Legend in Elizabethan England: A Study of the Development of Anti-Hispanism." (Masters thesis, Duke University, 1965); "The Black Legend in England, 1558-1660" (Unpublished Ph.D. dissertation, Duke University, 1967).

11. La Fuente, *Historia de las universidades*, II, 27.

12. Richard Konetzke, *El Imperio Español: orígenes y fundamentos* (Madrid, 1946), pp. 146, 165.

13. George M. Addy, *The Enlightenment in the University of Salamanca* (Durham, N. C., 1966), p. 42.

14. *Ibid.*, p. 82.

15. Lanning, *The Eighteenth-Century Enlightenment*, pp. 3-7.

16. *Ibid.*, pp. 26, 92, 350.

17. Joseph Townsend, *Journey through Spain* (3 vols.; London, 1792), III, 282. See also John Tate Lanning, *Academic Culture in the Spanish Colonies* (New York and London, 1940), pp. 103-104.

18. Lanning, *Academic Culture*, pp. 34-58.

19. *Constituciones de la Real y Pontificia Universidad de México* (Mexico City, 1775), p. 119, n. 22.

20. La Fuente, *Historia de las universidades*, III, 161.

21. A.G.I., Audiencia de Lima, 337: el claustro de la Universidad de San Marcos al rey, Lima, s.f.

22. La Fuente, *Historia de las universidades*, II, 36.

23. John Tate Lanning, "Legitimacy and *limpieza de sangre* in the Practice of Medicine in the Spanish Empire," *Jahrbuch für Geschichte von Staat, Wirtschaft und Gesellschaft Lateinamerikas*, IV (Cologne, 1967), 43-46.

24. *Constituciones, y ordenanzas antiguas, añadidas, y modernas de la Real Universidad, y Estudio General de San Marcos de la Ciudad de los Reyes del Perú* (Lima, 1735).

25. *Constituciones de la . . . Universidad de Mexico*, tít. 17, const. 246, p. 132.

26. A.G.N., Universidad, Vol. 81. Informaciones de limpieza de sangre desde 1701 hasta 1780, *passim*.

27. A royal *cédula* (Madrid, August 3, 1801) set up the terms for these concessions. (A.G.I., Ultramar, Legajo 733.)

28. Lanning, "Legitimacy and *limpieza de sangre*," *Jahrbuch* . . . , IV, 52-53.

29. James Ferguson King, "The Colored Castes and American Representation in the Cortes of Cádiz," *Hispanic American Historical Review*, XXXIII (1953), 33-64.

30. John Tate Lanning, ed., *Reales cédulas de la Real y Pontificia Universidad de San Carlos de Guatemala* (Guatemala, 1954), pp. 193-195.

31. *Constituciones de la . . . Universidad de México*, p. 4.

32. John Tate Lanning, *The University in the Kingdom of Guatemala* (Ithaca, N. Y., 1955), p. 147.

33. La Fuente, *Historia de las universidades*, II, 69.

34. *The Commonwealth of Learning* (London, 1705).

35. *The Exemplary Novels of Miguel de Cervantes Saavedra: To Which Are Added El Buscapié, or, The Serpent; and La Tía Fingida, or, The Pretended Aunt* (London, 1855), p. 477.

36. Addy, *The Enlightenment in the University of Salamanca*, pp. 50-51.

37. La Fuente, *Historia de las universidades*, II, 72-73.

38. Lanning, *The University in the Kingdom of Guatemala*, pp. 177-179.

39. *Ibid.*, pp. 81-85.

40. John Tate Lanning, ed., *Las reales cédulas de la Real y Pontificia Universidad de Mexico de 1551 a 1816* (Mexico City, 1946), pp. 219-222, 227-228. Real cédula al rector de la Real y Pontificia Universidad de México, Aranjuez, 19 de abril de 1770; *idem.*, Aranjuez, 21 de mayo de 1771.

41. Archivo de la Real Audiencia de Quito, Cuerpos Docentes. Manuel Rodríguez al presidente Carondelet, Quito, 1 de marzo de 1804.

42. John Addington Symonds, trans., *Wine, Women, and Song* (London, 1907), p. 54.

43. Vicente Espinel, *Vida de Marcos Obregón* (2 vols.; Madrid, 1922-1923), I, 194 (trans. in Addy, *The Enlightenment in the University of Salamanca*, pp. 52-53).

44. Real cédula al rector y claustro de la Universidad de Guatemala. San Ildefonso, 24 de agosto de 1788. John Tate Lanning, ed., *Las reales cédulas de la Real y Pontificia Universidad de San Carlos de Guatemala* (Guatemala, 1954), pp. 227-228.

45. Lanning, *The University in the Kingdom of Guatemala*, pp. 227-234.

46. Lanning, *Academic Culture*, p. 54.

47. La Fuente, *Historia de las universidades*, IV, 154.

48. Luis A. Eguiguren, *Catálogo histórico del claustro de la Universidad de San Marcos, 1576-1800* (Lima, 1912, pp. 7-45.

49. La Fuente, *Historia de las universidades*, IV, 153.

50. Lanning, "The Illicit Practice of Medicine," pp. 178-179. See n. 6 above.

51. Addy, *The Enlightenment in the University of Salamanca*, pp. 23-24.

52. Lanning, *Academic Culture*, pp. 56-57.

53. Lanning, *The University in the Kingdom of Guatemala*, p. 49.

54. Lanning, "Old World Background of Latin American Culture," *The Kennecott Lecture Series, 1959-1960*, pp. 23-24.

55. Benito Jerónimo Feijóo y Montenegro, *El Teatro crítico universal* (8 vols. and supplement; Madrid, 1726-1740), I, Discurso V, pp. 94-61.

56. Lanning, *Academic Culture*, pp. 85-89.

VII

Luther's Importance for Anthropological Realism

Lewis W. Spitz
Stanford University

Such an elaborate and kindly introduction as that which Professor John Headley has just given me is designed less for the benefit of the audience than of the speaker. It is intended to prevent a last-minute failure of nerve on his part in the presence of such a distinguished group of scholars. When I consider us *Wandervögel* of the academic world on the Chatauqua circuit the lines of Hilaire Belloc come to mind: "We circulate throughout the Land / The second rate, and second hand!" The English humorist Potter defined the art of lecturemanship as the art of getting people to take notes even when you don't know what you are talking about. There is many a man, says the pundit, who does not need an introduction but who could certainly stand some good conclusions, so I may turn to Professor Headley later in the hour for further assistance.

Jacob Burckhardt had a point when he refused to "hawk" his lectures beyond the gates of Basel, for if a lecture is what it should be, it takes a man's energy. Dour Burckhardt disapproved of academic conferences where scholars "come to sniff each other out" like dogs in a pack. Hopefully he would at least approve of today's enterprise, for we shall play with ideas through the centuries in a style for which he set a brilliant precedent.

Though anthropological realism may suggest *African Genesis* or *The Naked Ape*, the fact is that Luther will perform more like a highbrow Alley Oop who lived in the sixteenth century, but had an important impact upon the nineteenth-

and twentieth-century anthropological realists. This undertaking is difficult, for the *Einflusz* problem is one of the most difficult in intellectual history. Renaissance scholars are well aware of the pitfalls, for they recall the way in which Petrarch and Dante were exploited as symbols of cultural nationalism and natural superiority in the *risorgimento* and Fascist periods of Italian history. The outsized men of history may live again (*vir redivivens*) as their ideas, understood as they intended, stir up the minds of a later generation. Their ideas may be misunderstood with regrettable results, or by a *felix culpa* may be misinterpreted with fortunate results. Their thought may be vulgarized, understood on a lower level or transferred to a different context in such a way as to do violence to their inner essence. These are the hazards involved in the study of influence.

A single example will serve as a caveat. Socrates, a figure relatively neglected or sublimated during the Renaissance, or perhaps merely overshadowed by his great pupil Plato, received singular attention during the nineteenth century. But how different were the responses to his thought and reaction to his person! Hegel found Socrates to be subversive, for he not only cultivated subjectivity at the expense of the objective nature of truth, but he undermined the authority of the state by challenging the presuppositions upon which its concept of law depends. Jacob Burckhardt thought Socrates pitiful in that, as an exercise in futility, he actually tried to improve men. Nietzsche criticized Socrates for introducing a questioning criticality, a compunction for self-analysis which sapped the natural instincts and spontaneity of man. Sören Kierkegaard came closest to a positive evaluation of Socrates, appreciative above all of his contribution to the "concept of irony." Like Socrates, Luther, too, nearly became all things to all men. He was less remote, spoke to issues directly and with great urgency, but his influence emerged nevertheless in varying modalities. As in the case of Socrates the "reception" depended in no small part on the receivers. What games people play!

I. *Luther and Idealism*

Luther's impact upon modern thought was strangely bifurcated. On the one hand, he figured as a major influence upon and as a cultural symbol for the *Aufklärung* and German idealism. On the other hand, his religious thought and specifically his anthropology was of enormous importance as source and resource of anthropological realism. This dual thrust resulted less from opposing elements in his thought than from the fact that different aspects of his theology came into play as the modern intellectual configuration shifted and contributed to the change.

Luther belonged to the top-level tradition of Christian rationalism in the sense that he considered man's reason to be the most wondrous and majestic of God's creations. Even after the fall of man, reason remains a kind of god, a beautiful light, a sun, and a divine thing to rule over everything in this world. Some of Luther's expressions in praise of natural reason impress a man of our times as extravagant, unreal, and even naive. For in a day in which men understand all too well the obstacles to rational behavior and the dark forces of the subconscious, they are less apt to laud the powers of reason. In a post-Freudian, highly empirical, almost anti-intellectual society, men are less likely to rely with any great sense of security upon reason even in temporal things. With Pareto's reminders in *Mind and Society* how many decisions are made and actions taken simply in response to "derivations and residues," in accordance with learned or inherited responses, fully cushioned by rationalizations, men are a bit cautious about extolling the powers of *ratio* as Luther did. For Luther natural reason, as God created it, was king of creation.

Nevertheless, for Luther reason was not absolute; in matters having to do with God and man's relation to Him reason is blind and a false guide. It cannot show the way or find the path that leads from sin and death to righteousness and life. It remains in darkness. In religion the fond conceit of reason sets itself up as judge over what can and cannot be God's will. This "rationalism" of arrogant reason is inevitably inclined toward moralism. As the devil's harlot it tempts man to rely upon his own good works as though he were in a position to make demands upon God rather than acknowledging that he is in every respect a debtor to God. Compared with the light of God's Word in religion man's reason is but a candle in the sun. In commenting upon Psalm 119:105 ("Thy word is a lamp unto my feet, and a light unto my path"), Luther wrote:

> Reason, too, is a light, and a beautiful light. Yet it cannot point to or find the way or the foot that will lead from sin and death to righteousness and life, but remains in darkness. Just as our tallow and wax candles do not illuminate heaven or earth but the narrow nooks in houses. The sun, however, sheds light on heaven, earth, and everything. In just that way God's Word is the true sun which gives us an eternal day in which to live and to be happy. Such a Word is given richly and sweetly in the Psalms. Blessed is the man who delights in it and gladly sees this light, for it shines gladly. But moles and bats, that is, the world, do not like it.[1]

Luther uses the word "reason" in yet a third way as "regenerate reason." The man whose trust (*fiducia*) in God has been awakened by the Holy Spirit has a new, alive, hopeful outlook on life. His perspective on life is radically altered because of his new relationship to God. Reason for such a man is the "best instrument" for ordering a life of love for his fellow man in accordance with the Word and will of God. In the *Table Talks* Luther explained in clear and simple words how regenerate reason serves the man of faith.

Before faith and the knowledge of God reason is darkness in divine matters, but through faith it is turned into a light in the believer and serves piety as an excellent instrument. For just as all natural endowments serve to further impiety in the godless, so they serve to further salvation in the godly. An eloquent tongue promotes faith; reason makes speech clear, and everything helps faith forward. Reason receives life from faith; it is killed by it and brought back to life.[2]

Enlightened reason does not have the capacity to discover new truths in natural theology independently of revelation.

Rather, it orders life willingly in accordance with the requirements of the Word, in the footsteps of the Master. The *ratio theologica* is the reason of the *homo theologicus*. Here, too, the formula *simul justus et peccator* applies; for the regenerate reason, too, is at one and the same time justified, considered holy in God's eyes, while remaining imperfect, deficient in sanctification as a present reality.

Luther's use of the term "reason" was complex and his expressions must always be read in context. Nor can it be asserted that he was always careful to define and distinguish, but was perfectly capable in rhetorical outbursts of mixing various uses of the term together in the same passage. Reason can be used in an instrumental sense as the ability to draw logical conclusions. It can be considered a cultural factor in the secular realm. It can serve as a principle or criterion of a total world view in a philosophical or natural-religion sense.[3] Luther's main concern, however, was theological, that "the thing itself be distinguished from its abuse." A distinguished Reformation scholar, Brian Gerrish, has in a recent book spelled out the three-fold distinction which Luther made between natural reason ruling within its own proper domain of worldly matters, natural reason illegitimately carrying over into the domain of spiritual matters certain propositions derived from the secular realm (e.g., the virtues are rewarded), and regenerate reason working legitimately within the domain of spiritual matters by humbly adopting presuppositions derived solely from the "Word."

The natural reason which deals with mundane affairs is, as Luther's language often seems to suggest, a 'practical reason,' approaching at times our own notion of "common sense"; and to this extent natural reason, even within its proper boundaries, may appear to be a material as well as a formal conception, since it implies the adoption of certain concrete attitudes of mind. When the natural reason trespasses on the domain of spiritual matters, it is unambiguously a concrete, material attitude of the unregenerate man; here we have seen, *ratio* is a certain definite *opinio*. The regenerate reason, finally, is in the main a formal conception; reason here is a tool, an instrument, an organ. But since regenerate reason tends to coalesce with the notion of faith, in this context also *ratio* may sometimes take into itself a certain material content.4

It is quite obvious that Luther normally employs synecdoche, using reason for the whole man. Thus natural reason is really the reason of natural man and regenerate reason is actually the reason of regenerate man. Beyond this he frequently does hypostatize reason in a substantial and material sense, while at other times it retains a purely formal aspect.

In terms of the impact of Luther's distinctively Christian rationalism upon enlightenment and idealist thought, it was fortuitous that Luther associated an appeal to reason with the demands of conscience in his dramatic address at the Diet of Worms:

> Since then your serene majesty and your lordships seek a simple answer, I will give it in this manner, neither horned nor toothed: Unless I am convinced by the testimony of the Scriptures or by clear reason (for I do not trust either in the pope or in councils alone, since it is well known that they have often erred and contradicted themselves), I am bound by the Scriptures I have quoted and my conscience is captive to the Word of God. I cannot and I will not retract anything, since it is neither safe nor right to go against conscience.5

The *ratio evidens* to which Luther appeals seen in context as well as in the light of other references is the reason of regenerate man informed, as is his conscience, by the Word of God.6 In earlier centuries, however, the *ratio* in this famous reply was understood to mean magisterial reason, just as conscience was understood to be the subjective sensitivity of an autonomous individual asserting his freedom from heteronomous controls. Luther as the protagonist of reason, conscience, and freedom—this was the Luther who appealed to the men of the Enlightenment and the transcendental idealist philosophers.

There is a discernible difference in the way in which the English and French Enlightenment intellectuals and the German *Aufklärung* thinkers related to Luther's Reformation. Hume and Gibbon were contemptuous of the theological concern of the reformers. It is a curious development to find that in England many of the Victorians in the next century were critical of "Luther's rationalism and Erastianism."[7] Voltaire despised the Reformation as a "quarrel of monks" and sneered that "one cannot read without a mixture of contempt and pity the manner in which Luther treats all his opponents and particularly the Pope." The men of the *Aufklärung* were critical of Luther, but by no means contemptuous. They were critical of the medieval remains in his thought, but they were appreciative of his battle for the freedom of conscience, which for them was the essence of the Reformation. In Luther the gold of religious and ethical autonomy was still mixed with slag. They considered further purification and the completion of what Luther had begun to be their task. It was no mere theatrical gesture, therefore, or act of hypocrisy, when the men of the *Aufklärung* constantly called upon the name of Luther, for they considered him to be the leader of the first attack wave, while they constituted the phalanx of hoplites which would win the final victory of reason over superstition and the forces of darkness. "Reformation" became one of their favorite words, "reformation" as freedom and "reformation" as cultural reform and resurgence. They staged "reformations" of dogmatics, jurisprudence, orthography, the book trade, hymnbooks, and of Lutheranism itself. The majestic Goethe in the *Frankfurter gelehrten Anzeigen* in 1772 mocked the "iconoclastic Zeal" of the "enlightened reformers" of his day. Hamann commented ironically on the "epidemic reformation swindle" and the fact that "reformation" was such a favorite word in the *Aufklärung*.[8]

German transcendental idealism inherited certain basic ways of interpreting Luther's importance for humanity and higher culture. The idealists in general valued his contribution to the full development of individual personality and the "deepest inwardness," the critical role of private conscience and conscientiousness, and the advancement of liberty. The great Luther scholar Karl Holl, in an essay on the cultural

significance of the Reformation, commended the positive influence which Luther had upon Kant and Fichte, who, in the
spirit of Luther, deepened the Leibnizian idea of personality.[9]
Along with the concept of an unconditioned law, he argued,
they received the concept of sin.

In advancing from the narrowness of naturalism to the
breadth of an ethical understanding of man, Fichte believed
that he had arrived at the essence of man's reality. The nub
of his anthropology is presented in his *Die Bestimmung des
Menschen* which he published in 1800. Dealing with doubt,
knowledge, and faith, Fichte struggled with the question of
the doubt which the human self feels about its own reality
when confronted by the external world, a doubt with which
the naturalistic or "scientific" point of view threatens to over-
whelm man. He wished to assert the validity of the knowledge
of self and faith as the action by which the self affirms itself as
the sole reality. What is real is the knowing mind of man,
which gives to the external world such reality as it has. Through
the exercise of freedom the self determines what it is. The determination of the self does not lie in knowledge alone, but in
action in accordance with that knowledge. In the third book,
entitled "Faith," Fichte exhorted: "'Your determination does
not lie in mere knowledge but in action in accordance with
your knowledge: this message rings aloud in my inmost soul as
soon as for a moment I collect myself and look into myself.
You exist not merely for the purpose of idle self-contemplation
or brooding over pious feelings. No, you are there to act; your
action and your action alone decides your worth."[10] Man becomes sure of the world surrounding him because it is the
sphere and the object of his dutiful action, his ethical conduct.
Man does not act because he knows, but he knows because he
is called to act—as a member of two orders of life, the spiritual
in which man prevails by the effect of a pure will and the sen-
sual in which he participates through individual actions.

The heart of Fichte's anthropology is that man through an
act of will transcends the limitation of natural determination
to the sphere of his true freedom. Fichte's philosophy has been

glorified as the "'philosophy of freedom," for central to his thought is man in his moral aspect and therefore in the light of human freedom. Fichte's absolute subjectivism and argument for the autarchy of man are subject to a variety of serious criticisms from both naturalistic and theological positions, but a critique is not the purpose here. The point to be made is that when Fichte said, "One decision and I rise above nature," he was generally understood to be expressing the same confidence as Luther in personal liberty and the right to make ethical decisions in the world of action. Man has the ability to tear himself free from what he is by nature and to raise himself into the freedom of the spirit. The intellectual world of idealism took Fichte's message in the same sense as the literary world understood the popular poet and dramatist Schiller. When Schiller emboldened Western man with his slogan "Du kannst, denn du sollst." (You can, for you should), he, too, was believed to be reflecting Luther's view of man's moral essence. The individual freed from heteronomous controls of an ecclesiastical or regimental kind must make and is able to make free moral decisions. In June, 1790, Fichte wrote to his bride: "I shall always be called a heretic for that is certain . . . I know very well how I think; I am neither a Lutheran nor Reformed, but a Christian. And if I must choose, since a Christian congregation really exists nowhere, that congregation is dearest to me where one can think the most freely and live most tolerantly."[11] In spite of this protest of his independence, Fichte was indebted to the reformers as a theologian and in no small part because of the influence of Kant, his great master. On July 4, 1791, Fichte as a thirty-year-old theologian met Kant face to face in Königsberg. Under Kant's protection and influence he wrote his first book, *Critique of All Revelation*, which Kant later publicly spoke of as a "bad book."

Kant, as the most brilliant exponent of high idealism, was known as "the Protestant philosopher." On first examination, his transcendental criticism of the traditional metaphysical arguments concerning the soul, the universe, and God seemed diametrically opposed to Luther's theology, arriving at an agnostic position so far as human understanding as a basis for a priori synthetic judgments is concerned. But what Kant took away in his *Critique of Pure Reason* he sought to restore in his *Critique of Practical Reason.* The moral law is supreme and the individual is more certain of the moral imperative "I ought" than of any other fact of experience. Consideration of pleasure or of interest must give way to the demands of conscience, for nothing can gainsay the voice of conscience, although the individual is free to obey or to disobey the universal and necessary moral law. The moral law implies the existence of a Law Giver. Christ was the exemplification of the highest moral perfection. Historical faith is the vehicle of rational faith.

Energetic efforts have been devoted to analyzing the dogmatic sources of Kant's religious thought.[12] He seems to have known among Luther's writings only the small catechism. Nevertheless, a generic relationship between Kant and Luther's thought is discernible. Both were opposed to speculative religious metaphysics, for they agreed that precise scientific statements about God and transcendent reality were not possible for speculative reason. For Kant the postulates of practical reason, for Luther the faith experience were firmer grounds for establishing religious reality. Although Kant did not know the depth of sin and radical evil as the primal experience of man (*Urerlebnis*) as did Luther, he acknowledged the feeling of guilt. An ethic of intention was common to both; but for Kant the law, the duty to love the neighbor as oneself, informed and quickened conscience; for Luther the God of justice stood back of that law. The God of mercy and forgiveness meant nothing to Kant and everything to Luther.

In view of the fundamental differences between Luther and Kant it is fascinating to observe how the younger idealists loved to link Kant with the Luther of *On the Liberty of the Christian Man.* They were seen as partners in the promotion of freedom, education, liberalism, the sovereignty of conscience, and idealism. Whoever wanted to be a Christian had to be an idealist. Even in later scholarship, Kant was frequently described as having successfully put Luther's ethical religious feeling upon the foundation of reason.[13] The way in which later scholars, including such great minds as Karl Holl and Wilhelm Dilthey, analyzed Luther's thought using Kantian concepts provides a further demonstration of how in the idealist tradition Kant and Luther were linked together as intellectually of the some genre.

For nearly four decades the transcendental idealists were concerned about the relationship of Kant's phenomenal and the noumenal world. They shared a common metaphysical vision of the ultimate unity of thought and being. In the mystery of feeling, in an encounter with the divine, or in speculative thought, man transcends himself to understand, experience, or feel the ultimate unity of reality. This vision served for a time as an epistemological ground for the knowledge of God and served as a support for religion.[14]

Hegel in particular emerged as a patron and protector of religion. He went beyond Kant's critique not by a strict epistemological analysis but on the basis of his own metaphysical vision of the identity of thought and being, idea and reality. Hegel's early theological writings were heavily influenced by Luther. In his maturity he still considered himself to be a Christian thinker and a Lutheran. He was throughout many of his major works preoccupied with Christian themes. The process of reconciliation for Hegel was essentially the process in which the implicit unity of the divine and human natures becomes explicit. This process must take place in rational consciousness; thought and knowledge and the reconciling work of Christ must be understood in those terms. The unity of the divine and human natures is known insofar as it is embodied in the real immediate event of the incarnation. This unity is known ". . . in no other way than for this unity to manifest itself in a completely temporal, perfectly common appearance in the world in one of these men—in this man, who at the same time becomes known as the divine Idea, not as a teacher, not only as a higher being in general, but as the highest, as God's Son."[15]

Hegel stressed repeatedly that the historical incarnation was essential for man to gain an immediate certainty of the truth. If truth is "to become certain to men, God must appear in the flesh in the world." In writing on the incarnation Hegel reiterated that it is man's destiny to know the identity of his own nature with God. This Hegelian reading of Christianity set the stage for a first-rate tragicomic production, the left-wing Hegelian inversion which precipitated a major crisis in religious thought. Proceeding from Hegel's system, with its many affinities to Luther's theology, Bruno Bauer, David Friedrich Strauss, Ludwig Feuerbach, and Karl Marx turned against it and confronted Christianity with a modern challenge more fundamental than had the philosophers of the Enlightenment. The nineteenth-century "realists" identified Christianity closely with idealism. Belief in God was associated with the realm of the spirit, the supersensory, supernatural realm. This is the meaning of Nietzsche's devastating thrust: "Christentum ist Platonismus fürs Volk."

Lutherus redivivus! Intellectual history at this point unveiled one of Clio's little surprises, for at this very critical juncture in Western thought Luther's theology became a central focus of discussion. Luther scholasticized, moralized, catechetically domesticated, tamed, could be employed by the idealists for their purposes. But there was another side to Luther available for exploitation. Aldous Huxley once referred to the reformers as "sweaty realists" in their view of man. Realism in the nineteenth-century context meant thinking anthropologically. Man is the central reality, and through the understanding of man, man is enabled to interpret the realities of nature and religion around him, for they are not beyond him. Man does not begin with the world outside or a system of thought provided objectively by reason. Through an understanding of man, as his experience has shaped him, man as the prime reality comes to understand what it is necessary for him to understand about reality. The battle between idealism and realism has long since been decided in favor of realism, anthropological realism and not that of mere empiricism. Luther participated in the operation.[16] Erasmus once said of Luther: "God has given us a radical physician!"

II. *Luther's Anthropological Realism*

As the key witness in the case of the anthropological realists against the idealists' spiritualization of Christianity, Luther's understanding of man is of critical importance. Luther, much more so than Calvin or Zwingli, linked together the *cognitio dei et hominis.* Man is a central concern for Luther precisely because man is a central concern for God. God is the highest concern for Luther just as he should be for everyman. The God who loves man and whom man can in turn love is known in the God-man, Christ, alone. The incarnation is the focus of both theology and anthropology.

It will be useful to rehearse the basic elements of Luther's view of man before exploring in greater detail two points of crucial importance for the nineteenth-century realists' reading of Luther, namely, his giving priority to experience and being over thought and action and his intense concentration upon God in the human Jesus. While Luther's anthropology is in the main-line Western Christian tradition, formally acknowledging, for example, the body/soul dichotomy, immortality of the soul, man's rationality, and the like, he deviates in both emphasis and substance on important matters. There is no mistaking the ways in which he differs from the Renaissance Platonic idealization of man. The humanists, rationalists, and idealists agreed in their own times that Luther had a "too dark and pessimistic view of man."

Luther did not feel comfortable operating with the dichotomy of a body/soul division or the trichotomy of body/soul/spirit. He was too thoroughly Hebraic, thanks to his intense study of the Old Testament, to read Saint Paul through Hellenistic eyes. He objected strenuously to Erasmus' exegesis of Saint Paul's epistles interpreting "spirit" as that ethereal side of man which draws him upward toward God while "flesh" is the bodily side of man that keeps him earthbound. "In my temerity," Luther declared, "I do not distinguish body, soul, and spirit, but present the whole man unto God." Just as he controverted the humanist Erasmus, so he directed a major apologetic against the scholastic Latomus on the very question of sin and righteousness in man.[17] Against this "sophist," who had defended the University of Louvain's condemnation of Luther's theology, Luther explained his position that man in the flesh is entirely sinner and that man in the spirit is the man of faith who is entirely forgiven by God. The man of faith is at the same time justified and righteous in God's eyes, while in reality he remains spotted with sin, as he and his neighbor know (*simul justus et peccator*). In the course of his argument Luther comments as follows upon Romans 7:21 ("I find then a law, that, when I would do good, evil is present with me"): "For it is no one else," Luther explains, "who wishes to do the good than he to whom the evil clings. The spiritual man wishes to do the good as a whole man (*totus homo*) but the fleshly man hangs on to him as not entirely a whole man (*minus totus*)."[18]

This emphasis upon the *totus homo* is in line with Luther's exegesis in his *Lectures on Romans*, where in commenting on Romans 7:25 ("Therefore I with the mind serve the law of God, but with the flesh, the law of sin"): "This is the most telling passage of all," Luther writes. "Notice that one and the same man serves both the law of God and the law of sin, that he is righteous and at the same time he sins. He does not say: 'My mind serves the law of God,' nor 'My flesh serves the law of sin,' but he says, 'I, this whole man (*totus homo*), this person here, stand in this double servitude.' He therefore gives thanks that he serves the law of God and he asks for mercy that he serves the law of sin."[19] This concept of man as a single unity, a *totus homo*, was an important development away from the Platonic conception of the soul as prisoner in the body, so common to the medieval ascetic and Renaissance metaphysical doctrine of man.

Secondly, Luther's realism is evident in his stress upon sin as man's primal experience (*Urerlebnis*). He deepened the conception of sin by describing it as the root condition of man, a state of unspirituality in which man is estranged from God. Sin is not a simple single transgression of the law, but a state of indifference and hostility to God which makes even "good" works, which in structure conform to the law, sinful.[20] It is not merely a matter of deficiencies or individual flaws, as Horace described man in the *Satires* (I, iii, 68): "No one is born free from vices." It is a total, all-comprehending state of the total man. Man's natural condition is to be self-loving, self-seeking, self-serving, for man is by nature turned in upon himself (*incurvatus in se*).[21] Man in this condition is not a mere automaton, one who against his will or with no will at all lives out his life condemned to an inherited state of spiritual death. Luther distinguishes *necessitas* and *coactio*, for while man is necessarily as natural man engulfed in this condition of unspirituality, he is not coerced. His is a religious necessity, not a metaphysical determinism. His predicament is more desperate precisely because he willingly lives out his life in an abyss of self-centeredness in which he does not wish to love God above all things or his neighbor as much as himself. The enslaved will (*servum arbitrium*) remains *arbitrium, voluntas*, will. Man in this condition remains man with a potentiality for spiritual liberation. He is not, says Luther to Erasmus, a goose or a stone. He is a person fitted (*aptus*) with a disposition (*dispositiva qualitas*) and passive aptitude (*passiva aptitudo*) for a spiritual awakening or rebirth. The man in whom the Holy Spirit works faith in God is thereby given a freed will (*arbitrium liberatum*), a will which can desire and perform acts of love pleasing to Him, for they are done in a state of spiritual life. Royal liberty (*libertas regia*) is the happy possession of men who have come to trust in God.

Thirdly, Luther's realism is evident in his assessment of man's anxiety in living toward death. Man, spiritually dead, lives in a constant state of anxiety (*angst*), for away from God life is meaningless and empty. Man thrown into the world lives out his life toward death in dread. "Indeed," Luther commented in 1519, "death is on all sides, whatever they [men] see and feel. They are stretched out between life and death:

They dread death; they do not have life."[22] That is the message of his *Sermon on the Preparation for Death*, 1519,[23] and of the somber *Invocavit* sermons preached during Lent in 1522.[24] His theme in the discourse on Psalm 90, delivered in 1534, was "In the midst of life we are in death" (*Media vita in morte sumus*). Man is afflicted with calamities, miseries, brevity of life, torments of afflicted conscience, desperation, temporal and eternal death. The author of the psalm is a "most Moses Moses, that is, a severe minister of death, of the wrath of God and of sin."[25] Life taken as a whole is like a besieged city surrounded on all sides by death. Man lives constantly in a "border situation" (*Grenzsituation*—a *sein zum Tode*) and on the razor's edge between life and death. Life's very transiency is its most disconcerting feature.

Luther saw the reality of death with clear eyes. A close brush with death had triggered his decision to enter the monastery, and he never forgot that death is man's nextdoor neighbor. The world is on a daily and continuous march toward death. The death of an animal, the death of a heathen, the death of a Christian are three kinds of death. The death of a Christian is the most poignant, for beyond the physical end of life, the question of the man's relation to God comes into play. There is no greater power on earth than death, for the world itself will one day come to an end.[26]

Luther's anthropological realism was stark realism. Also Christian existence is subjected to constant shattering. The theologian is made by living, dying, being damned, not by understanding, reading, or speculating.[27] The believer is sustained by a theology of hope. Everyone must do his own believing, Luther constantly asserts, just as everyone must do his own dying.

Fourthly, Luther's anthropological realism is evident in the interior theological context in that he insists upon the reality of faith as experienced and the priority of suffering to being, of being to thought and action. Luther abhorred speculation in theology and stressed the immediate, concrete, and personal dimension of religion. The most important words in religion, he once observed, are the personal pronouns, the "I," "Thou," and "he," my brother. His theology was marked by a strange dynamic concreteness. Faith is *fiducia* or trust in God, not *credulitas* or credulous acceptance of particular propositions about God. His writings are studded with statements that to trust is instantaneously to possess the object of faith. "As you believe, so you have!" he exclaimed.[28] "You have as much as you believe (on account of the promise of Christ)," he repeated time and again.[29] At times he seems almost to hypostatize faith. Faith is the *vita cordis*, the very life of the heart, and a *vita experimentalis*, the experimental or experiential life of the spiritual man.

The relationship of faith and experience is a subtle question related directly to the problem of being preceding action. On the one hand, Luther divorces faith from subjective human feelings and assumptions. Faith is invisible and hidden, even insensible.[30] Faith lives in darkness and may even be described as "blind."[31] Luther exerts every effort to direct faith to an objective ground in the Word outside the self's own feelings, which so readily deceive and are subject to sudden change. On the other hand, Luther does not really wish to divorce faith from experience, but wants merely to underline the fact that the experience of faith is an experience of another kind. It is the work of the Holy Spirit and should not be confused with emotions or mystical experiences of any other kind. Where a man has experienced something of God's goodness and love, where holy joy fills the heart, there the Holy Spirit has been the teacher.[32] The experience of faith in this sense is truly an experience which contrasts markedly from the experience of natural man who lives without the awakening of faith.[33] The content of faith, the Word, may be objectively understood, but must be subjectively apprehended. The story of Redemption remains speculation, theory, mere idle historical knowledge, unless a man believes that his cause was involved and that all was done for him.

Not only is the experience of struggle and the release of faith essential for the believer, but is indispensable to the theologian, if he is to understand his subject. "Experience alone makes the theologian," Luther reiterated.[34] The true theologian is not the one who knows great things and teaches many things, but the one who lives in a holy and "theological" way.[35] Luther's scholastic master Gabriel Biel had asserted that "reading [Scriptures], meditation and prayer" make the theologian.[36] Already in 1513 Luther substituted *experientia* as the third component in the right formula. In the preface to the first part of his German writing of 1539 Luther coined his oft-cited definition: "Prayer, meditation, and the experience of struggle [*tentatio*] make a theologian." The way in which a theologian understands the Word depends upon his prior disposition.[37]

The power and persuasive thrust of Luther's theology was a result of a subtle fusion of his own personal religious experience and the product of his scientific labors as an exegete. Interestingly enough he at times associates personal experience with conscience, while the Scriptures serve as both source and norm of truth. In 1530 he wrote in a *Rhapsodia* about justification:

The miracles of my teaching are experiences, which I prefer to the resurrection of the dead. . . . Since this experience is more certain than life itself, it is not a deceiving sign for me, but serves instead of many thousands of miracles, since it agrees with the Scriptures in all things. You have two most faithful and invincible witnesses, namely Scripture and conscience, which is experience. For conscience is a thousand witnesses, Scripture an infinite number of witnesses.[38]

Theology is real and concrete, involving the whole man. It is therefore not to be confused with the abstractions of metaphysics or scholastic distinctions. This drive away from an intellectualized scholastic theology toward a theology of experience emerged powerfully in his crucial *Lectures on Romans* of the years 1515-1516. In a striking passage Luther hits at the religiously irrelevant word games of the scholastic theologians and presses for an understanding of man's deeper needs. His reflections on Romans 8:19 ("For the expectation of the creature waits for the revelation of the sons of God") are to this point:

The apostle philosophizes and thinks about the things of the world in another way than the philosophers and metaphysicians do, and he understands them differently from the way they do. For the philosophers are so deeply engaged in studying the present state of things that they explore only what and of what kind they are, but the apostle turns our attention away from the consideration of things as they are now, and from what they are as to essence and accidents, and directs us to regard them in terms of what they will be. He does not speak of the "essence" of the creature, and of the way it "operates," or of its "action" or "inaction," and "motion," but, using a new and strange theological word, he speaks of "the expectation of the creature." By virtue of the fact that his soul has the power of hearing the creature waiting, he no longer directs his inquiry toward the creature as such but to what it waits for. But alas, how deeply and painfully we are caught up in categories and quiddities, and how many foolish opinions befog us in metaphysics! When shall we learn to see that we waste so much precious time with such useless studies and neglect better ones?[39]

In commenting on Romans 8 he carries on his argument according to the *analogia fidei* rather than the *analogia entis*:

Would it, then, not be sheer madness on our part to sing the praises of philosophy? For is it not so that while we think highly of the science of the essences and actions and inactions of things, the things themselves loath their essences and their actions and inactions and groan under them? . . . The apostle is therefore right when, in Colossians 2:8, he speaks up against philosophy and says: "Beware lest any man cheat you by philosophy and vain deceit according to the tradition of man." If the apostle had wanted to understand any philosophy as something good and useful, he certainly would not have condemned it so unequivocally! We conclude, therefore, that anyone who searches into the essences and functionings of the creatures rather than into their sighings and earnest expectations is certainly foolish and blind. He does not know that also the creatures are created for an end. This passage shows this clearly enough.[40]

Luther's powerful emphasis upon experience, the soul-struggle and the effect of God's grace upon man through the gift of faith was central to his whole theology. His basic ground of objection to scholastic theology was the failure of the doctors to deal adequately with sin and grace. They do not weigh the seriousness of sin as heavily as they should, acting as though sin could be removed by the flick of an eyelash, as darkness is by light. Unlike the fathers such as Augustine and Ambrose, the scholastics follow Aristotle instead of Scriptures. In his *Nicomachean Ethics* Aristotle bases sinfulness and righteousness and the extent of their actualization on what a person does.[41] Luther declares that it is God's grace that makes a man righteous, grace understood as a benignity, when God forgives a man his sin at a particular time and place. The man thus justified in God's eyes does good works. Luther explained this point with epigrammatic brevity and force:

Indeed, neither the works which precede nor those which follow make a man righteous—how much less the works of the law. Not those which precede, for they only prepare a man for justification; nor those which follow, for they require that justification be already accomplished. For we are not made righteous by doing righteous deeds. But we do righteous deeds because we are righteous. Therefore grace alone *(sola gratia)* justifies.[42]

Such was the religious ground upon which he objected to Erasmus' way of interpreting *Romans*, as though Saint Paul with *law* meant merely the ceremonial laws. In a letter to Spalatin, October 19, 1516, dating from the time of his preoccupation with *Romans*, Luther explained that Erasmus was wrong in his interpretation, for it is not as Aristotle thought that we are made righteous by doing righteous deeds, but by having become and being righteous we do righteous deeds. It is "first necessary that the person be changed, then the works." "I do this," Luther concluded, "for the sake of theology and the salvation of the brethren."[43] In fact, Luther emphasized this very crucial idea that man's condition determines the spiritual quality of his thought and action in his exegesis of

Romans 1:17, which he frequently described as the "great breakthrough" for his Pauline theology.[44] In asserting that "the good tree brings forth good fruit," in that sequence, Luther could, of course, appeal to authority higher than his own. In his commentary on Ecclesiastes Luther carried this argument over to the case of the skeptic. His despair, Luther stressed, is not the result of the vanity of all things in themselves or merely the transiency of life. Rather, it is the result of the anterior condition of the inner man which determines his negative perception of the world outside.

Luther spelled out the sequence of events in the marginal gloss to Romans 12:1 following, it is curious to note, the Aristotelian *progressio a non esse ad esse,* the progression from non-being to being, which is familiar also from scholastic theology. Luther explains:

So far the apostle has spoken about what it means to become a new man, and he has described the new birth which bestows the new being (John 3:3ff). But now he speaks about the works of the new birth; one who has not yet become a new man presumes that he is doing them—but in vain. For being comes before doing, but being-acted-upon comes even before being. Hence, becoming, being, acting, follow one another.[45]

In the corollary Luther gave this sequence of five stages in natural growth according to Aristotle (privation, matter, form, operation, and passion) a theological application. In the case of the Spirit, he explained, not-being is something without a name, and man in sin; becoming is justification; being is righteousness; acting is to act and live righteously; to be acted upon is to be made perfect and complete. These five are somehow always in motion in man.[46] "I do not have vision," Luther argued, "because I see, but because I have vision therefore I see."[47] Neither the external piety of a priest nor the human imitations by a monkey make them essentially righteous human beings.[48]

The initiative in man's justification lies with God. The

Holy Spirit changes the will or "inner spirit" of man. One cannot answer the question why it is I who is *re*born anymore than one can answer the question why it is I who was born. Luther cites Augustine's *De Spiritu et Litera* to establish that it is God himself who gives what he commands of man.[49] "Now, this sublime power that is in us is not, so the apostle asserts," writes Luther, "a product of our own, but it must be sought for from God. This is why it is *shed abroad* and in no way brought forth from us or originated by us. And thus *by the Holy Spirit*; it is not acquired by moral effort and habit as the moral virtues are. *In our hearts*, i.e., deep down in the innermost parts of the heart and not on the surface of the heart in the way foam lies on water."[50] Such is the divine initiative!

A fifth and final aspect of Luther's anthropological realism is his stress upon the hypostatic union of the divine and human natures in Christ. His stress upon Christ's humanity and the communication of divine attributes to Christ's human nature sets him apart not only from humanism and scholasticism but, in emphasis, even somewhat from the other magisterial reformers. His exalted view of the human nature of Christ brought into focus God's unbounded love for man. Luther's sacramental teaching of the ubiquity of Christ and real presence is dependent upon his high Athanasian Christology. Moreover, Christ was proof of what man as man could have been, were it not for the fall of man. He followed Saint Paul in seeing Adam as the archetype of fallen man and Christ as the archetype of perfect man. All this is known and very well understood by those who know and understand Luther at all. But it is necessary to raise a special question at this point, for it became a vital issue at a later time. Luther was impressed, as was Calvin after him, with man's ingenious ability to create religions. Man's resourcefulness is unlimited in making gods of all sorts and of seeing in those idols the very qualities which man would most like to see there. With respect to the High God, man projects upon God the terror or love which in reality is in his own heart. Luther was no religionist and an old German monograph is entitled *Luther's Criticism of All Religion!*[51] How does one determine whether when a natural man to whom the gospel story is mere history sees God in Christ beckoning him, he is not merely projecting his own exalted view of man upon a divine Christ?

As a man believes, he has! Luther plunges ahead without dreaming or caring what use would be made of his words. In his exposition of the first commandment in the *Large Catechism*: "How often I have said that the trust and faith of the heart alone make both God and idol. If the faith and the trust is right, then your God is right, and, contrariwise, where the trust is false and wrong, there the right God is also not present." "So it is," says Luther, "with our faith and unbelief: whoever portrays Him in his heart as merciful or angry, sweet or sour, he has Him just that way."[52] One of Luther's least guarded expressions reads: "Just as I think about God, so he is to me!"[53] Such statements occur in his scholarly as well as in his popular writing. In his key exegetical work, the *Commentary on Romans*, for example, he offers his corollary to Romans 3:5 ("But if our unrighteousness commend the righteousness of God, what shall we say? Is God unrighteous who taketh vengeance? [I speak as a man]"):

> God is mutable to the highest degree. This is obvious, because one can justify and judge him, according to Psalm 18, 26: "With the elect thou wilt be elect, and with the perverse thou wilt be perverted." For as everyone is in himself, so God is to him objectively. If he is righteous, God is righteous; if he is pure, God is pure; if he is unjust, God is unjust, etc. So he will appear as unjust to those who are eternally damned, but to the righteous, as righteous, and so he is in himself. This change, however, is extrinsic. This is plainly implied in the word "Thou wilt be judged." For as God is judged only from the outside, on man's part, so he is also justified only from the outside. Hence, one can necessarily say only extrinsically of God: "That thou mayest be justified."[54]

Luther's intention is perfectly clear, but his vulnerability to exploitation is all too obvious from our vantage point.

iii. *Anthropological Realism and Luther*

The great Protestant philosopher of the *Aufklärung*, Immanuel Kant, in his work *Religion Within the Limits of Reason Alone* (1793) introduced a thought "concerning the universal subjective ground of the religious illusion" which seemed to subvert the independent authenticity of revelation and thereby to anticipate the realists' criticism of religion. He wrote:

> Anthropomorphism scarcely to be avoided by men in the theoretical representation of God and His being, but yet harmless enough (so long as it does not influence concepts of duty), is highly dangerous in connection with our practical relation to His will, and even for our morality; for here *we create a God for ourselves*, and we create Him in the form in which we believe we shall be able most easily to win Him over to our advantage and ourselves escape from the wearisome uninterrupted effort of working upon the innermost part of our moral disposition.[55]

Kant went on to argue that it is in no way reprehensible to say that every man *creates a God* for himself, for he must always compare any revealed God with his own ideal in order to judge whether he is entitled to regard and honor it as God. All the artificial self-deceptions in religious matters have a common base, Kant concluded.[56] Among the three divine moral attributes, holiness, mercy, and justice, man habitually turns directly to the second in order to avoid the forbidding condition of conforming to the requirements of the first! Kant was getting uncomfortably close to depth-psychologizing *sola gratia*.

But even if Kant in his old age had not moved in this direction, another child of the *Aufklärung*, illegitimate and romantic, Johann Gottfried Herder, would have turned Western thought down such a road. In his *Ideas* (1784) on history Herder put the whole ponderous thought into a single capsule: "Religion is man's humanity in its highest form."[57] Even when looked upon solely as an exercise of the understanding, this ordained Lutheran minister went on, it is the most sublime

flowering of the human soul. He gives the following account of
the origin of this precious blossom:

As soon as man learned to use his understanding when stim-
ulated ever so slightly, as soon, that is, as his vision of the world
became different from that of the animals, he was bound to sur-
mise the existence of invisible, mighty beings which helped or
harmed him. These he sought to make his friends, or to keep as
his friends, and thus religion, whether true or false, right or wrong,
became the teacher of mankind, the comfort and counsel of a life
so full of darkness, danger and perplexity.[58]

He went on to describe religion as a "childlike service of God,
an imitation of the highest and most beautiful qualities in the
human image, and hence that which affords the deepest satis-
faction, and most effective goodness and human love."[59]

Neither Kant nor Herder, of course, thought that their psychological, phenomenological, or evolutionary historical explication of religion and its origins really brought into question
the objective reality of a transcendent Deity. The noumenal
world could not be touched by phenomenological explanations.
When, however, the moment came that a radical materialist
entered the ring armed with such argumentation, a "fatal mu-
tation" suddenly occurred. That moment was the publication
in 1841 of Ludwig Feuerbach's *The Essence of Christianity*.
How fascinating that Feuerbach should come from left-wing
Hegelianism, for Hegel had in his great synthesis sought to
combine rationalist and romantic elements, Kant and Herder,
into one harmonious system. In writing on the incarnation
Hegel had pontificated that it is man's destiny to know the
identity of his own nature with God. An inversion of this
hypothesis was easy enough and not long in coming. It was
God's destiny in the year of our Lord 1841 to learn of the
identity of His own nature with man. Compared with Hegel's
grand system, Feuerbach's thought seems simple, unilinear,
trifling. But Feuerbach needed only one spade, an ace, with
which to undermine and topple Hegel's proud tower.

In his *The Essence of Christianity* Ludwig Feuerbach

shocked the intellectual world with the radical assertion that all religion is anthropology. Years later in his *Lectures on the Essence of Religion* he provided a summary of his own doctrine:

I now come to those of my writings which embody my doctrine, religion, philosophy, or whatever you may choose to call it, and provide the subject matter of these lectures. This doctrine of mine is briefly as follows. *Theology is anthropology*: in other words, the object of religion, which in Greek we call *theos* and in our language God, expresses nothing other than the essence of man; man's God is nothing other than the deified essence of man, so that the history of religion or, what amounts to the same thing, of God—for the gods are as varied as the religions, and the religions are as varied as mankind—is nothing other than the history of man.[60]

Christianity differs from the religions of uncivilized peoples only in transforming the phenomena that arouse man's fear not into special gods, but into attributes of one God. God is the epitome of all realities or perfections, a compendious summary devised for the benefit of the limited individual, an "epitome of the generic human qualities distributed among men, in the self-realization of the species in the course of world history."[61] His most radical phrase was: "Man and man, the unity of I and Thou, is God." *Homo homini deus est*! Now in arguing that not the attribute of divinity but the divinity of the attribute is the first truly divine being, Feuerbach did not consider himself to be an atheist, but rather the discoverer of the true wealth of religion, for the only true atheist is the man to whom these attributes mean nothing. Feuerbach's notorious "Der Mensch ist was er isst" (man is what he eats) was intended to express not a materialistic theory of human nature, but simply a plea in favor of the human right of healthy survival.[62] If theology is anthropology, it remains that a high regard for man's being is reflected in theology. In God as subject man can only perceive that which is a predicate or quality of himself. Humanism is raised to the level of religion. "The beginning, middle, and end of religion is man."[63] In the divinity of Christ the believer sees projected the best qualities of collective man.

"Thus Christ," Feuerbach stated enthusiastically, "as the consciousness of love, is the consciousness of the species. He therefore who loves man for the sake of man, who rises to the love of the species, to universal love, adequate to the nature of the species, he is a Christian, is Christ himself."[64]

Feuerbach thus offered an analysis not only of the metaphysical idea of God as the absolute, but also of the personal God as revealed in the Scriptures. The idea of a personal God is the ultimate religious idea, for in the personal God man has arrived at the most perfect possible projection of himself. Luther as the great preacher of the "Word made flesh" naturally intrigued Feuerbach, who recognized Luther and Augustine to be "the two great matadors" of Christendom.[65] He thought of Luther as "der erste Mensch" of Christendom and often used to say humorously of himself, "Ich bin Luther II." In later years Feuerbach repeatedly said that his work *The Essence of Christianity* really presupposed his study of *The Essence of Faith According to Luther*, even though the *Luther* came several years later (1844).[66] Although he assured his publisher that it was the "deepest thing that has ever been written on the essence of Luther,"[67] he was far from satisfied with it. In a letter of May 13, 1844, to his friend Christian Kapp, he described it as too casually written, brief where ideas still needed explication and repetitious where ideas had already been expressed.[68] In a newly discovered fragment of a draft of a letter to Arnold Ruge in Paris, April, 1844, Feuerbach referred to Luther as the "Essence of Christianity on German soil," the well-grounded German resolution of the "deepest and most powerful essence of mankind." His book, he confided, is studded with citations to gain the respect of the learned crowd.[69]

Feuerbach considered his book to be as much pro as anti-Luther, a contradiction which lies in the nature of the situation.[70] As an idealism the Christianity which Luther espoused was a source of alienation, in turning man's attention away from the individual men. Yet in emphasizing the triumph of God's merciful forgiveness coming from His heart over the wrath against sin which comes from His moral essence, Luther offered the loftiest concept of eternal, changeless, fatherly love. Christ as the daily mirror and true picture or image of God reflects the best that is in mankind. Feuerbach knows his Luther well and exploits effectively those unguarded statements about having the God one believes in. Luther is proof for his thesis that faith in the goodness of God is the form in which man affirms himself, the way in which each man makes Luther his contemporary. Feuerbach exploited (1) Luther's conception of faith; (2) his Christology, especially the communication of attributes (*communicatio idiomatum*) of the divine to the human nature of Christ; and (3) his conception of the real presence in the Sacrament.

While Luther did come exceedingly close to Feuerbach in some of his expressions, he would have been horrified at the idea that Christ as true God was merely the objectivized essence of the human species. Rather, he believed faith itself to be the work of God who has created both man and his consciousness of God. Man in nature cannot know or of his own reason and strength come to trust in the God of love. God must create the new man of faith. Luther even seems to have anticipated Feuerbach's approach in his commentary on the *Magnificat* and other passages presenting his *theologia crucis* when he confesses that the form which God's self-disclosure took is precisely not the form which man would have anticipated or desired. In the introduction to a sermon on Luke 24:13-25, which Luther preached in the city church in Wittenburg in 1534 he emphasized, as he consistently did, that the Scriptures are not a depository for human notions about God, but the vehicle which God uses to address man.

It is a fascinating spectacle to observe the way in which the greatest theologian of our day, Karl Barth, reacted to the Luther-Feuerbach concatenation on theology proper. Karl Barth in his early years was alarmed, not to say terrified, at Luther's earthy way of portraying God's consanguinity with man through the incarnation. Luther did not provide safeguards against the reversibility of his propositions as they were turned about by Feuerbach. Lutheran theology, he warned solemnly, has "guarded itself perhaps all too rigidly against the Calvinist corrective."[71] After all, Hegel had emphatically declared that he was a good Lutheran, and so did Feuerbach, in his own way and upon his own level. Barth himself thought it necessary with respect to his thought about God's own being to go to school with Anselm.[72]

Barth thought that the experience-theology of the early nineteenth century was immediately vulnerable to Feuerbach's manipulation. Feuerbach, he explained, sought to take Hegel and Schleiermacher seriously, completely seriously, at the point where they concurred in asserting the nonobjective quality of God. He wanted "to turn theology, which itself seemed half-inclined towards the same goal, completely and finally into anthropology; to turn the lovers of God into lovers of men, the worshippers into workers, the candidates for the life to come into students of the present life, the Christians into complete men; he wanted to turn away from heaven towards the earth, from faith towards love, from Christ towards ourselves, from all, but really all, supernaturalism towards real life."[73] Barth conceded that what appears to be a weakness in Feuerbach's position, namely the sensory and natural quality of his thought might also be its particular strength.

Beyond the usual criticism of Feuerbach, especially that he did not consider nature as *extra nos* (outside of us) and stubbornly resistant to an anthropomorphic explanation, Barth advanced two lines of objection to his thought. First, he believed that Feuerbach's conception of "Man's essential being" or the "consciousness of the species" which he made the measure of all things and in which he thought he saw man's true divinity might very well be a fiction just like Hegel's "Reason" or any other abstraction. The true man, conceived in real existential terms, is the individual man. Secondly, he believed that Feuerbach did not take cognizance either of man's wickedness or of his mortality. Thus his abstraction of the divinity of man in general is much less impressive when considered concretely in the individual case.[74] Barth makes the same criticism as Marx, that Feuerbach in following the left-wing Hegelian line of Max

Stirner is too abstract, too ideal, too far from concrete reality, for the unique individual is important. Before God we are liars. We can lay claim to His truth, certainty, salvation only by grace.[75] Barth considered Feuerbach as basically a man of one idea, trivial and superficial, but one who, because of his impact on modern thought, had to be reckoned with seriously.[76]

Barth is a big man, capable of executing reversals with grace and charm. Among the surprising turns in his thought is his new appreciation of Luther's Christology, taming down his own stress upon God as being "wholly other." He is very ingenious in explaining that on Renaissance grounds of "man the measure" theology had been unable to give an effective answer to Feuerbach, when, invoking Luther's sanction, he theorized that statements of the Christian faith are in reality statements of more or less profound human needs and desires projected into the infinite. For that reason early in his career Barth stressed the disjunction of the divine and human. Now (1956), *mutatis mutandis*, Barth announces a great turning point in his own thought, a *Wendung*! The prevailing theological interest in the existence of the believing man would not necessarily have been erroneous had it been a matter of shift in tone and emphasis for serious and pertinent reasons. The Scriptures, after all, speak emphatically enough of the commerce of the believing Israelites and the believing Christians with God. How else, Barth asks, could they testify on behalf of Him who was very God and very man? Then he with great temerity asserts: "The theologians should not have hesitated so long to appeal to Luther, especially the early Luther, and to the early Melanchthon! And how much assistance and guidance could they have received had they paid any attention to Kierkegaard! There is no reason why the attempt of Christian anthropocentrism should not be made, indeed ought not to be made."[77]

No sooner had Feuerbach published his book on *The Essence of Christianity*, than that brilliant "maker of modern history" Karl Marx perceived that Feuerbach could very well use Luther in support of his thesis. In January, 1842, Marx wrote his brief comment on *Luther as Umpire between Strauss and Feuerbach,* which he sent off to the *Deutschen Jahrbücher* in November for publication. David Friedrich Strauss had on a platform of radical historical skepticism and religious illusionism argued against the reality and utility of miracles. Feuerbach had written on miracles and had used Luther's picture of the world as a drunken peasant who when pushed into the saddle of a horse from one side falls off the other. Thus the intellectual world having been helped up from a one-sided rationalism has toppled over into historicism and empiricism. Miracles, as Luther appreciated, tell us something profound about man. Luther knew that all the works of nature are miraculous, just as is the real presence of God under the bread in the sacrament.[78] At this juncture in the debate Marx intervened with his decisive judgment in favor of Feuerbach. He quoted a long passage from Luther's commentary on Luke 7 in which he treats the miracle of resurrection from the dead and concluded:

> In these few words you have an apology for the whole Feuerbach writing—an apology for the definitions of providence, omnipotence, creation, miracle, faith as they are presented in this writing. Oh, shame yourselves, you Christians, shame yourselves that an *antiChrist* had to show you the essence of Christianity in its true unconcealed form! And you speculative theologians and philosophers, I advise you: free yourselves from the concepts and prejudices of speculative philosophy, if you wish to come in another way to things as they are, that is, to the *truth.* And there is no other way for you to *truth* and *freedom* except through the *Feuer bach* [stream of fire]. Feuerbach is the purgatory of these times.[79]

Marx and Engels moved rapidly beyond Feuerbach, however. In *The Holy Family,* 1845, a wicked attack on Bruno Bauer "and company," Marx criticized Feuerbach's cult of the abstract man and urged that it be replaced by the science of real men and their historical development. In *The German Ideology,* completed in 1846, Marx and Engels devoted Part One to Feuerbach, but their reference to him was oblique and they used him more as an occasion for presenting their materialistic philosophy rather than for offering a thorough critique of his thought. Later Engels criticized Feuerbach severely in his *Ludwig Feuerbach and the Outcome of Classical German Philosophy* for ignoring the new knowledge about man and nature provided by modern science and for not pursuing consistently the implications of materialism. The new immense advances in science, Engels believed, were making possible in an approximately systematic form a comprehensive view of the interconnection of the different spheres in nature, of which Feuerbach seemed to be unaware.[80] Engels even speaks of Feuerbach's "astonishing poverty" when compared with Hegel in the doctrine of moral conduct and philosophy of law.[81]

But perhaps the most damning charge which Marx and Engels leveled against Feuerbach was that he was like the idealist philosophers, who were speculative rather than relevant and active in effecting change. Marx had been born a Jew, but when Karl was six years old his father Heinrich embraced Christianity and, with his wife and children, was baptized and became a member of the Evangelical State Church (Lutheran combined with Reformed). Marx rebelled against that church as a devotee of the *status quo*, although he was grateful that his father's conversion had freed him of the burden of Judaic legalism. Marx articulated his impatience with Feuerbach's "half-way" ideology in his famous *Theses on Feuerbach*. Thesis XI reads: "The philosophers have *interpreted* the world in various ways; the point, however, is to *change* it."[82]

Another development in nineteenth-century anthropological realism related to an important aspect of Luther's thought may be tagged "voluntarist." The great pessimist Arthur Schopenhauer and the irrepressible Friedrich Nietzsche with their stress on the priority of will and the will to power as the mainsprings of human action acknowledge Luther, rightly or wrongly, as a predecessor on the road to this great insight. Luther's overall assessment of human nature, of course, was a more likely antecedent than the optimism of some of Luther's contemporaries or of the official philosophy of the Enlightenment. But it was rather the facet of Luther's anthropology having to do with the priority of suffering or becoming to being, and being to thought and action to which they attached themselves. This assumption was clear in Feuerbach's thought—in fact, was necessary to his conclusions. Man necessarily thinks and acts as he is. On the loftiest plane, when he thinks about God, he unconsciously thinks about him as he himself is. He creates him in the image of man. Schopenhauer called on Luther to support the psychology on which he based his voluntarism.

In his major work *The World as Will and Idea* Schopenhauer repeatedly cited Luther as an authority who favored determinism over freedom and will prior to reason, because being precedes thought and action. That the will is not free, he argued, is an original evangelical doctrine powerfully developed by Augustine against the platitudes of the Pelagians. Luther made it the main point of his book *De servo arbitrio*. Grace effects faith; faith receives rightcousness as a gift; it comes upon us from outside and is not a product of our free will.[83] Good works, Luther declares in his book *De libertate Christiana*, follow freely from faith and do not produce rewards.[84] That Saint Paul, Augustine, and Luther taught that works cannot justify a man, Schopenhauer argues, is a result in the final analysis of the fact that *operari sequitur esse*, doing follows upon being. Hence men who are in essence all sinners cannot do good works.[85] In acting we merely experience what we are, a depressing thought in Schopenhauer's context. This association of his own key dogma with Luther's thought was no mere sport or device on the melancholy German's part. For in his early prize-winning essay on *The Freedom of the Will*, crowned by the royal Norwegian Society of the Sciences in 1839, Schopenhauer had already declared: "Especially do I call upon Luther who in his book written for that express purpose, the *De servo arbitrio*, fought against freedom of the will with all his might."[86]

Nietzsche moved on to the will to power. As a "realist" Nietzsche mocked Christianity as the "Platonism of the masses." In his early years Nietzsche knew and admired Luther as a great German, a religious and cultural giant to be revered like Schiller and Goethe. In his later years Nietzsche became a bitter assailant of Luther, who had revitalized Christianity with its slave morality and inhibited man in his quest to break through beyond himself.[87] Despite this rejection, Nietzsche could not rid himself of certain attitudes and hypotheses absorbed in his youth and associated with Luther. "We Germans are still very young," he wrote, "and our last achievement is still Luther and our sole book is still the Bible. The Germans have never moralized."[88] He continued to value Luther's German modesty, a virtue Wagner did not possess.[89] Luther is an artist, pure and selfless.[90] Schopenhauer is simple and honorable, but crude, like Luther.[91] He observed Luther's identification with the lower classes and thought that Luther would shake up the propertied classes in the modern world.[92]

Moreover, many aspects of Nietzsche's thought are reminiscent of Luther's, such as his view of history as the arena in which the powers of this world struggled for mastery. But more relevant to the question of anthropological realism is the fact that on several occasions when Nietzsche discussed ethics, he reverted to Luther's analysis of being and action, and did so consciously. In answer to such basic questions as How deep is the ethical? Does it merely belong to that which is acquired by learning? Is it a means of expression? all deeper men are unanimous in their opinion. Luther, Augustine, Paul come to mind, for they agree that our morality and its accomplishments are not to be explained in terms of our conscious will, in brief, that the explanation as the basis of utilitarian purposes is not adequate.[93] Citing Luther with approval in this point was not necessarily very flattering, coming from Nietzsche. Luther, Augustine, Paul teach the absolute depravity of man, lack of freedom to do good, eventually grace, for sick men look for a cure.[94] Luther "belonged," for the world is an *Irrenanstalt*, a madhouse.

For Nietzsche, as for Luther, thought and action are secondary manifestations of man's inner self. Nietzsche believed man to be driven by the will to power, not to be confused with the individual's empirical will, which only indirectly and partially gives expression and an outlet to the basic driving will inherent in every action, the will to power. Man cannot transcend what he is. Like Feuerbach, and in a special way, Marx, and Schopenhauer, Nietzsche accepted the premise that *operari sequitur esse*.

What a marvelous spectacle! Luther's influence in evidence not only upon transcendental idealism, but also upon anthropological realism! In his commentary on Psalm 14:4-6 Luther declared that he was no prophet, but was sure of his message. The more people despise him, he warned, and honor themselves, the more they must fear that he is a prophet.[95] He was a prophet in that he "proclaimed" that in the final analysis man can understand what he really is in a primary or ultimate context only if word comes to him from outside himself. Anthropology in the most fundamental sense is dependent upon theology. He was a prophet in that he unknowingly "foretold" developments in intellectual history which have unfolded gradually in modern times.

That Luther's world of thought should have shaped the thought-world of the German idealists and realists was in a way inevitable, for they were conditioned by a culture based upon the Reformation experience and the Christian tradition. Luther's theology, with its paradoxes, could when taken in part rather than as a whole, which is impossible for philosophy, provide an intellectual thrust in the direction of either idealism or realism. In a good many passages our moderns seem to be blissfully unaware of how new insights have been suggested by or conditioned by the religious base and component of their thought. Like Cyrus of old men are used in a way unknown to them. In his autobiography *To Have Lived These Days* Harry Emerson Fosdick offers a portion of the book under the caption "Ideas that Have Used Me."

In some cases it is clear that a happy misunderstanding (*felix culpa*) of Luther's thought helped to propel a modern ideology forward. By taking his stand and thereby introducing religious pluralism, Luther certainly made decisive a historical contribution to the liberal option in subsequent human history. But the way in which the Enlightenment understood his idea of conscience and Christian liberty as a mandate for the autonomous individual to oppose tradition, authority, and community was clearly a misapprehension and misapplication of his ideas. Similarly, the way in which the realists applied his theological premise of an unfree will as though he were a metaphysical determinist was clearly a case of misunderstanding. The transposition of the priority of being to thought and action, which Luther in the first instance derived from the *sola gratia* polemic against salvation by good works, from the theological realm to a general ontological context could more easily be justified, for Luther leaves the possibility for such a transfer open and even suggests it himself.

Feuerbach and Schopenhauer in certain passages seem to be exploiting the authority of Luther to support unorthodox positions in a conscious way. This is a case of the tyranny, as Lord Chesterfield once put it, which the living exercise over the dead. It is like Kaiser Wilhelm quoting John Knox to the effect that "one man with God is always a majority." Luther contributed to, but was also used by, idealists and realists alike. Both groups failed to appreciate his deepest concerns, the primal anxiety and dread (*Urgrauen*) which oppresses mortal man, the concern to find gracious the God who is the final ground of being, the conviction that the divine initiative changes man's being, makes of him a new creature, the theology of hope and joy. Other moderns, the existentialists and post-liberal theologians have been able to wrestle more seriously with Luther's thought in its third and fourth dimensions.

Ever since Copernicus, Nietzsche observed, man has been falling from the center of the universe toward an X. Lacking a precisely defined cosmology, religious thinkers, idealists such as Kant and realists such as Feuerbach, have been forced to retreat to the domain of man's inwardness.[96] Biblical imagery has been internalized, the principle of analogy between heaven and earth has given way to a dialectic of identity or alienation between Creator and creation, and a language characterized by the free associative interplay of imagery.[97] Evidence of Luther's precocity and one clue to his impact on post-Reformation thought is the fact that while the Copernican cosmology was still intact, he replaced a synthetic with an antithetical dialectic, the *theologia crucis*. Luther's biblical realism in anthropology has remained disconcertingly relevant down to present times.

Notes

1. *Weimar Ausgabe* (*W.A.*), 48, 76, No. 100, ll. 1-12, Cf. *W.A.* 6, 291, 8-14: "The effort to establish or defend the divine order with human reason, unless it has already itself been grounded and enlightened by faith, is as pointless as throwing light on the bright sun with a dark lantern or resting a rock on a reed. For Isaiah in chapter 7 makes reason subject to faith and says: Unless you believe, you will not be understanding and reasonable. He does not say: Unless you are reasonable, you will not be believing."
I am grateful to the National Endowment for the Humanities for providing with a senior fellowship the sustained time for preparing this lecture for publication, which at the time of delivery was neither written out nor thought out.

2. *W.A.Ti.* 3, 104, No. 2938a, 24-29: "optimum instrumentum." *W.A.* 40I, 412, 20: "Alia ratio generatur quae est fidei."

3. Half a century ago Hans Preusz distinguished these three uses of *ratio* by Luther, "Was bedeutet die Formel 'convictus testimonüs scripturarum aut ratione evidente' in Luthers ungehörnter Antwort zu Worms?" *Theologische Studien und Kritiken*, 81 (1908), 62 ff.

4. Brian Gerrish, *Grace and Reason* (Oxford, 1962), p. 168. Gerrish's analysis is substantially in agreement with a work done independently by Bernhard Lohse, *Ratio und Fides: Eine Untersuchung über die ratio in der Theologie Luthers* (Göttingen, 1958).

5. *Career of the Reformer*, II, 113, in *Luther's Works*, George Forell, ed., Vol. XXXII (Philadelphia, 1958).

6. See Berhard Lohse, "Luthers Antwort in Worms," *Luther: Mitteilungen der Luthergesellschaft* (1958), No. 3, pp. 124-134.

7. I owe this observation to Professor William Baker, a close student of English historiography in the Victorian age.

8. Fritz Blanke, "Hamann und Luther," *Lutherjahrbuch*, X (1928), 28-29. See Horst Stephan, *Luther in den Wandlungen seiner Kirche* (2nd ed.; Berlin, 1951), pp. 35-67.

9. Karl Holl, "Die Kulturbedeutung der Reformation, 1911," *Gesammelte Aufsätze zur Kirchengeschichte*, I: *Luther* (6th ed.; Tübingen, 1932), 468-543, 531; translated as *The Cultural Significance of the Reformation* (New York, 1959), p. 134.

10. Fichte, *Die Bestimmung des Menschen*, Book 3: *Glaube, Sämmtliche Werke*, II (Berlin, 1845), 249; translated in Karl Barth, *Church Dogmatics*, III, part 2 (Edinburgh, 1960), 99.

11. Cited in August Messer, *Fichtes religiöse Weltanschauung* (Stuttgart, 1923), p. 21. It is interesting to note that a recent not very ecumenical Catholic study of Luther's theology criticizes Luther's concern with self and individual salvation for its subjectivism and personalism, almost as though Luther had been a Fichtean, or at least a Methodist, distorting spirituality; see Paul Hacker, *Das Ich in Glauben bei Martin Luther* (Graz, 1966).

12. See, for example, Joseph Bohatec, *Die Religionsphilosophie Kants in der "Religion innerhalb der Grenzen der bloszen Vernunft"* (Hildesheim, 1966).

13. See Bruno Bauch, *Luther und Kant* (Berlin, 1904), p. 169; Ernst Katzer, *Luther und Kant* (Gieszen, 1910).

14. Joseph C. Weber, "Feuerbach, Barth and Theological Methodology," *Journal of Religion*, 46, No. 1 (January, 1966), 24.

15. Hegel, *Philosophie der Geschichte*, III1, 131, Johannes Hoffmeister, ed., *Vorlesungen über die Philosophie der Weltgeschichte* (Hamburg, 1955), cited in Stephan Crites, "The Gospel According to Hegel," *Journal of Religion*, XLVI,

No. 2 (April, 1966), 254. The entire article, pp. 246-263, is excellent and offers a useful corrective to Walter Kaufman, *Hegel* (New York, 1965), sec. 65.

16. Georg Wünsch, *Luther und die Gegenwart* (Stuttgart, 1961), p. 99.

17. *Rationis Latomianae pro incendiariis Lovaniensis scholae sophistis redditae, Lutheriana confutatio, 1521, W.A.* 8, 43-128.

18. *W.A.* 8, 122, 22-25.

19. *W.A.* 56, 347, 1-7; trans. Wilhelm Pauck, *Luther: Lectures on Romans* (London, 1961), p. 208. A monograph on the subject which would benefit from supplemental scholarship is Erdmann Schott, *Fleisch und Geist nach Luthers Lehre unter besonderer Berücksichtigung des Begriffes "totus homo"* (Leipzig, 1928).

20. *W.A.* 101, 1st half, 508, 20.

21. *W.A.* 56, 356, 4-7: "Et hoc consonat Scripturæ Quæ hominem describit incuruatum in se adeo, ut non tantum corporalia, Sed et spiritualia bona sibi inflectat et se in omnibus querat. Quæ Curuitas est nunc naturalis, naturale vitium et naturale malum."

22. *Operationes in Psalmos, W.A.* 5, 207, 32-34.

23. *W.A.* 2, 685-697: *Eyn Sermon von der bereytung zum sterben.*

24. *W.A.* 10III, 1-64: *Acht Sermone D.M. Luthers von ihm gepredigt zu Wittenberg in der Fasten.*

25. *W.A.* 40III, 484-594: *Enarratio psalmi XC per D.M. Lutherum in schola Witenbergensi anno 1534 publice absoluta.*

26. See Carl Stange, *Luthers Gedanken über die Todesfurcht* (Berlin, 1932) p. 8: Luther: "Denn Auf Erden kann nichts Höheres begegnen weder der Tod, da die Welt und alles miteinander musz aufhören." *Erlangen Ausgabe* 142, 133; *W.A.* 37, 535, 23-24.

27. *W.A.* 5, 163, 28-29: "Vivendo, immo moriendo et damnando fit theologus, non intelligendo, legendo aut speculando."

28. *W.A.* 40I, 444, 14: "Quia sicut credit, sic habet," *W.A.* 18, 769, 17-18; "Atque ut credunt, ita habent," *W.A.* 18, 778, 13-14.

29. *W.A.* i, 543, 8-9: "tantum habes, quantum credis"; 595, 5: "tantum habes quantum credis."

30. Cf. *W.A.* 18, 633, 7: "Altera est, quod fides est rerum non apparentium Ut ergo fidei locus sit, opus est, ut omnia quae creduntur abscondantur"; *W.A.* 5, 86, 33-35: "Atque ita oculus fidei in tenebras interiores et caliginem mentis suspicit nihilque videt, nisi quod attenuatur suspiciens in excelso expectansque, unde veniat auxilium ei." *W.A.* 5, 623, 40-624, 2: "Agat ergo secundum fidem, idest insensibilitatem, et fiat truncus immobilis ad has blasphemias, quas in corde suo suscitat satanas."

31. *W.A.* 7, 551, 19-21: "Sein geist ist *sanctum sanctorum*, gottis wonung ym finsternn glauben on liecht, denn er glawbt, das er nit sihet, noch fulet, noch begreiffet." See Walther von Loewenich, *Luther als Ausleger der Synoptiker* (Munich, 1954), pp. 83-88, on this problem of faith and existential experience.

32. *W.A.* 7, 548, 10-11: "Unnd da ist denn der heilig geyst, der hat solch uberschwenklich kunst und lust ynn einem augenblick ynn der erfarung geleret." So also *W.A.* 9, 98, 21, in which Luther commends Tauler's theology as being "sapientia experimentalis et non doctrinalis. Quia nemo novit nisi qui accipit hoc negotium absconditum."

33. *W.A.* 18, 605, 32-34 (the famous lines of the *De servo arbitrio*): "Spiritus sanctus non est Scepticus, nec dubia aut opiniones in cordibus nostris scripsit, sed assertiones ipsa vita et omni experientia certiores et firmiores."

34. *W.A.Ti.* 1, 16, No. 46, 1. 12.

35. *W.A.* 5, 26, 18-20.

36. Heiko Oberman, " 'Justitia Christi' and 'iustitia dei.' Luther and the

scholastic doctrines of justification," *Harvard Theological Review*, 59 (January, 1966), 1-26.

37. *W.A.* 4, 511, 13: ". . . Qualis tu es in dispositione, tale est [verbum] tibi."

38. *W.A.* 30ᴵᴵ, 672, 37-673, 13-17.

39. *W.A.* 56, 371, 2-14; trans. Wilhelm Pauck, *Luther: Lectures on Romans*, pp. 235-236.

40. *W.A.* 56, 372, 5-25; trans. Wilhelm Pauck, *Luther: Lectures on Romans*, p. 237.

41. *W.A.* 56, 273, 8-9.

42. *W.A.* 56, 255, 15-19.

43. Wilhelm de Wette, *Briefwechsel*, I (Berlin, 1825), ep. 22, p. 40: "prius necesse est personam esse mutatam, deinde opera."

44. *W.A.* 56, 172, 9-11: "Sicut Aristoteles 3. Ethicorum manifeste determinat, secundum quem Iustitia sequitur et fit ex actibus. Sed secundum Deum precedit opera et opera fiunt ex ipsa." This is a major theme in Luther's works, repeated in his *Sermon on Good Works, The Liberty of the Christian Man*, and elsewhere.

45. *W.A.* 56, 117, 25-29; trans. Wilhelm Pauck, *Luther: Lectures on Romans*, p. 321, n. 1.

46. *W.A.* 56, 441, 23-442, 1-5; trans. Wilhelm Pauck, *Luther: Lectures on Romans*, p. 322. *W.A.* 56, 441, n. 23, explains that the terms are derived from Aristotle via such medieval handbooks on physics as Ockham, *Summule in lib. physicorum*, c. IX, c. XXV f. Cf. *W.A.* 4, 113, 14-15: "Ratio omnium est haec regula, quod nos justi non sumus ex operibus, sed opera justa ex nobis primo justis."

47. *W.A.* 4, 19, 21-24, incorrectly cited in Erich Seeberg, *Luthers Theologie: Motive und Ideen*, I (Göttingen, 1929), 107, n. 3, as *W.A.* 7, 19.

48. *W.A.* 56, 248, 27-33; *W.A.* 56, 249, 1-11.

49. *W.A.* 56, 264, 5-8.

50. *W.A.* 56, 307, 16-21; trans. Wilhelm Pauck, *Luther: Lectures on Romans*, p. 162.

51. Herbert Vossberg, *Luthers Kritik aller Religion* (Leipzig, 1922).

52. *W.A.* 37, 589, 35-57.

53. Cited in Georg Wünsch, *Luther und die Gegenwart*, p. 117.

54. *W.A.* 56, 234, 1-9; trans. Wilhelm Pauck, *Luther: Lectures on Romans*, pp. 84-85. Cf. G. Wünsch, *Luther und die Gegenwart*, p. 117.

55. Immanuel Kant, *Religion Within the Limits of Reason Alone* (Chicago, 1934), pp. 156-157.

56. *Ibid.*, p. 188.

57. Herder, *Ideen zur Philosophie der Geschichte der Menschheit* (2nd ed.; Leipzig, 1921), p. 153.

58. *Ibid.*, p. 154.

59. *Ibid.*, p. 155. These three Herder citations are taken from Karl Barth, *Protestant Thought: From Rousseau to Ritschl* (New York, 1959), pp. 213-214, who cites another edition of the *Ideen*.

60. Ludwig Feuerbach, *Lectures on the Essence of Religion* (New York, 1967), p. 17.

61. Ludwig Feuerbach, *The Essence of Christianity* (New York, 1957), p. xvi.

62. Melvin Cherno, "Ludwig Feuerbach and the Intellectual Basis of Nineteenth Century Radicalism" (dissertation, Stanford, 1955), p. 52.

63. *Essence of Christianity*, p. 184.

64. *Ibid.*, p. 269.

65. *Sämmtliche Werke*, XII (2nd ed.; Stuttgart-Canstatt, 1960–), p. 83.

[173]

66. *Das Wesen des Glaubens im Sinne Luthers* (1844), trans. Melvin Cherno, *The Essence of Faith According to Luther* (New York, 1967).

67. *Sämmtliche Werke*, XII, 108.

68. *Ibid.*, XIII, 136. He repeated the complaint in a letter of October 15, 1844, also to Kapp.

69. Werner Schuffenhauer, *Feuerbach und der junge Marx* (Berlin, 1965), p. 83.

70. *Sämmtliche Werke*, II, 405, cited in S. Rawidowicz, *Ludwig Feuerbachs Philosophie. Ursprung und Schicksal* (2nd ed.; Berlin, 1964), p. 16, n. 4.

71. Karl Barth, *Protestant Thought*, p. 359.

72. See Barth's very brilliant book *Anselm: Fides Quaerens Intellectum* (Richmond, Va., 1960), in which he argues that since Anselm was arguing within the "theological circle," assurance of God resting upon anterior faith, he was not vulnerable to the criticism of Aquinas and Kant, as they supposed.

73. Karl Barth, *Protestant Thought*, p. 355.

74. *Ibid.*, p. 359. See the excellent article by Joseph C. Weber, "Feuerbach, Barth, and Theological Methodology," *Journal of Religion*, 46, No. 1 (January, 1966), 24-36.

75. See the very perceptive introductory essay to Feuerbach's *The Essence of Christianity* (New York, 1957), pp. x-xxxii, criticisms, pp. xxvii-xxviii. Karl Löwith, ed., *Die Hegelsche Linke* (Stuttgart-Canstatt, 1962), p. 11, observes that Feuerbach and the young Hegelians worked up to a superficial level and provided further proof of Jacob Burckhardt's dour observation that after 1830 the world grew more "common."

76. Barth's criticism that Feuerbach did not take death seriously is both unfair and yet justifiable. In his thesis at Erlangen, *De Ratione una universali infinita* (1828), pp. 11-68, Feuerbach included thoughts on death and immortality, a theme to which he frequently returned. Nature brings death, immortality is a projection. Any ethic based on immortality is a miserable construction. See Feuerbach, *Sämmtliche Werke*, I: "Gedanken über Tod und Unsterblichkeit"; "Todesgedanken, 1830"; "Die Unsterblichkeit vom Standpunkt der Anthropologie, 1846-1866"; *Sämmtliche Werke*, XI, 69-324. At the same time Barth's criticism is justified from the point of view of Barth (and Luther), since Feuerbach did not take seriously sin as the "sting of death," viewing death merely in a naturalistic, not a theological context. For Barth's own anthropology the reader can profitably study his *Church Dogmatics*, III, part 2 (Edinburgh, 1960), chap. x: "The Creature," and IV, part 1 (Edinburgh, 1961), chap. xiv: "Jesus Christ, the Lord as Servant."

77. Karl Barth, *The Humanity of God* (Richmond, Va., 1960), pp. 24, 26. Of relevance is his small study *Christ and Adam: Man and Humanity in Romans 5* (New York, 1957). Walther von Loewenich, *Luther und der Neuprotestantismus* (Witten, 1963), p. 261, criticizes Barth for giving a distorted picture of the experience-theology of the nineteenth century, for it did not consider religious experience to be the only source of faith, but only a way of making certainty greater. Since the Holy Spirit must work through experience there is no point in ridiculing experience as subjectivism.

78. Feuerbach, "Ueber das Wunder" (1839), *Sämmtliche Werke*, VII, 1-41; *Lectures on the Essence of Religion*, p. 146.

79. Marx-Engels, *Werke*, I (Berlin, 1961), pp. 26-27. See Werner Schuffenhauer, *Feuerbach und der junge Marx*, 24-25. The embattled Strauss published his *Streitschriften zur Vertheidigung meiner Schrift über das Leben Jesu und zur Charakteristik der gegenwärtigen Theologie*, 3 vols., in 1837.

80. Frederick Engels, *Ludwig Feuerbach and the Outcome of Classical German Philosophy* (New York, 1941), pp. 18 ff, 28, 46.

81. *Ibid.*, p. 36.

82. Text translated in Engels, *Ludwig Feuerbach*, Appendix A, pp. 73-75. If this present discussion of Luther, Feuerbach, and Marx seems to be improbable, confer the relatively brilliant comparison of Pascal and Marx in Lucien Goldmann, *The Hidden God: A Study of Tragic Vision in the Pensées of Pascal and the Tragedies of Racine* (New York, 1964), pp. 278-282. There is, of course, a vast literature on Christianity and Marxism in general, of which at least one ambitious title merits special mention, Nicholas Lobkowicz, ed., *Marx and the Western World* (Notre Dame, 1967), in which the editor discusses Marx's attitude toward religion sympathetically and James L. Adams offers a distinctively Protestant point of view.

83. Schopenhauer, *Die Welt als Wille und Vorstellung*, I (Wiesbaden, 1965), 480.

84. *Ibid.*, p. 482. On p. 621 Schopenhauer refers to Luther's ethic of selfless love.

85. Schopenhauer, *Die Welt als Wille und Vorstellung*, II (Wiesbaden, 1961), 693, from chap. 48: "Zur Lehre von der Verneinung des Willens zum Leben."

86. Schopenhauer, *Parerga, Sämmtliche Werke*, III (Frankfurt am Main, 1962), 583-584. In chap. iv of the *Über die Freiheit des Willens* he discusses Luther as his forerunner.

87. Cf. the closely documented articles by Heinz Bluhm on Nietzsche and Luther: "Das Lutherbild des jungen Nietzsche," *PMLA*, 58 (1943), 246-288; "Nietzsche's Idea of Luther in *Menschliches Allzumenschliches*," *PMLA*, 65 (1950), 1053-1068; "Nietzsche's View of Luther and the Reformation in *Morgenröthe* and *Die Fröhliche Wissenschaft*," *PMLA*, 68 (1953), 111-127. See also Emanuel Hirsch, "Nietzsche und Luther," *Lutherjahrbuch*, II-III (1920/1921), 61-106.

88. Nietzsche, *Werke*, XIII (Leipzig, 1903), 333.

89. *Ibid.*, X, 441.

90. *Ibid.*, p. 433.

91. *Ibid.*, p. 301.

92. *Ibid.*, pp. 290, 307.

93. *Ibid.*, XIII, 215, No. 506.

94. *Ibid.*, pp. 301-303.

95. *W.A.* 7, 373, 17-29. Luther compares himself with Balaam's ass which God chose to use even though there were enough other asses around.

96. Jacob Taubes, "Dialectic and Analogy," *Journal of Religion*, 34 (1954), 111-119, 115. See also Paul Wernle, *Allegorie und Erlebnis bei Luther* (Bern, 1960).

97. See the intriguing study by Friedrich Karl Schumann, "Gedanken Luthers zur Frage der Entmythologisierung," *Wort und Bestalt* (Witten, 1956), pp. 165-178.

Appendix

Statement of Objectives

The Southeastern Institute of Medieval and Renaissance Studies is established for the advancement of scholarship and the improvement of teaching, primarily in the southeastern region. Through the Institute the resources of Duke University and the University of North Carolina—particularly staff and library holdings—are made available to scholars and teachers throughout the region. Participation is invited from students of all areas of medieval and renaissance studies, including (among others) art, aesthetics, history, literature, music, philosophy, and religion. The individual seminars of the Institute may combine several of these interests.

The Institute consists of several informal seminars (seven in 1968), each one concerned with a topic of special interest to students of the medieval and renaissance periods. Each seminar is led by a Senior Fellow, a scholar selected for eminence in his field, and has an enrollment of not more than six participants, designated Fellows. Auditing of the seminars is strictly limited and is dependent upon the consent of both the Senior Fellow and the Executive Committee of the Institute. A standard fellowship of $500.00 is awarded each Fellow and is normally increased by a matching or smaller research award from his own institutions. The typical seminar meets twice a week for one or two hours, but schedules are kept flexible to permit arrangements best adapted to the needs of the seminar. Each Fellow participates in one seminar only and thus has ample free time to devote to his own research. In addition to the seminars, the Institute sponsors a public lecture by each of the Senior Fellows, as well as other occasional lectures by distinguished visiting scholars, and holds a daily coffee hour and informal discussion period for those Institute members who wish to attend.

The sessions of the Institute alternate annually between the campuses of Duke University and the University of North Carolina at Chapel Hill. The fourth session, from July 20 to August 24, 1968, was held on the campus of Duke University.

Seminars and Fellows, Fourth Session

1. STUDIES IN RENAISSANCE ALLEGORY

Senior Fellow: Dr. Don Cameron Allen, Sir William Osler Professor of English Literature, Johns Hopkins University. ACLS Fellow (1935-36); Fulbright Fellow (Oxford, 1950-51); Johnson Research Fellow in the Humanities (Wisconsin, 1961-62). Baskerville Lectures (Brown, 1946); Taft Lectures (Cincinnati); Scott Lectures (Washington University, 1953). Carpenter Professor (Chicago, 1949). Vice-President, Modern Language Association (1965-66). Visiting Professor, Ohio University (1938), Northwestern (1947), Illinois (1949), New York University (1950), University of Colorado (1957, 1961, 1963). Editor, *ELH, Isis, MLN, ELN, SEL, RLM*; on editorial committee, *PMLA* (1946-61). Editor, Francis Meres' *Treatise Poetrie* (1935); Francis Meres' *Palladis Tamia* (1938); Dekker's *Owles Almanacke* (1943); Sir William Cornwallis, *Essayes* (1946); *A Strange Metamorphosis of Man* (1949); *That Soueraine Light* (1952); John Hall, *Paradoxes* (1956); *Studies in Honor of T. W. Baldwin* (1958); *Four Poets on Poetry* (1959); *The Moment of Poetry* (1962). Author, *The Star-Crossed Renaissance* (1941); *The Legend of Noah* (1949); *The Harmonious Vision* (1954); *Image and Meaning* (1960); *Doubt's Boundless Sea* (1964); etc.

Scope: Classical interpretation and English literary method.

Description: The seminar was concerned with Renaissance interest in the moral and physical interpretations of Homer, Vergil, Ovid, and the Classical mythologies. The interpretive methods of Renaissance antiquaries were also considered. An attempt was made to see whether or not the methods can be applied to the reading of English poets of the sixteenth and seventeenth centuries. An ability to read Latin prose was required.

Fellows: James Earl Applegate (Wilson College); Claude Graveley Arnold (University of St. Thomas); Mrs. Alice Blitch (Western College for Women); George Wilson Boyd (Millsaps College); Julian Ward Jones, Jr. (College of William and Mary); Anne Kingsbury LeCroy (East Tennessee State University); John James Mulryan (St. Bonaventure University).

2. THE TRANSMISSION OF BIBLICAL TEXTS IN THE MIDDLE AGES AND THE RENAISSANCE

Senior Fellow: Dr. Kenneth W. Clark, Professor Emeritus of New Testament, Duke University. Fulbright Research Fellow, University of Manchester, England (1954-55) and University of Athens, Greece (1961-62). Secretary (1946-50), Vice-President (1964), President (1965), Society of Biblical Literature; Co-Director and Executive Editor, International Greek New Testament Project; Director, microfilming expeditions to St. Catherine's Monastery (Mt. Sinai) and the Orthodox Patriarchal Library, Jerusalem (Old City). Editorial Board of *Novum Testamentum* (Leiden), Editorial Committee of *Journal of Biblical Literature*, Advisory Board of Editors for *Peake's Commentary on the Bible*. Author: *Descriptive Catalogue of Greek New Testament Manuscripts in America* (1937); *Eight American Praxapostoloi* (1941); "The Transmission of the New Testament," *The Interpreter's Bible*, XII (1957), 617-627; "The Textual Criticism of the New Testament," *Peake's Commentary* (1962), pp. 663-670; "The Theological Relevance of Textual Variation in Current Criticism of the Greek New Testament," *Journal of Biblical Literature* (1966); "Today's Problems with the Critical Text of the New Testament," University of Chicago Divinity School centennial volume (forthcoming).

Scope: Interdisciplinary: history, literature, manuscripts and incunabula, principles and methods of textual restoration.

Description: It was proposed to illumine this aspect of medieval culture in a combination of projects devised by the member-Fellows of the group. Suggestions: examination of the Hebrew or the Greek resources for the Biblical texts; interplay between Byzantium and the medieval West; ecclesiastical controversies engendered by textual criticism; special attention to any one of the emerging European versions; critique of the significance of textual emendation; comparison of Catholic and Protestant textual traditions. Primary materials exist in the special collections at UNC and Duke (manuscripts in Greek *et al.*, incunabula, early printed Bibles, various translations).

Fellows: David Dwight Burr (Virginia Polytechnic Institute);

Appendix

Charles Edmund Lewis (University of Virginia); John Barton Payne (Randolph-Macon Woman's College); Lorenzo Pierce Plyler (Methodist College); Loy Hahn Witherspoon (University of North Carolina at Charlotte).

3. SPANISH LITERARY AND INTELLECTUAL HISTORY TO 1700

Senior Fellow: Dr. Otis H. Green, Professor of Romance Languages, University of Pennsylvania. Visiting Professor, University of Colorado, summers of 1934, 1936, 1948, 1949, 1950. Guggenheim Fellow, 1964-65. Co-Editor of *Hispanic Review*. Comendador de la Orden de Isabel la Católica. First Vice-President, Modern Language Association of America, 1961 and 1966; President, 1967. Member of the Council, Renaissance Society of America. Author: *The Life and Works of Lupercio Leonardo de Argensola* (1927; Spanish language edition, 1945); *Courtly Love in Quevedo* (1952; Spanish language edition, 1955); *Spain and the Western Tradition: The Castilian Mind in Literature from El Cid to Calderón* (4 vols.; 1963-66: Spanish language edition, 1967-68).

Scope: Interdisciplinary: literature, history, philosophy, religion.

Description: The seminar concerned itself with Spanish literary and peripherally literary works which help to provide the key for understanding the Spanish culture pattern, the *Denkformen*. It deepened the perceptions brought forth in Dr. Green's *Spain and the Western Tradition*, and extended the field of inquiry into the eighteenth century. In addition to Dr. Green's four volumes, three recent works provided starting points: Luis Rodríguez Aranda, *El desarrollo de la razón en la cultura espanola*; Monroe Z. Hafter, *Gracián and Perfection: Spanish Moralists of the Seventeenth Century*; José Antonio Maravall, *Antiguos y modernos: La idea de progreso en el desarrollo inicial de una sociedad*.

Fellows: Ricardo Arias y Arias (Queens College, N.Y.); Frank Brantley (Memphis State University); J. Martinez de Bujanda (Université de Sherbrooke); Frank Halstead (University of Mississippi); William David Ilgen (University of North Carolina at Chapel Hill); James Allan Parr (Murray State University).

4. STUDIES IN MEDIEVAL CRITICISM

Senior Fellow: Dr. O. B. Hardison, Jr., Professor of English, University of North Carolina, Chapel Hill. Fulbright Fellow, Rome,

Italy, 1953-54; Folger Library Summer Fellow, 1958; Guggenheim Fellow, 1963-64. Chairman (1965), Co-Chairman (1966), Southeastern Institute of Medieval and Renaissance Studies. Haskins Medal, Medieval Academy of America (1967). Editor, *Studies in Philology,* 1966-. Author, *The Enduring Monument: The Idea of Praise in Renaissance Literary Theory and Practice* (1962); *Christian Rite and Christian Drama in the Middle Ages* (1966). Editor, *Modern Continental Literary Criticism* (1962); *English Literary Criticism: The Renaissance* (1963); editor, with Frank Warnke and Alex Preminger, *The Encyclopedia of Poetry and Poetics* (1965); SIMRS *Medieval and Renaissance Studies,* I (1966); etc.

Scope: Medieval literature, history of criticism, history of rhetoric, aesthetics, comparative literature.

Subject: The seminar considered significant documents of literary criticism from the period extending roughly from the sixth to the fifteenth century. The Senior Fellow was especially concerned with the work of Euanthius and Fulgentius, but this emphasis in no way limited the Fellows in their choice of topics within the general framework of the seminar. A reading knowledge of Latin was required of all Fellows.

Fellows: James Roderick Banker (University of North Carolina at Raleigh); Jeffrey Alec Helterman (Vanderbilt University); Robert Eugene Lucas (University of North Carolina at Greensboro); Roger P. Parr (Marquette University); William Bruce Parrill (Southeastern Louisiana College); Leslie George Whitbread (Louisiana State University at New Orleans).

5. LUTHER'S BIBLE TRANSLATION: INTENSIVE STUDY OF SELECTED PASSAGES

Senior Fellow: Dr. John G. Kunstmann, Professor Emeritus of German, University of North Carolina, Chapel Hill. Member, Department of Germanic Languages and Literatures, University of Chicago, 1927-55. Visiting Professor, Columbia University, 1947; University of North Carolina, 1954; Duke University, fall semester, 1965. Founder of Lutheran Reformation Festival, University of Chicago, 1946. President, American Assn. of Teachers of German, 1960-63; Life Member of Lutheran Academy for Scholarship (and Director of Research, 1949-57). Editor of and contributor to *Proceedings of the First Institute on the Church and Modern Cul-*

ture, 1951. Contributor to *Studies in Philology* (UNC), 1939–. Author, *The Gurley Psalter of the University of Chicago*, 1951; "And Yet Again: 'Wes das Herz voll ist, des gehet der Mund über,'" 1952. Member, Editorial Board, *Modern Philology*, 1952-55; *Annuale Mediaevale*, 1960–; *PMLA*, 1962-67. Recipient of *Festschrift*, 1959, and of Great Cross of Merit, Order of Merit, Federal Republic of Germany, 1961.

Scope: Literature, religion, theory of translation, linguistics, cultural history.

Description: Primary concentration on the text of Luther's version, with correlative studies of sources and comparison with other renderings. Such a study presupposed a reasonably good knowledge of Early New High German AND of Latin, Greek, and (hopefully) Hebrew-Aramaic. The precise direction of study was determined, in each case, by the amount of linguistic preparation brought by the Fellow.

Fellows: James Vincent McMahon (Emory University); Arlene Adrienne Miller (Stanford University); Roy Kinnear Patteson (Peace College); David Gerhard Schmiel (St. Paul's College, Mo.); Jeremiah J. Smith (Bellarmine College).

6. THE RENAISSANCE AND THE SPANISH CONQUEST ("DOMINACIÓN") OF AMERICA

Senior Fellow: Dr. John Tate Lanning, James B. Duke Professor of History, Duke University. Fellow, Guggenheim Foundation (1930-31), ACLS (1932), Rosenwald Foundation (1946). Elected member of *Sociedad Cubana de Estudios Historicos e Internacionales* (1942); *Sociedad de Geografia e Historia de Guatemala* (1946). Recipient of Herbert Eugene Bolton Memorial Prize, American Historical Association (1956); Serra Award, Academy of American Franciscan History (1958). Lecturer, University of Chile (1931); University of Córdoba (1931); Seminar Conference on Latin America, George Washington University (1935); Trumbull Lecturer, Yale (1943); Kennecott Lecturer, University of Arizona (1960). Chairman, Conference on Latin American History of the American Historical Association (1952, 1958). Associate Managing Editor (1935-39) and Managing Editor (1939-45), *Hispanic American Historical Review*; Member, Board of Advisory Editors, *Hispanic American Historical*

Review, Americas, Latin American Review. Author, *The Spanish Missions of Georgia* (1953), *Academic Culture in the Spanish Colonies* (1940), *Reales Cédulas de la Real y Pontificia Universidad de México* (1946), Dr. *Narciso Esparragosa y Gallardo, Varon ilustre de Venezuela* (1953); *Reales cédulas de la Real y Pontificia Universidad de San Carlos de Guatemala* (1954), *The University in the Kingdom of Guatemala* (1955); etc.

Scope: History, education, arts and sciences. Range determined by interests of the Fellows.

Description: The seminar studied Spanish universities, contrasting the classic Salamanca with Alcalá de Henares at the time of the Conquest—the moment when Spanish universities reached the peak of their glory. From a major emphasis upon the establishment and promotion of universities as a part of the sixteenth-century inheritance of Spaniards in America, the seminar then moved into academic subjects that were also broad aspects of the social and intellectual life of the Spanish colonies: medicine, law, architecture, astronomy.

Fellows: Elbert Daymond Turner (University of North Carolina at Charlotte); Thomas Blossom (Old Dominion College); Robert Louis Fiore (Michigan State University); Charles Russell Reynolds (North Carolina State University at Raleigh).

7. THE REFORMATION IN HISTORICAL THOUGHT

Senior Fellow: Dr. Lewis W. Spitz, Professor of History, Stanford University. Recipient of Fellowships from Guggenheim Foundation, Huntington Library, ACLS; Harbison Award of the Danforth Foundation for Outstanding College Teaching. Fulbright Professor, Institute for European History, Mainz, Germany (1960). Member, Council of the Renaissance Society of America; Past President, North California Renaissance Conference; Past President, American Society for Reformation Research. Author: *Conrad Celtis the German Arch-Humanist* (1957); *The Religious Renaissance of the German Humanists* (1963); *Life in Two Worlds—William Sihler* (1967). Editor: *Career of the Reformer,* IV, *Luther's Works,* XXXIV (American ed., 1960); *The Reformation—Material or Spiritual?* (1962); (with Richard Lyman) *Major Crises in Western Civilization* (2 vols.; 1965); *The Protestant Reformation* (1966); etc.

Appendix

Scope: Interdisciplinary: intellectual history, philosophy of history, historiography.

Description: A significant clue to the mentality of an age is to be found in its conception of its own place in history. The seminar explored the historical self-consciousness of the third generation of northern Renaissance humanists who contributed so much to the Reformation. Basic attitudes and central themes were then traced through the subsequent historiographical tradition to such contemporary schools of thought as the Marxist, Psychoanalytical, Catholic, and Neo-orthodox.

Fellows: William J. Baker (Tusculum College); Thomas H. Clancy (Loyola University, New Orleans); William James McGill (Alma College); W. D. White (St. Andrews Presbyterian College); Frank Junior Wray (Berea College).